ROBERT A. HEINLEIN

Science-Fiction Writers

ROBERT SCHOLES, GENERAL EDITOR

H. Bruce Franklin: *Robert A. Heinlein: America as Science Fiction*

ROBERT A. HEINLEIN
America as Science Fiction

H. Bruce Franklin

New York   Oxford
OXFORD UNIVERSITY PRESS
1980

Copyright © 1980 by Oxford University Press, Inc.

Library of Congress Cataloging in Publication Data

Franklin, Howard Bruce.
  Robert A. Heinlein: America as science fiction.

  (Science-fiction writers series)
  "Checklist of works by Robert A. Heinlein": p.
  Bibliography: p.
  Includes index.
    1. Heinlein, Robert Anson, 1907–   2. Authors,
  American—20th century—Biography.   I. Series.
  PS3515.E288Z67   813'.54   80-13756
  ISBN 19502746-9
  ISBN 19502747-7 pbk.

Rights to reproduction of cover art from *The Avalon Hill General* for Starship Troopers granted by The Avalon Hill Game Company, Baltimore, Maryland.

Cover designs and drawings from *Astounding* are Copyright © 1940, 1941 by Street & Smith Publications, Inc.; Copyright © 1968, 1969 (renewed) by The Condé Nast Publications, Inc.; used by permission of The Condé Nast Publications, Inc.

Photograph of Robert Heinlein used by permission of Jay Kay Klein.

The illustrations for *Sixth Column, Time for the Stars, Stranger in a Strange Land, Glory Road,* and *Farnham's Freehold* are Copyright © 1976 by Midamericon; they appeared originally in the *1976 Midamericon Program Book* and are used by permission of Midamericon and those artists who could be located. I wish to thank Paul Rivoche for permission to use his illustration of *Sixth Column,* Ron Miller for permission to use his illustration of *Time for the Stars,* Jackie Causgrove for permission to use her illustration of *Stranger in a Strange Land* and Doug Potter for permission to use his illustration of *Farnham's Freehold.* Persistent efforts to reach Herb Arnold have been unsuccessful.

Printed in the United States of America

To my mother
and in memory
of my father

EDITOR'S FOREWORD

For the first eight decades of this century critics of fiction have reserved their highest praises for novels and stories that emphasize individual psychology in characterization, unique stylistic nuances in language, and plausibility in the events presented. It is an interesting feature of literary history that during this same period of time a body of fiction has flourished which privileges the type over the individual, the idea over the word, and the unexpected over the plausible event. This body of work, which has come to be called—with only partial appropriateness—"science" fiction, has had some recognition from serious critics but still hovers between genuine acceptance and total dismissal in literary circles.

Schools now offer courses in science fiction—either because one zealous teacher insists upon it or because "the kids read that stuff." But it is rare to hear of works of science fiction integrated into "regular" courses in modern literature. The major reason for this is that as long as the dominant criteria are believed to hold for *all* fiction, science fiction will be found inferior: deficient in psychological depth, in verbal nuance, and in plausibility of event. What is needed is a criticism serious in its standards and its concern for literary value but willing to take seriously a literature based on ideas, types, and events beyond ordinary experience.

The *Science-Fiction Writers* series of critical volumes is an attempt to provide that sort of criticism. In designing the

series we have selected a number of authors whose body of
work has proved substantial, durable, and influential, and we
have asked an appropriate critic to make a book-length study
of the work of each author selected, taking that author
seriously enough to be critical and critically enough to be
serious.

In each volume we will include a general view of the author's life and work, critical interpretations of his or her major
contributions to the field of science fiction, and a biographical
and bibliographical apparatus that will make these volumes
useful as a reference tool. The format of each book will thus be
similar. But because the writers to be considered have had careers of different shapes, and because our critics are all individuals who have earned the right to their own interpretive
emphases, each book will take its own shape within the limits
of the general format. Above all, each volume will express the
critical views of its author rather than some predetermined
party line.

The present volume, Bruce Franklin's study of Robert Heinlein, is an important contribution to American studies in general. If we can accept the notion of mythology made popular
by Claude Lévi-Strauss, then Heinlein must be regarded as a
major American mythographer. For Lévi-Strauss and other
structuralist critics, myth provides a reconciliation in fictional
form of cultural oppositions too painful to be considered rationally. In ancient Greece, for example, the knowledge that
human beings are born through the sexual union of their
parents was in conflict with the taboo against incest. How
could one man and one woman (like Adam and Eve) be the
ancestors of a whole race without the incest taboo having been
violated and all that race being accurst? The answer to the
problem is provided by a myth in which large numbers of new
human beings are said to have sprung up from the earth without parents, like plants from seeds. The myth "solves" the rational problem by displacing it. We still solve many of our
problems in this same way.

A writer who expresses the values of his culture as power-
fully as Heinlein thus becomes an important object of study.
He expresses and tries to reconcile all our conflicting hopes

and fears by various mythic displacements. Our desires for freedom and order, our longing for frontiers and high technology, our impulses to universal brotherhood and our passionate distrust of foreigners, the American male's wish that his womenfolk would be both equal and submissive—all these and many more of the fundamental contradictions of our culture are the very stuff out of which Heinlein's fiction is made. As in many myths, in Heinlein's works we find these opposites apparently reconciled. Only a rational dissection of them will reveal just how deep the conflicts actually are.

In some ways Bruce Franklin is the ideal critic to perform that dissection. His pioneering study of American science fiction of the nineteenth century (*Future Perfect*, Oxford University Press, 1966, 1978) opened many eyes to the fact that science fiction in America was a genre with a past, and that our finest writers (Poe, Hawthorne, Melville, Twain) had not ignored it. His military experience (with the Strategic Air Command) has also given Franklin an important perspective on Heinlein, whose commitment to military values is everywhere acknowledged. But more important is the fact that Franklin approaches the criticism of American culture as a Marxist.

Though Heinlein has often been seen as a radical of the right, from Franklin's perspective he is at the very center of the system of beliefs and values that characterizes American capitalism. Franklin's book is thus a critique of American values *through* the work of a writer who presents those values—with all their internal contradictions—in a clear and vigorous manner. It is a critique, however, and not a pointless exercise in hostility, because Franklin is respectful of Heinlein's skill as a writer, and thus reads his work with the care and attention it deserves. Science fiction is more tendentious, more engaged, more overtly ideological than our traditional modernist fiction with its emphasis on individual psychology. The clash of values is an important dimension of the whole field and must be an important part of its critical study as well. In this book Heinlein and Franklin enact that clash for us, bringing it into the foreground, where it belongs.

July 1980   R.S.

ACKNOWLEDGMENTS

The biographical and bibliographic research for this book received generous help from: Arlene R. Rockwood, Librarian of the Butler Public Library in Butler, Missouri; Alma Vaughan, Reference Specialist of the State Historical Society of Missouri in Columbia; Rita Bottoms, Head of Special Collections, The University Library, University of California, Santa Cruz; J. D. Oliver of the Alumni Association of the United States Naval Academy; R. L. Lewis, Recorder of Deeds for Bates County, Missouri; Lurton Blassingame; Eleanor Wood; and Sam Moskowitz. Virginia Gerstenfeld Heinlein took the trouble to check through the entire list of Heinlein's writings published prior to 1979.

Robert A. Heinlein most graciously and hospitably spent a day talking with me in his home. He also read through the manuscript, saved me from some embarrassing errors, and even argued me out of a point or two.

Kim Lewis has been an exceptionally thorough editor, and the editorial suggestions of John Wright have been very helpful. Parts of the manuscript benefited from the suggestions of Yvonne Crowley, Martin Karcher, and Carolyn Karcher, who also assisted with biographical research.

Karen Franklin, Gretchen Franklin, and Robert Franklin each read through the entire manuscript, and each gave many splendid suggestions and invaluable criticisms. Jane Morgan Franklin participated in every stage of the development of the book, but no formal acknowledgment could possibly express what I owe to her.

H.B.F.

CONTENTS

The Reverend Foster . . . had an instinct for the pulse of his times stronger than that of a skilled carnie sizing up a mark. The culture known as "America" had a split personality throughout its history.

Stranger in a Strange Land

ROBERT A. HEINLEIN

Robert A. Heinlein as guest of honor at the 34th World Science Fiction Convention, held in Kansas City, 1976. Photo by Jay Kay Klein.

1
ROBERT A. HEINLEIN:
His Time and Place

The phenomenon of Robert A. Heinlein expresses, among other things, the extraordinary quality of the everyday experience of our century. Heinlein is certainly our most popular author of science fiction, easily the most controversial, and perhaps the most influential. And science fiction has moved inexorably toward the center of American culture, shaping our imagination (more than many of us would like to admit) through movies, novels, television, comic books, simulation games, language, economic plans and investment programs, scientific research and pseudo-scientific cults, spaceships real and imaginary.

The most rapid and profound changes in human history have taken place in the twentieth century. Our time and our space have been transmuted by such now mundane contrivances as the automobile and the airplane, electric power grids and electronic computers, radio and television. The human race has become aware of itself as a single species inhabiting a planet, has fought for control of that planet in what have been called "world wars," and has now become capable of flight beyond that planet.

Our new technology has allowed us to peer deeply into the macrocosmic and microcosmic dimensions of our universe. A general theory of this material universe has been developed. We seem to have verified that theory experimentally, releasing inconceivable energy from the forces that constitute matter,

and we have observed and measured events hypothesized in
that theory, including astronomical occurrences from several
hundred million years back in time and radiation released
within a second or two of the explosion of the primeval fire-
ball that is now thought to have generated our universe perhaps fifteen to twenty billion years ago.

We have manufactured weapons capable of destroying our
species and we have developed productive resources capable
of satisfying all the material needs of our species, though by
1970 there were more than twice as many people on the
planet as there had been when the century opened. The relations between the sexes are being radically transformed by the
changing material conditions of existence. Some of the most
visionary dreams of the nineteenth century now seem possibly
attainable within the lifetime of people alive today: political
and economic equality between women and men, and between white and non-white peoples; a doubling of the average
life expectancy and nearly universal literacy on this planet;
human beings walking on another planet. Nightmares almost
beyond the imagination of the nineteenth century also seem
possible, including universal destruction through biological,
chemical, or nuclear agents released accidentally or deliberately.

As the ever-accelerating pace of scientific and technological development has constantly revolutionized the material
conditions of existence, social and political upheavals have
turned this into the century of global revolution. It is no
wonder then that science fiction has kept pushing closer to
the core of twentieth-century culture. For science fiction is a
vital form of imaginative experience in the actual world we
inhabit, a world in which science and technology constantly
reshape our existence so that our imagined shapes of the future more and more determine the present.

What is so special about Robert Heinlein's role in science
fiction? In 1939, Heinlein published his first story, and within
two years he was already being acclaimed by some as the most
popular living writer of science fiction. By the mid 1960s,
Heinlein had an audience of millions. His works have been
translated into twenty-eight languages. All but one of his
thirty-five published books (twenty-six novels and nine collec-

tions of shorter fiction) are presently in print in mass-market paperbacks. He is customarily called "the Dean of science fiction."

Heinlein is the only author who has won the Hugo Award (the World Science Fiction Convention's prize for the best novel of the year) four times. He was the first writer of hardcore science fiction to break into general circulation magazines. He is a leading figure in the development of the modern science-fiction movie, science-fiction television serials, and the modern science-fiction juvenile novel. Words coined in Heinlein's fiction have become part of our language.

Heinlein is many things to many people, as we can see in the use of some of his coinages. Engineers call a certain kind of servomechanism a *waldo*, a term he invented in 1942. His 1961 verb *grok* became part of the youth movement of that decade and is now widely diffused. TANSTAAFL ("There ain't no such thing as a free lunch"), coined in 1966, has become a shibboleth for the libertarian movement, which has made him one of its standard bearers. Although one of his novels was a living bible for some participants in the counterculture of the 1960s, Heinlein is also a respected figure in military circles, chosen to address the United States Naval Academy and to fly in the B-1 bomber.

If you glance at the criticism of his work or chat with a few people who have read him at all, you will learn one thing: Robert Heinlein induces very strong reactions. There are many people who detest him, and there are millions of dedicated Heinlein fans. He has been praised as a master craftsman and celebrated as a visionary leading the human race into a glorious destiny. He has also been ridiculed as an "infantile" self-indulgent eccentric obsessed with "pre-Oedipal" power fantasies, a "dull" and "boring" hack who presents "indistinguishable" characters in a "banal" style. The political content of his works has been labeled conservative, radical, militaristic, iconoclastic, populist, anarchist, libertarian, and fascistic.

No critic of Heinlein can pretend to be neutral or emotionally uninvolved. When I was asked to do this book, the main question in my own mind was whether I could be fair to the man and his achievement. As I considered this question, I began to realize that Heinlein, though of course quite exceptional in some ways, must be understood as a very representative American. Because he embodies the contradictions that have been developing in our society ever since the Depression flowed into the Second World War, to understand the phenomenon of Robert Heinlein is finally to understand the culture that is the matrix for ourselves.

The people born in the first decade of our century and attaining a normal life span have lived through those revolutionary changes I have outlined. Robert Anson Heinlein is one of those people, and the course of his life, even more than most, is intertwined with those transformations of our epoch.

Heinlein was born on July 7, 1907, to Rex Ivar Heinlein and Bam Lyle Heinlein in the small town of Butler, which lies in the heart of southern Missouri farming country. Less than fifty years earlier, sporadic Civil War skirmishes swept through Butler's streets and most of the buildings in the town were burned to the ground by Union cavalrymen trying to prevent Confederate sympathizers from harboring rebels. After the war, Butler had been gradually rebuilt and was now a peaceful farming and livestock center, with a population of three thousand, large enough to make it the seat of Bates County. The biggest events were the livestock auctions held twice a week and the annual Little Bit and Bridle horse show. One of the largest enterprises in town was a hardware and general store filling a whole block, owned by Oscar Heinlein, Rex's uncle. The most famous citizen of the local region was Cole Younger, who had just returned to Missouri in 1903, after his parole and pardon, to lecture about his adventures with his brothers and Frank and Jesse James in the most notorious band of outlaws in American history.

Heinlein's parents, childhood sweethearts who graduated together in the Butler High School class of 1896, had married in 1899 and gone to live in the home of the bride's father, Alva E. Lyle, an early Missouri settler, now a practicing physician in Butler. Heinlein has referred to Dr. Lyle (in one of his rare comments about his family background) as "a horse-and-buggy doctor, who strongly influenced me."[1] Heinlein's father Rex went to work in Uncle Oscar's general store.

This was the period when the heartland of America was about to be transformed by modern industrialism, which replaced the family farm with mechanized agribusiness, sweeping people off the countryside into the booming new cities. In the year 1900, Samuel E. Heinlein, Rex's father, was working as a traveling salesman for the Kansas-Moline Plow Company of Kansas City, Missouri, one of the fastest-growing of the new midwestern cities. Within three years, Samuel had left Butler and moved up to Kansas City, where he worked as a "traveler" and assistant manager for Midland Manufacturing Company, a producer of agricultural implements. In 1906, Samuel became manager of Midland. The following year, when Samuel moved into a larger house, Rex moved from Butler to begin a series of positions as clerk and cashier with Midland Manufacturing, living briefly in his father's house while he located a home for his family. This was the year of Robert's birth.

The early years of Robert's life were the time when he was strongly influenced by Grandfather Lyle, who died in 1914. Robert spent several summers back in Butler, and his father also worked in a bank there for several months in 1909. Heinlein still remembers going with the doctor on his rounds in his horse-drawn buggy. In his 1973 novel, *Time Enough for Love*, the main character, reliving his boyhood days in pre-1914 Missouri, thinks: "Papa: He is away now. I had forgotten what he looks like—I had forgotten all their faces except Gramp," and recalls that he "had always been closer to his Grandfather . . . than to his father; not only had his father often been away on business, but also Gramp had been home in the daytime and willing to spend time with him."[2] According to the portrait of Grandfather Lyle in *Time Enough for Love*, that horse-and-buggy doctor from the old times in southern Missouri seems in young Robert's eyes to have incarnated the virtues of that time and place: resourcefulness, shrewdness, boldness, vigor, physical and moral toughness. Yet Heinlein himself did not personally share much of the experience of this farming community that had recently been a part of America's frontier, and the voice of Dr. Lyle was a voice from the past.

When Robert moved up from Butler with his family, he entered a city that embodied the next stages of America's development: Kansas City, site of the stockyards, rapid industrialization, urban machine politics, and the growing dominance of giant corporations over the small productive enterprises that represented the urban half of the American dream, the counterpart of the family farm. Just as the family's move from country to city made it part of the mainstream of American life, so the fortunes of the family in the big city replayed in microcosm a typical early twentieth-century American story.

Samuel's becoming manager of Midland Manufacturing Company apparently had encouraged his son Rex to try his own fortune in the big city. In 1910, the company, now known as Midland Implements, Jobbers of Implements & Vehicles, went out of business. The following year, Samuel and his brother Harvey Wallace Heinlein set up their own company, Heinlein Brothers, Agricultural Implements, across the street from the defunct Midland company. Rex and several other members of the Heinlein family now switched their employment to Heinlein Brothers. The future must have looked bright to the family. But this dream of a family enterprise lasted only a year. By 1912, Heinlein Brothers no longer existed. Harvey Heinlein was now a "traveler" for the Elite Post Card Co., where Rex worked as a bookkeeper, while his father Samuel was reduced to being a "traveler" and "salesman," first for the Elite Post Card Co., then for a variety of small companies during the last seven years of his life. The small-fry businesses attempting to capitalize on the booming market in agricultural equipment were being inexorably displaced by a growing giant—the International Harvester Company of America. In 1913, Rex got employment as a bookkeeper for International Harvester, where he was to work as cashier, bookkeeper, collector, correspondent, and clerk until 1937.

So Robert, with his two older brothers, younger brother, and three younger sisters grew up as a child of Kansas City, with all its ruthless energy and humdrum daily routines. The Kansas City of World War I, and of the postwar years of boom and bust (such as the crash in farm prices of 1920–21), of Prohibition and the Jazz Age, with its speakeasies wailing out the famous Kansas City blues, must have seemed eons away from Butler. Heinlein retained his dreams of Missouri's frontier past, just as he was being caught up in the forces of the future that were transforming the midlands of America. Heinlein's only published comment about his years in Kansas City public schools notes that one of his schoolmates at Greenwood Grammar School was Sally Rand,[3] who was to go on to fame as a fandancer. (The name and figure of Sally Rand appear frequently in his fiction, beginning with the female lead of his 1940 story " 'Let There Be Light,' " who has a "figure like a strip dancer, lots of corn-colored hair, nice complexion, and great big soft blue eyes" that all make her "look so much like Sally Rand.") He graduated from Central High School in 1924, and that yearbook's list of his high-school activities tells us quite a bit about him: "National Honor Society, '23, '24; Major, R.O.T.C.; President Central Officers Club; Captain Negative Debate Team; President Central Shakespeare Club; Student Council; Inter-Society Council; Boys' High School Club; Kelvin Club; Central Classics Club; Rifle Club." His classmates obviously considered him a studious youth, for they voted him "Worst Boy Grind." They also showed startling insight in the little tag line they added to sum up his character: *"He thinks in terms of the fifth dimension, never stopping at the fourth."* He spent the following year at Kansas City Junior College. Up to this point, his formal education seemed to reinforce his boyhood reading, which was a powerful influence in shaping his aspirations and determining his future.

Robert Heinlein was part of a relatively new reading audience created by the rise of industrial capitalism, which had triumphed in the Civil War and dominated the final decades of the nineteenth century. Transportation was being revolutionized by the development of the railroad (construction of the first transcontinental railroad had begun during the Civil War) and the steamship. Agriculture was being revolutionized by the invention of the harvester, the disc cultivator, the reaper, and the mowing machine, the machines producing that ever-accelerating flow of people from the countryside into the cities, in which Heinlein's family participated. Industry itself was being revolutionized by three nineteenth-century inventions: industrial steel, vulcanized rubber, and portland cement. These hallmarks of modern times were all on hand: dynamite, the rapid-fire pistol, the repeating rifle, barbed wire, and the machine gun. Such nineteenth-century inventions as the electric battery, the electromagnet, and the cathode ray tube were preparing the path for even faster technological development. The history of capitalism itself was being recorded and registered by other inventions of the nineteenth century: the adding machine, the calculating machine, the punch time clock, the cash register, the stock ticker, and punch-card accounting. The means of communication and artistic creation were being transformed by still other nineteenth-century inventions: photography, the phonograph, the typewriter, the telegraph, the telephone, radio, and the movies.

Industrial capitalism demanded a vast pool of skilled workers, technologists, and scientific personnel. Free public education was now not a luxury but a necessity: it had won out (against fierce resistance) in the industrial states in the 1830s and 1840s; it had been implemented throughout the South by the Reconstruction governments led by former slaves and poor whites in the late 1860s and early 1870s; it had been carried to the level of higher education by the land-grant college movement begun by the first Morrill Act of 1862 and accelerated by the second Morrill Act of 1890. So now there were millions of literate and ambitious boys and young men aspiring to careers in technology and science, hoping to be perhaps one of the great inventive geniuses—such as Thomas Alva Edison—held out to them as a model and ideal. And of course there had to be a literature aimed at this audience: the first great wave of science fiction intended for a mass audience—the science-fiction dime novel. This was the literature that first fired the youthful imagination of Robert Heinlein.

From the Civil War until World War I, the dominant literary form in America was the dime novel, with many hundreds of millions of copies flooding the newly created mass audience. As E. F. Bleiler has written, ". . . the dime novel was big business. Never before or since has book publishing held a larger share of the gross national product. The first mass-produced entertainment industry of importance, it stood in the same relation to the average young American as television does today."[4]

The first science-fiction dime novel, Edward Sylvester Ellis's *The Steam Man of the Prairies*, appeared in 1865. This seminal work combined four of the great formative myths of America, myths that we shall trace through the works of Heinlein himself: the myth of the frontier, the myth of boundless individual opportunity, the myth of the lone inventive genius, and the emerging myth of a technology capable of solving all problems. Ellis created in *The Steam Man of the Prairies* the figure who was to dominate the science-fiction dime novel: the lone genius in the form of a teenaged boy. His fifteen-year-old hero designs and builds, all by himself, a ten-foot tall robot driven by an internal steam engine, capable of pulling a horseless carriage along at nearly sixty miles an hour. The boy inventor, along with a grizzled old hunter and gold miner, take the steam man out to the Wild West, where they use this marvelous invention to help kill scores of "treacherous redskins" while making their fortune in a virgin gold strike.

The youthful genius embodying the highest aspirations of the boys and young men in the new reading audience was soon appropriated by Harry Enton's 1876 steal, *Frank Reade and His Steam Man of the Plains*. In the 1880s emerged the most important author of science-fiction dime novels, Lu Senarens, often called "the American Jules Verne," though Verne lifted more from him than he did from Verne.[5] Senarens retired Frank Reade to a farm run by steam-powered machines, and made his son, Frank Reade, Jr., the hero of the best-selling series of them all. Competing with Frank Reade, Jr., for fame, fortune, and readers was a host of other boy inventors, including Tom Edison, Jr., Tom Swift, Jack Wright (another Senarens creation), and Electric Bob. This core of lone geniuses created veritable assembly lines of new inventions, particularly robots and vehicles such as different types of flying machines and submarines, to conquer the air, the seas, and the lands of the world.

As a boy, Heinlein was an avid reader of the Frank Reade, Jr., and Tom Swift science-fiction dime novels, and there are still copies of them in his library. His reading gradually moved on to authors with deep ties to this literature, including Verne, Edgar Rice Burroughs, and H. G. Wells, as well as the science fiction and other works of Mark Twain, Rudyard

Kipling, and Jack London. He was also engrossed by the optimistic visions of the future projected in Edward Bellamy's *Looking Backward: 2000–1887* and *Equality*. Technology and science promised great things for America and for him: "Science of all sorts and astronomy in particular were my hobby as a boy and I planned to become an astronomer."[6]

Heinlein's life took a somewhat different path, when he managed to wangle what he has called a "political appointment" to the United States Naval Academy:

> "Our family was always in politics. I worked two years writing letters and applications and finally got the appointment through a Boss Pendergast man, Jim Reed. I would have taken West Point as readily, but the only opening was the Academy. I was always honored by Reed because I was the first of his appointees that ever graduated."[7]

This gives us a brief glimpse of another side of the contradictions that make up America. Tom Pendergast, whose reign is described, rather idyllically, in *Time Enough for Love*, was not only the political boss and probably the crime boss of Kansas City but also the man behind the political careers of both Jim Reed, the United States Senator who led the successful fight to keep America out of the League of Nations, and Heinlein's fellow Missourian Harry Truman. And the patronage system that gave Heinlein his opportunity to become a high-ranking military officer has also been one of the main links between America's highest political leaders and its highest military leaders.

At Annapolis, Heinlein had a fairly distinguished career, including becoming a champion with the dueling sword. He graduated in 1929, twentieth in a class of 243, as an ensign with very bright prospects. Of course this was not a year of bright prospects for America, at least not after the stock-market crash that fall and the beginning of the great Depression.

Heinlein served first on destroyers and a battleship. Then he was transferred to an environment that made the science fiction of the Frank Reade, Jr., series seem antiquated, one of the world's first modern aircraft carriers, the USS *Lexington*, just completed in 1927. On the *Lexington*, he was a gunnery officer, and he also had opportunities to fly in the back seat of some of its aircraft. Then in 1934, just as the first battles of what was to become World War II were opening in China and Africa, Heinlein's bright naval career ended abruptly. He contracted tuberculosis and retired, on lifetime medical disability, as a lieutenant, junior grade. He has never stopped thinking of himself as a United States naval officer, as he made clear in a 1973 speech at the Naval Academy, and he has used his experience as a gunnery officer extensively in several novels.

Married just after graduation from the Naval Academy, Heinlein now found himself in the middle of the Depression with a wife but without a career. Going back to the path he had looked forward to in his youth, he began doing graduate work in physics and mathematics at the University of California at Los Angeles. But once again his health failed, and he was forced to go to Colorado to recuperate. During these years he tried many things, including architecture and selling real estate. He acquired an interest in a silver mine, the Shively & Sophie Lodes, Silver Plume, Colorado. While in California, he even had a fling at politics, running in the Democratic primary to unseat Charlie Lion, a state representative; Heinlein came in second.

All during the 1920s and 1930s, he kept absorbing popular science fiction, now reading the successors to the nineteenth-century dime novel, the "pulps" (referring to the quality of their paper) which began just before World War I and blossomed in the period following. Then in 1939, Heinlein saw an ad in *Thrilling Wonder Stories*, offering a prize of $50 for the best amateur story. After writing his first science-fiction tale, he found out that *Astounding Science-Fiction* was paying a penny a word. Since his story ran to 7,000 words, he sent it to *Astounding*. They bought it for $20 more than he would have won in the contest, and Robert Heinlein, at the age of thirty-two, began his lifetime career.

Astounding regularly conducted polls of its readers to determine which stories they liked best. Soon the most popular writer was Robert A. Heinlein, often rivaled only by "Anson MacDonald," a Heinlein pseudonym.

Heinlein's new career halted temporarily after America formally entered World War II in December 1941. He returned to the employment of the Navy, now as a civilian engineer in the

Naval Air Material Center at the Philadelphia Navy Yard, where he worked in the designing and testing of materials associated with naval aviation, including plastics for aircraft and high-altitude pressure suits. During this period his only known publications are technical monographs, such as *Testing in Connection with the Development of Strong Plastics for Aircraft* (1944). One of his co-workers was Navy Lieutenant Virginia Gerstenfeld, a test engineer and chemist, whom he was to marry in 1948 (after a postwar divorce from his first wife) and who was to be an important influence on his later work, sometimes virtually as a full collaborator.

After World War II, Heinlein tried his hand at several kinds of writing—detective stories, girls' stories, articles warning about the dangers of nuclear war—before settling down to science fiction exclusively. But by 1947, the second period of his science fiction, as well defined chronologically as the first, had already begun. That year he began publishing two series of stories, both glorifying space travel, one goal of the aerospace industry that had emerged from the war. One of these series opened in the *Saturday Evening Post*, thus leading the breakthrough of science fiction into the "slicks." The other, beginning with *Rocket Ship Galileo*, was a best-selling series of juvenile space novels. In 1950, he helped turn *Rocket Ship Galileo* into what is often called the first modern science-fiction movie, *Destination Moon*. His second juvenile novel, *Space Cadet* (1948), became the basis for the first modern science-fiction television serial, *Tom Corbett: Space Cadet*. His tremendous productive burst, begun in 1947, ended in 1959. In this period he published twenty-six short stories, sixteen novels, three extensively revised versions of earlier novels, two screenplays, more than a dozen articles, and uncounted radio and television scripts.

The third well-defined period in Heinlein's writing career began in 1961, with a novel that has sold over two million copies, has created millions of partisans for and against him, and, even without his other works, has established him as a central figure in modern American culture—*Stranger in a Strange Land*. Abandoning the short story, the form that had made him such a dominant presence in science fiction, he

Robert A. Heinlein, L. Sprague de Camp, and Isaac Asimov (left to right) when all three were working on the same floor of the Naval Air Material Center of the Philadelphia Navy Yard between 1942 and 1945. Photo: U.S. Navy, 1944.

now brought forth in quick succession another four controversial novels, ending this new burst of productivity in 1966.

Then came a fourth period, again neatly marked off, consisting of just two massive novels, the first published in 1970, the second in 1973, each generating a fresh storm of enthusiasm and outrage. A fifth period opened, appropriately enough in 1980, with *The Number of the Beast*—, a whimsical apocalypse.

From 1939 on, the major events of Robert Heinlein's biography are the works he was creating in these five distinct periods of his career as an author of science fiction. But these works of science fiction are themselves inseparably intertwined with the major historical events that define the late Depression, the Truman-Eisenhower years, the 1960s, the 1970s, and perhaps the 1980s. These five periods of Robert

Heinlein's creativity, as I shall try to show, can best be understood as five stages of America projected in science fiction.

NOTES

1. *Something about the Author*, ed. Anne Commire (New York: Gale, 1979), Vol. 9, p. 103. Practically all previously published biographical writing on Heinlein has apparently been based almost entirely on his own statements in interviews and brief autobiographical notes for standard reference works. My account is based mostly on original research in primary documents and materials, such as the *City Directory for Kansas City, Missouri*, 1900–1939; U.S. Census Reports; yearbooks from Heinlein's graduating class at Central High School and the United States Naval Academy; birth and marriage certificates; regional histories. This has been augmented through correspondence and interviews, including a day-long interview most graciously granted by Heinlein.

2. *Time Enough for Love* (New York: Berkley Publishing, 1974), pp. 488, 493.

3. Alfred Bester, "PW Interviews: Robert Heinlein," *Publishers Weekly*, July 2, 1973, p. 44.

4. E. F. Bleiler, *Eight Dime Novels* (New York: Dover Publications, 1974), p. vii. My comments on the science-fiction dime novel also owe much to the trailblazing chapter in Sam Moskowitz, *Explorers of the Infinite* (Cleveland: World Publishing, 1963).

5. See Moskowitz, pp. 115–17.

6. *More Junior Authors*, ed. Muriel Fuller (New York: Wilson, 1963), p. 109.

7. Bester, p. 45.

2

FROM DEPRESSION INTO WORLD WAR II: The Early Fiction

"—during the '30's almost everyone, from truck driver
to hatcheck girl, had a scheme for setting the world right
in six easy lessons; and a surprising percentage managed
to get their schemes published."

Robert Heinlein
"The Roads Must Roll," June 1940

In 1938 the atom was split. That did not seem such big news
to many people, for in 1938 the Japanese were extending their
invasion of China, the Italian Fascist army was trying to wipe
out the stubborn partisan resistance in Ethiopia, Franco's
forces opened their decisive offensive against the Loyalist
government of Spain, Franco's ally Adolf Hitler invaded Aus-
tria, and Czechoslovakia was divided up by Germany,
Hungary, and Poland. In early 1939, the Soviet Union crushed
an attempted invasion by Japan. In late 1939, Germany successfully invaded Poland. At some point, World War II had
begun.

Meanwhile, in April of 1939, the New York World's Fair
opened, in futuristic splendor, with visions of "the World of
Tomorrow" presented by hundreds of corporations and
dozens of states and countries. The Long Island Railroad
promised to take you there swiftly from Manhattan: "From the
World of Today to the World of Tomorrow in ten minutes for
ten cents." Four months later, in a world plunging from the
Great Depression into a global holocaust, *Astounding Science-
Fiction* printed Robert Heinlein's first story.

Heinlein's first three published stories are all celebrations of the individual genius—lonely, misunderstood, but leading humanity forward to new frontiers of time and space. This lone superior individual, alienated but true to his own unprecedented destiny, is to become the central character-type of Heinlein's fiction for the next third of a century.

The hero of "Life-Line" (August 1939), his first story, is Dr. Hugo Pinero, the kind of lonely scientific genius who had haunted the pages of nineteenth-century science fiction from Victor Frankenstein through H. G. Well's Time Traveller. Pinero has invented a marvelous machine that determines with chilling accuracy the time of a person's death. Ridiculed by the scientific establishment, but hailed by the media as "The Miracle Man from Nowhere," he sets up a lucrative business, "Sands of Time, Inc.," so successful that it begins to threaten the profits of the giant insurance corporations.

Determined to crush the little upstart, Amalgamated Life Insurance attempts to destroy Dr. Pinero's business with an injunction. But they encounter a judge who delivers a most revealing lecture, obviously expressing the views of Robert Heinlein, whose family's farm-equipment business had been superseded by an emerging monopoly and whose own recent small-business ventures had been unable to compete, in this era of life-and-death struggle between corporate monopoly and small enterprise. This judge denounces the "strange doctrine" that because a "corporation has made a profit out of the public for a number of years, the government and the courts are charged with the duty of guaranteeing such profit in the future, even in the face of changing circumstances and contrary to public interest."* He denies the demand of Amalgamated Life Insurance "that the clock of history be stopped, or turned back."

Like many in his social class, Heinlein clung tenaciously to the belief that the main vehicle of progress was free enterprise, a vehicle sometimes willfully sabotaged by the giant

---

* Unless otherwise noted, all references are to the original publication, as identified in the text. Page references will not be given for short stories. For longer works published in serial form, page references will be given parenthetically and will include month and page number; where it will be more convenient for the readers, and where no ambiguity will be thus created, references will be made by chapter number.

corporations. This is an overt theme in several of his stories during this period. In "Life-Line," Amalgamated Life Insurance shows its true nature after it is frustrated in court: it hires gangsters who carry out their assignment of murdering Dr. Pinero and wrecking his wonderful equipment. Then the leading scientists, earlier labeled by Pinero the "Barbarians! Imbeciles!" who "have blocked the recognition of every great discovery since time began," fulfill their part on the job by burning all the documentary evidence of Pinero's brilliant results.

Although the corporations and the academic establishment are the main enemy of the lone genius in "Life-Line," Pinero expresses as much scorn for "the little man in the street" as for "you little men" of the Academy of Science. Yet despite all this exaltation of rugged individualism, there is a detectable countercurrent: a yearning to be part of a collective, a yearning so intense that it threatens to overwhelm individual identity. Pinero's theory and his machine are based on the assumption that each individual life is a continuity in space-time that can be compared to "a long pink worm, continuous through the years." In explaining his theory, Pinero argues that these pink worms are not, despite all appearance to the contrary, really discrete individuals:

> "As a matter of fact there is a physical continuity in this concept to the entire race, for these pink worms branch off from other pink worms. In this fashion the race is like a vine whose branches intertwine and send out shoots. Only by taking a cross-section of the vine would we fall into the error of believing that the shootlets were discrete individuals."

This sense of the individual as part of a human collective, organically joined to a death-defying timeless racial identity, is the other side of an unresolved contradiction that branches throughout all of Heinlein's work.

"Misfit," Heinlein's second story, published in *Astounding* in November 1939, dramatizes the lone genius as a kind of ugly duckling who, unlike Dr. Pinero, achieves acceptance in the human family. Like "Life-Line," "Misfit" can also be read as a product of the Depression. In fact, its teenaged hero, Andrew Jackson Libby, is recruited into a twenty-second-century version of the New Deal's Civilian Conservation Corps. This

C.C.C. of the future is the Cosmic Construction Corps, employing young misfits to convert asteroids into space stations. Libby, "a thin, gangling, blond lad," turns out to be a supergenius. When the ballistic calculator fails at a crucial moment, Libby takes its place, saving the mission. Like the nineteenth-century science-fiction dime novel, "Misfit" allows its readers to identify with a boy genius who wins the admiration and gratitude of the adult world.

The first of Heinlein's stories with a juvenile hero, "Misfit" foreshadows his juvenile novels of 1947–58.[1] In fact, *Starman Jones* (1953) has an extended replay of Libby's superhuman computations in space. The figure of Libby himself continues to haunt Heinlein's imagination and to appeal to his readers. In *Methuselah's Children* (1941) Libby singlehandedly invents and builds the "space drive" that allows trips into deep space, in this and many later tales. In *Time Enough for Love* (1973) one of the ritual quests performed by the novel's deathless mythic hero is to voyage backward in time to bury the orbiting body of his old friend Andrew Jackson Libby. In *The Number of the Beast*—(1980) Libby is resurrected as a beautiful woman, Elizabeth Andrew Jackson Libby Long, cloned from his original body and preserving his memory.

"Misfit" also introduces another theme of growing importance in Heinlein's later fiction: love and interchangeability between a human being and a thinking machine. Libby is assigned to the ballistic calculator, "three tons of thinking metal." The emotional response of this boy who had never felt "needed" is intense: "He loved the big machine. . . . Libby subconsciously thought of it as a person—his own kind of person."

The lone genius in Heinlein's third story, "Requiem" (*Astounding*, January 1940), is Delos D. Harriman, an old man about to die. Bearing the name of the nineteenth-century railroad magnate, Harriman is the crafty, visionary, ruthless, heroic capitalist who has (as we learn in a later story) almost singlehandedly built "the Company" that all by itself explored and colonized the moon; he has also created the Harriman Foundation which finances space travel in many later tales. Prohibited by rules laid down by the bureaucracy of "this damn paternalistic government" and his own company from traveling to the moon, Harriman nevertheless roguishly buys his final trip to die on that remote place of his youthful dreams.

In describing these dreams, Harriman eloquently paints a picture of the boys and young men who made pre-World War II science fiction—both those who read it and those who wrote it. This picture is a wonderful self-portrait of Robert Heinlein:

". . . I believed—I believed. I read Verne and Wells and Smith, and I believed that we could do it—that we *would* do it. I set my heart on being one of the men to walk the surface of the Moon, to see her other side, and to look back on the face of the Earth, hanging in the sky."

". . . I just wanted to live a long time and see it all happen. I wasn't unusual; there were lots of boys like me—radio hams, they were, and telescope builders, and airplane amateurs. We had science clubs, and basement laboratories, and science-fiction leagues—the kind of boys that thought there was more romance in one issue of the *Electrical Experimenter* than in all the books Dumas ever wrote. We didn't want to be one of Horatio Alger's get-rich heroes either; we wanted to build space ships."

For these technologically oriented boys and men, stimulated by the visions of science fiction, technology tends to be the focus of romance, love, and even sex. Harriman's wife "had not shared his dream and his need." As he dozes on his voyage to the moon, he imagines her voice calling "Delos! Come in from there! You'll catch your death of cold in that night air." The ship itself seems more alluring: "He noted with a professional eye that she was a single-jet type with fractional controls around her midriff." He scans her controls "lovingly"; "Each beloved gadget was in its proper place. He knew them—graven in his heart." On the voyage he finds himself between two sensual beauties:

The Moon swung majestically past the viewport, twice as wide as he had ever seen it before, all of her familiar features cameo-clear. She gave way to the Earth as the ship continued its slow swing, the Earth itself, as he had envisioned her, appearing like a noble moon, eight times as wide as the Moon appears to the Earthbound, and more luscious, more sensuously beautiful than the silver Moon could be.

Throughout Heinlein's fiction, Earth is beautiful only when viewed from a distance, when people and their civilization cannot be seen.

Despite the vision of "the World of Tomorrow" projected by the 1939 World's Fair, the Depression had shattered the dreams of millions of Americans. Looking back, we can see that this economic catastrophe signaled the collapse of the free-enterprise system, which was rapidly being replaced by monopoly and state capitalism as the dominant form of the American political economy. Robert Heinlein's social and political outlook was shaped within this historical drama. Again and again throughout his writing career, we see him posing the old beliefs in "free trade" and "free enterprise" against the growing monopolies and bureaucracies of the giant corporations and the state controlled by these impersonal forces.

In the pre-World War II stories, the struggle often takes the classic form of the small businessman, the inventor, or the small factory owner fighting directly against the corporate monopolies, which sometimes are seen as already dominating the government. Two striking examples are stories published in 1940, " 'Let There Be Light' " and "The Devil Makes the Law," the first a hard-core science-fiction tale published in the May issue of *Super Science Stories*, the second a wild fantasy published in the September *Unknown*.

The hero of " 'Let There Be Light' " is Dr. Archie Douglas, a young physicist doing research in a laboratory set up in the factory owned by his father. While awaiting a visit from the illustrious biologist Doctor M. L. Martin, Archie tries to pick up a beautiful blonde with a "dumb pan" and a figure like fan-dancer Sally Rand's. She turns out to be the famous M. L. Martin ("Mary Lou to her friends") and Heinlein's first significant female character.

Mary Lou, who has been experimenting with the biology of fireflies, teams up with Archie to invent a device to turn electric power into light with minimum power loss. Then Archie's father explains that he is about to be driven out of business by the utility monopoly, which has "bought" both houses of the legislature "body and soul" in order to keep exploiting "power that actually belongs to the people." So the two geniuses reverse their process and invent a solar power generator, promising "Free power! Riches for everybody!"

Now they have to struggle against the monopoly, whose political and economic power is explained to naïve Archie by worldly-wise Mary Lou, who cites the preface to George Bernard Shaw's *Back to Methuselah*[2] in describing "the combined power of corporate industry to resist any change that might threaten their dividends." She tells of the ruthless methods industry uses to suppress inventions, including the super carburetor (an American folk legend that I personally have heard from at least a dozen mechanics in different sections of the country), and of the commitment of American industry to produce commodities "just as bad as the market will stand" so that they will wear out as soon as possible. Using feminine wiles to massage his male ego, she attributes their inventions solely to him and warns that "You threaten the whole industrial set-up."

Since they cannot safely profit from the inventions, Mary Lou proposes that they release the secret to everybody: "Free power! You'll be the new emancipator." So finally the theme of the lone Promethean genius is blazoned forth in a newspaper headline: "GENIUS GRANTS GRATIS POWER TO PUBLIC." The publicly acclaimed GENIUS of course is Archie, who now persaudes Mary Lou to marry him "to make an honest man of me." It is interesting to note that the anti-monopoly if not downright anti-capitalist message of this story is expounded by Mary Lou, who allows her own scientific and practical roles to be concealed from the public, and that the story is the first Heinlein published under a pseudonym (Lyle Monroe), thus concealing his own identity from the public.

"The Devil Makes the Law" is, as its title suggests, an allegory. The setting is a typical American town where, as elsewhere in this fantastic world, all the businessmen routinely use magic in their trades, manufacture, and professions. The protagonist is another Archie, Archibald Fraser, Merchant and Contractor in the construction business. His small business, like all the others in town, is threatened by a ruthless monopoly named Magic, Inc. When the businessmen take their struggle to the statehouse, an old "mass of masonry" which "seemed to represent something tough in the character of the American people, the determination of free men to manage their own affairs," they are dismayed to discover that Magic, Inc. is already in control of their own state government and those of other states across the country.

Archie and his friends—including a small manufacturer who uses witches to produce the garments made in his factory, an African witch-doctor, and a fiercely independent old witch-lady—are forced to take their fight directly to the source of this infernal monopolistic conspiracy: Hell itself. There, with the help of an FBI agent working for the anti-monopoly division and disguised as a demon, they unmask and defeat the boss of the monopoly, one of Satan's own lieutenants.

Heinlein's loathing of monopoly develops into the most radically "left" story of his career, "Logic of Empire," published in *Astounding* in March 1941. Here, as in much of his post-World War II fiction, "the Company" has stretched beyond Earth to become an enormous interplanetary monopoly, tyrannizing over farflung colonies which are moving toward a replay of the 1776 American Revolution.

The story begins with two prosperous gentlemen, lawyer Humphrey Wingate and his wealthy friend Sam Houston Jones, whom Wingate accuses of being a "parlor pink," drinking and arguing about whether the "labor clients" of the Venus Development Company are actually slaves. Wingate vociferously champions the Company, with its "obligations to its stockholders," and condemns the lazy workers, "a class of people that feel that the world owes them a living." The argument ends in a drunken decision to sign a contract for six years of indentured labor on Venus, and they wake up incarcerated in a spaceship.

Heinlein then dramatizes the conditions of labor on Venus as a combination of indentured labor in the eighteenth-century American colonies, Black chattel slavery on nineteenth-century American plantations, and wage slavery and debt peonage in the factories and on the farms of twentieth-century America. Once off the spaceship that resembles a slave ship, the "clients" are sold to "patrons" in a slave auction. As soon as Wingate, our point-of-view character, begins laboring on a plantation, the narrative begins to sound like a future version of nineteenth-century narratives of escaped slaves, such as the *Narrative of the Life of Frederick Douglass, An American Slave*. There are overseers, an addictive drink used to narcotize the slaves, and even threats made against recalcitrant slaves "to sell you South" to more "factory-like plantations."

Cover design by Hubert Rogers for "Logic of Empire."

Technically, the status of the Company's "labor clients" most closely resembles a combination of the conditions of the two main groups of workers in pre-World War II America: the debt peonage characteristic of the majority of Black rural workers and the wage slavery typical of mine and factory labor.

Wingate discovers "that while he was free theoretically to
quit, it was freedom to starve on Venus, unless he first worked
out his bounty and his passage both ways."

Even more devastating is Wingate's discovery that the conditions of labor are deadening his consciousness; in a passage
echoing Frederick Douglass's picture of his own degradation,
Wingate realizes that "he was becoming one of the broken
men," whose mind is relaxing into "slave psychology." And
like Douglass, Wingate reawakens the freedom of his mind by
resolving upon bold action based on the belief that "No slave
is ever freed, *save he free himself.*" So he and two other slaves
attack their owner and escape.

The fugitives discover one of the "runaway slave camps,"
where they gain admittance by identifying themselves with
the code name "Fellow travelers." This turns out to be the
first of many examples in Heinlein's works of a vigorous frontier cultural outpost, the antithesis of the decadent monopolistic tyrannies of Earth. This "rough frontier culture" gives
Wingate still another course in his re-education. He is surprised to find "that fugitive slaves, the scum of Earth," were
able to build a viable society, just as "it had surprised his ancestors that the transported criminals of Botany Bay should
develop a high civilization in Australia."

Wingate, now almost totally awakened to social reality,
begins writing "a political pamphlet against the colonial system." He then encounters a character soon to be familiar to
Heinlein readers, a cranky old mouthpiece for the author, in
this case a university professor fired for his political views
(under a pretext very similar to Stanford University's for firing
Thorstein Veblen). "Doc" ridicules Wingate's "devil
theory"—although the pamphlet seems tame compared with
"The Devil Makes the Law"—explaining that "bankers,"
"company officials," "patrons," and "the governing classes
back on Earth" are not "scoundrels" but products of social
necessity and their own class outlook: "Men are constrained
by necessity, and then build up rationalizations to account for
their acts." Doc gives Wingate a key lesson in Heinlein's economic theory: "Colonial slavery is nothing new; it is the in-
variable result of imperial expansion, the automatic result of
an antiquated financial structure—." Later, back on Earth, this

message is reiterated by Sam Houston Jones, who has bought himself and Wingate out of slavery:

> "I've been wondering how long it would take you to get your eyes opened. . . . It's nothing new; it happened in the Old South, it happened again in California, in Mexico, in Australia, in South Africa. Why? Because in any expanding free-enterprise economy which does not have a money system designed to fit its requirements the use of mother-country capital to develop the colony inevitably results in subsistence-level wages at home and slave labor in the colonies."

Finally, Wingate, who has renounced "the empty, sterile bunkum-fed life of the fat and prosperous class he had moved among and served," realizes his inability to produce another *Uncle Tom's Cabin* or *Grapes of Wrath* and seems resigned to Sam's pronouncement that "Things are bound to get a whole lot worse before they can get any better."

Tacked on to the end of "Logic of Empire" is a note from editor John Campbell, informing readers of *Astounding* that "all of Robert Heinlein's stories are based on a common proposed future history of the world." Two months later, in May 1941, *Astounding* printed Heinlein's chart of this future history. Modeled on the charts of macrohistory included in Olaf Stapledon's *Last and First Men* (1930), and sharing Stapledon's vision of a spiral of progress moving upward through cyclical rises and falls, Heinlein's chart provided a framework for much of his prewar fiction, an independent display of his historical ideology, and a new pleasure for his growing throng of readers, who could now anticipate the missing pieces of the puzzle. Campbell's introductory essay, "History To Come," perceptively noted what many subsequent critics have agreed is the most engaging quality of Heinlein's fictions of the future: their sense of being "lived-in," as opposed to the "stage setting" environments of stories that have to create their future environments from scratch. Heinlein's fans thus had the comfort of entering a somewhat familiar projected history where they could recognize an occasional old friend, while at the same time experiencing the thrill of the unexpected.

Heinlein made minor revisions of this chart of future history until 1967, adding new tales as they were written and occasionally deleting an old one. Most of the stories sub-

sequently included were published before World War II; those
eventually added or subtracted made no fundamental change,
except to delete references to all years before 1975 and to ex-
tend the future from 2140 to 2600. The principal addition was
a cluster of nine short stories, published between 1947 and
1950, sketching the early days of space exploration shortly
before and after the year 2000. Most of the Future History was
published in three volumes: *The Man Who Sold the Moon*
(1950), *The Green Hills of Earth* (1951), and *Revolt in 2100*
(1953). In 1967, Heinlein published *The Past Through Tomorrow*, billed as the "Future History Stories Complete in One
Volume," and including a publisher's note telling how "Heinlein created a gigantic chart—filling an entire wall of his
study—to keep track of his future world and the progress of its
peoples and civilizations." The latest revised chart is published in each collection.

Besides itemizing and dating the stories, the chart draws
the "life-lines" of some of the characters, prophesies technical
development, and provides sociological summaries of the
main events in human history for the next centuries. Other
works loosely interconnect with the projected future. Gaps are
filled in by a postscript to *Revolt in 2100* called "Concerning
Stories Never Written" and by the novel *Time Enough for
Love*. From the 1941 chart to the latest revision in 1967, the
outline of the Future History remains consistent.

In the immediate future lies the "Collapse of Empire" and
"the CRAZY YEARS" of the middle twentieth century: "Consid-
erable technical advance during this period, accompanied by a
gradual deterioration of mores, orientation, and social institutions, terminating in mass psychoses in the sixth decade, and
the Interregnum." Then comes the strike of 1960, the "FALSE
DAWN" of 1960–70, with the first rocket reaching the moon in
1978: "The Interregnum was followed by a period of reconstruction in which the Voorhis financial proposals gave a temporary economic stability and a chance for re-orientation. This
was ended by the opening of new frontiers and a return to
nineteenth-century economy." This crucial quest in Heinlein's
fiction—for "new frontiers" that will lead back to free-
enterprise capitalism—is embodied in the Future History conception by Harriman's Lunar Corporation, the foundation of

Luna City, and the development of the "PERIOD OF IMPERIAL EX-PLOITATION, 1970–2020." But "the short period of interplanetary imperialism" is ended by three revolutions: Antarctica, the United States, and Venus.

Viewed in the context of the Future History, "Logic of Empire" can be read as a study of the conditions that lead to revolution. At the close of "Logic of Empire," Sam Houston Jones foresees the rise of "a rabble-rousing political preacher like this fellow Nehemiah Scudder" to overthrow the technocratic monopolies. This important event in the Future History is loosely sketched in "Concerning Stories Never Written." Scudder's revolt leads to a religious dictatorship in the United States, outlined in the Future History chart: "Little research and only minor technical advances during this period. Extreme puritanism. Certain aspects of psychodynamics and psychometrics, mass psychology and social control developed by the priest class."

Those words describe the scene at the opening of Heinlein's first long fiction, " 'If This Goes On—' " (*Astounding*, February, March 1940). The former United States is now under a theocratic dictatorship, headed by the latest incarnation of the Prophet, crushed under the weight of a vast military apparatus, and suppressed by omnipresent secret police, religious zealots employing hypnosis, torture, drugs, and the very latest methods of scientific thought control. Here is a perfect setting for Heinlein to explore what has long been one of his central themes: the relation between cultural conditioning and the possibility of human freedom.

If consciousness is determined by being, including the constantly reinforced values of a particular society or social class—and Heinlein sees all this as fairly obvious—then how is it possible for an individual, a social class, or a people to have true freedom, which depends upon the ability to transcend conditioning in order to arrive at true or at least accurate perception? In "Logic of Empire," Humphrey Wingate was thrown bodily into the social class whose existence he had so radically misunderstood, and he thus came to transcend the false consciousness of his own affluent class. Heinlein chooses as protagonist and narrator of " 'If This Goes On—' " a stolid, loyal, naïve young graduate of West Point, assigned to guard duty near the center of government at New Jerusalem. The story of the revolution is unfolded through the developing revolutionary consciousness of this one young man, John Lyle. But the problem remains, as we shall see, whether such a radical transformation of perception is possible for the people of the nation.

John Lyle falls in love with Judith, a nun-like Virgin about to be despoiled by the lascivious arch-hypocrite Prophet. It is this romantic attachment that literally drags Lyle to his initiation into the underground revolutionary Cabal. He rescues Judith, resists torture because the Cabal had hypnotically prepared him for it, assumes a new identity, escapes arrest, becomes the chief of staff of the commander in chief in the Cabal's enormous underground general headquarters, and takes command of the final victorious assault on New Jerusalem. Then at the end John Lyle decides to become a common citizen in the new system, marrying Judith and becoming a partner in a textile wholesaling firm.

Lyle had learned the truth about the dictatorship through his personal involvement at its evil core and through a long, intensive re-education administered to him by the Cabal. But what of the mass of orinary citizens, exposed from birth to a profound superscientific conditioning to accept their slave status under the holy and omnipotent state? How are they to become convinced that all they had believed is false?

This problem is posed directly by a member of the technological elite running the revolution, the "chief of psychodynamics," who argues that " 'We can seize power, but we cannot hold it!' ":

"Remember, my brothers, no people was ever held long in subjugation save through their own consent. The American people have been conditioned from the cradle by the cleverest and most thorough psychotechnicians in the world to believe in and trust the dictatorship which rules them. Since the suppression of our ancient civil liberties during the lifetime of the first Prophet, only the most daring and individual minds have broken loose from the taboos and superstitions that were instilled in their subconscious minds. If you free them without adequate psychological preparation, like horses led from a burning barn, they will return to their accustomed place." [March, p. 134]

John Lyle, hero of " 'If This Goes On—,' " is admitted into the ranks of the underground revolutionary Cabal. Drawing by Hubert Rogers in *Astounding*, February 1940.

This is the same problem faced by Hank Morgan in Mark Twain's *A Connecticut Yankee in King Arthur's Court*, when he attempts to establish a capitalist industrial republic amidst the religious darkness of feudal England. It is also one of the central problems of twentieth-century socialist revolution, which attempts to establish a new form of society, often in lands dominated by the most backward beliefs and most pervasive thought control, such as Russia in 1917, China in 1949, Cuba in 1959.

In " 'If This Goes On—' " Heinlein presents a solution to this intricate problem, one "concocted" by the technological geniuses in the "psychodynamics" section of the Cabal. This plan "to change the psychological conditioning of the people and make them aware that they really had been saved from a tyranny which had ruled by keeping them in ignorance, their minds chained" provides for "readjusting the people to freedom of thought and freedom of action" under the direction of the men from psychodynamics:

> They planned nothing less than mass reorientation under hypnosis. The technique was simple, as simple as works of genius usually are. [March, p. 141]

All that is involved is placing the masses of people under hypnosis and showing them an extremely sophisticated propaganda film. The technique had already been tested, and found "usually" successful:

> Usually it had worked, and the subjects were semantically readjusted to a modern nondogmatic viewpoint, but if the subject was too old mentally, if his thought processes were too thoroughly canalized, it sometimes destroyed one set of evaluations without providing him with a new set. The subject might come out of the hypnosis with an overpowering sense of insecurity which usually degenerated into schizophrenia, involute melancholia, or other psychoses involving loss of cortical control and consequent thalamic and subthalamic anarchy.

So the forces of the Cabal " 'had our work cut out for us!' ":

> More than a hundred million persons had to be examined to see if they could stand up under quick re-orientation, then re-examined after treatment to see if they had been sufficiently readjusted. Until a man passed the second examination we could not afford to enfranchise him as a free citizen of a democratic state. [March, p. 141]

There is not the slightest suggestion of the monstrous possibilities inherent in the technological elite's determining who thinks correctly enough to be allowed to vote, and no hint of irony in Lyle's description of their colossal task: "We had to teach them to think for themselves, reject dogma, be suspicious of authority, tolerate differences of opinion, and make

their own decisions—types of mental processes almost unknown in the United States for many generations."

Thirteen years after the original publication of " 'If This
Goes On—' " Heinlein revised it extensively for publication in
Revolt in 2100. In the new version a cantankerous old man
from Vermont, who looked like "an angry Mark Twain,"
arises to denounce the proposed mind-conditioning technique:

> "Free men aren't 'conditioned'! Free men are free because they
> are ornery and cussed and prefer to arrive at their own preju-
> dices in their own way—not have them spoonfed by a self-
> appointed mind tinkerer! We haven't fought, our brethren
> haven't bled and died, just to change bosses, no matter how
> sweet their motives."[3]

He goes on, articulating ideas that in the original version had
been presented by the head of psychodynamics in a postscript:

> "I tell you, we got into the mess we are in through the efforts
> of those same mind tinkerers. They've studied for years how to
> saddle a man and ride him. They started with advertising and
> propaganda and things like that, and they perfected it to the
> point where what used to be simple, honest swindling such as
> any salesman might use became a mathematical science that
> left the ordinary man helpless."

When challenged to provide a solution, this new avatar of
Mark Twain advocates simply restoring the old civil liberties
and the franchise to everybody: " 'If they mess it up again,
that's their doing—but we have no right to operate on their
minds.' " This position certainly seems less dangerous than
the one Heinlein had presented without challenge in the 1940
version. However, it merely evades the central problem of this
revolution, which according to the logic of the story itself
should not be able to succeed and certainly should not be able
to establish a new society capable of resisting the very forces
that had originally established the tyranny. Heinlein barely
covers the confusion by having the old man dramatically drop
dead and the Cabal then immediately accept his position. For
he remains stuck on the horns of an awkward dilemma that
grows from seeing only two choices: either have the elite in-
doctrinate the people into correct thinking or just pretend that

the problem will solve itself. The last words on the subject come from John Lyle: "I don't know who was right."[4]

This basic political and philosophic problem will reappear in many forms throughout Heinlein's works, for he will continue to see essentially just two alternatives: either the elite (the *good* elite) saves the day, which obviously contradicts democratic principles he sometimes espouses, or society succumbs to the ignorance and folly of the masses of common people. His concept of revolutionary social change imagines something created *by* an elite *for* the benefit of the people, usually quite temporarily. He seems incapable of believing that progressive social change could come through the development of the productive forces and consequent action by the exploited classes themselves. Thus Heinlein places himself consistently in direct opposition to the most powerful forces of social change in the twentieth century.

According to the chart of the Future History, the elite revolution we witness in " 'If This Goes On—' " does succeed in establishing "THE FIRST HUMAN CIVILIZATION," a society implicit in the sequel, "Coventry" (*Astounding*, July 1940). The new society is based on "the Covenant," a social "contract" guaranteeing "the maximum possible liberty for every person." The Covenant forbids "no possible act, nor mode of conduct" as long as the action does not "damage" another individual. Those who violate the Covenant are not punished; they are allowed to choose between undergoing "psychological readjustment" to remove their tendency to injure other people or being sent to Coventry, a bountiful land reserved for those who refuse to accept the Covenant.

Heinlein's story does not show us life in this rational libertarian utopia, although we learn that science has provided an extremely high standard of living, social harmony prevails, while "danger and adventure" are still available: "there is danger still in experimental laboratories; there is hardship in the mountains of the Moon, and death in the jungles of Venus." Instead Heinlein shows us life in the tooth-and-claw world of Coventry, the land of exile.

The faith in rugged individualism preached in much of Heinlein's post-World War II writing is here the object of scathing attack. The arrogant, conceited protagonist, David

"If This Goes On...," by Robert Heinlein

The final victorious assault on the religious dictatorship's stronghold. Cover design for " 'If This Goes On—' " by Hubert Rogers.

MacKinnon, refuses to accept the mutual obligations that constitute society, yet he whines that society should guarantee him some private property in Coventry. The guard at the Barrier to Coventry scorns him and the other such "rugged indi-

vidualists": " 'You've turned down our type of social co-
operation; why the hell should you expect the safeguards of
our organization?' " As he approaches the gate to Coventry,
deluding himself with his quest for a "Crusoe-like independence," MacKinnon fails to realize that even his personal pos-
sessions are the end products of "the cumulative effort and intelligent co-operation" of many people, living and dead.
What he finds in Coventry is a lawless social jungle of
vicious predators, as well as a conspiracy to overthrow the society of the Covenant. MacKinnon speedily learns his lesson.
He absorbs the virtues of self-sacrifice, and "cures himself" by
becoming responsible to an old man known as Fader (father?)
and to society. Fader turns out to be an undercover agent of
the Covenant society, and he and MacKinnon each manage to
return there with warnings of the dangerous plot brewing in
Coventry.

A similar message appears in "The Roads Must Roll" (Astounding, June 1940), set in 1970, the period of the "FALSE
DAWN" in the Future History. Automobiles have now been
replaced by high-speed rolling roads with their own restau-
rants and stores. The skilled workers who man the great underground apparatus powering the roads follow the leadership of a monomaniac who asks "why we technicians don't
just take things over." Heinlein denounces his ideology, developed from "the Bible of the Functionalist movement," a
treatise "published in 1930," "dressed up with a glib mechanistic pseudopsychology" and proclaiming that those with the
most indispensable function in advanced industrial society
ought to be its masters. The fallacy, as Heinlein notes, is that
in modern society many different functions are indispensable:
"The complete interdependence of modern economic life
seems to have escaped him entirely."

The other Future History story set in this period is
"Blowups Happen" (Astounding, September 1940), predicting
"the most dangerous machine in the world—an atomic power
plant." Here too the main theme is social responsibility. With
so much "responsibility for the lives of other people" in their
hands, the atomic engineers in the plant must be selected for
their "sense of social responsibility" and then they must be
ceaselessly observed by the finest psychiatrists. Even so, there

*"If you want to return, signal at the booth on the other side of the Barrier
—but be prepared to change your personality,"* the guard called after him.

David MacKinnon about to leave the society of the Covenant in "Coventry."
Drawing by Orban in *Astounding*, July 1940.

emerges the statistical inevitability of a catastrophic—perhaps
world-destroying—accident. The only solution, to place the
main power plant in orbit, is vigorously fought by the profit-
hungry Board of Directors of the Company (who talk just like
the management of the Three Mile Island nuclear power plant
which came close to a meltdown in 1979). But even they are
eventually pressured into accepting a socially responsible
role, the breeder reactor is on its way into orbit, and the
human race is on its way into space, in ships to be powered by
nuclear fuel.

" '—We Also Walk Dogs' " (Astounding, July 1941) was
later included in the Future History chart, someplace around
the year 2000. It is the tale of General Services, Inc., "the handy-
man of the last century, gone speedlined and corporate,"
doing anything its customers ask for, though disdaining "the
richly idle" who provide most of the business. Yet even the
superefficient operators of General Services, who can arrange
to have a lone genius invent an anti-gravity shield on order,
become lost in adoring contemplation of the timeless beauty
of the Flower of Forgetfulness, a Ming bowl they have lifted
from the British Museum.

The climax of the Future History comes in Methuselah's
Children (Astounding, July, August, September 1941), which
begins with the disruption of the Covenant society in the year
2125, traces Heinlein's history back through all the other Future History stories to a key event in 1874, and ends with the
"beginning of the first mature culture" in the middle of the
twenty-second century.

Back in 1874, a rich old man, fearing death, establishes the
Howard Foundation, designed to breed a strain of humans
with extreme longevity. The result is the Howard Families,
who clandestinely build their own culture in the United
States during the next two and a half centuries until they
number over a hundred thousand individuals, led by 183-
year-old Mary Risling (revised to Mary Sperling in the 1958
edition and the sequel, Time Enough for Love). The Families
have decided to reveal their existence to the larger society,
resulting in a frenzy of vicious envy that sweeps aside the
Covenant and launches a pogrom aimed at extracting the alleged "secret" of longevity by any means, including the Inqui-
sition of the old religious dictatorship.

The engineer stopped at the order. So, the psychologist had decided he was unstable—mad.

The inside of the atomic power plant as imagined in "Blowups Happen."
Drawing by Schneeman in *Astounding*, September 1940.

Although the individuals in the Families are supposedly of superior intelligence, richly enhanced by extraordinarily long and varied experience, we see most of them incapable of confronting this crisis and acting like "bird-brained dopes" (July, p. 42). So on one hand we witness the citizens of the most humane, rational, libertarian, and scientifically advanced society suddenly metamorphose into a ruthless, snarling horde of beasts, merely because some other people have attained longevity; while on the other hand we see a subsociety, allegedly superior to this superior society (not to mention such inferiors as us), behaving like sheep.

Since, according to Heinlein, the majority of people are incapable of determining their own collective action rationally, there can be only one solution: wise leaders must arise to manipulate the masses for their own good. As the crisis begins to unfold, a new leader of the Families suddenly appears: the most characteristic, enduring, and revealing of all Heinlein's heroes, the daring, individualistic, shrewd, tough, brilliant, resourceful swashbuckler born in 1912 as Woodrow Wilson Smith and now calling himself Lazarus Long.

The wise leader on the other side turns out to be the chief Administrator of the Covenant society, Slayton Ford, a genius at organization (as his last name suggests). Lazarus Long concocts a plan, secretly accepted by Slayton Ford, that decides the fate of the Families. Long's plan is to commandeer an enormous interstellar spaceship and transport every single member of the Families—without their consent—to some planet to be discovered beyond our solar system. Before Ford hears this plan, he himself reluctantly comes to the conclusion that there can be no solution to the problem posed by the existence of the Families, either on Earth or on any planet of our sun:

> The only matter as yet unsettled in his mind was the question of whether simply to sterilize all members of the Howard Families or to kill them outright. Either solution would do, but which was the more humane? [July, pp. 41–42]

These are not the thoughts, mind you, of some sinister maniac, but the calm reflections of a man who is later to be chosen for his wisdom and political incisiveness as the administrative leader of the Families themselves. Nor are these thoughts being published in an historical vacuum. This passage appeared in July 1941, while similar speculations about a "final solution" to the problem posed by the people of a subculture were being considered by the leaders of Germany, Bulgaria, Rumania, Hungary, and the other fascist powers. Heinlein himself had already explored, in 1940, the helplessness of the Jews in the concentration camps, as well as the genocidal urges of Adolf Hitler and Nazism, in the short story "Heil!" (*Futuria Fantasia*, Summer 1940). Zyclon-B, the gas eventually used in the death camps, was already being manufactured by Dow-Badische, the German branch of the Dow Chemical combine.

Ford accepts Long's plan with relief, but a practical question remains: How can all one hundred thousand people of the Families be kept safely in one place until the spaceship is stolen? As the summary in the August 1941 *Astounding* puts it: "But Long points out that the people of Earth will have to be deceived, or they won't release the Families. The Families must be deceived, or they won't have the necessary swift action and unanimity of movement." Long comes up with the brilliant solution: Ford is to carry out a "mass arrest" of all the Families and place them in a "concentration camp"! (August, pp. 64, 68).

The spaceship, duly stolen by Lazarus and most aptly named the *New Frontiers*, is soon off to the stars with all hundred thousand people, powered by a "space drive" singlehandedly invented—and built—by Andrew Jackson ("Slipstick") Libby, the calculating genius of "Misfit." "The work to be done is too urgent" for elections or other democratic social organization, so "democracy will have to wait on expediency" (August, p. 90). Slayton Ford, with them as a fugitive for his role in the adventure, now becomes their head of internal organization, in charge of a mass "indoctrination campaign" (p. 91), while overall dictatorial authority is invested in the Captain, aptly named Rufus King. Heinlein, with all his love of the first American Revolution, constantly seems drawn back toward the monarchy, at least aboard ship.

Eventually they land on an Earth-like planet inhabited by the Jockaira, a "completely gregarious" race. Everything is

fine until they discover that the Jockaira are under the rule of
mysterious superhumans they call "the gods," making them
domesticated animals in contrast with the wild beings from
Earth. The "gods" literally lift the Families from the planet
and send them, using inscrutable forces, thirty-two light years
away to a park-like Edenic planet with placid seas, low hills,
and calm breezes, inhabited by a race of Little People, apparently gentle, loving telepaths.

The Little People, who seem to be "simply Mother Nature's children, living in a Garden of Eden" (September, p.
147), see no need for buildings, machines, agriculture. "Why
struggle so for that which the good soil gives freely?," they
ask, and point to many trees bearing Earth's foods, indicating
"to eat therefrom" (pp. 146–47). But in fact they are another
kind of superior being, "masters in the manipulation of life
forms" (p. 148). Though individually they resemble "mor-
ons," it turns out that "the basic unit of their society was a
telepathic rapport group of many parts" and "collectively,
each rapport group constituted a genius which threw the best
minds the Earthmen had to offer into the shade" (pp. 148,
152). These group minds (derived from Olaf Stapledon's *Last
and First Men* and *Star Maker*), able to produce scientific mar-
vels "with a degree of co-operation quite foreign to men," are
a challenge to the human essence, as conceived by Heinlein.
In searching for an apt comparison, Heinlein again reveals the
outlook of his own social class, in his own society, during the
late Depression years when the doom of small enterprise and
perhaps of the entire system of free-enterprise capitalism was
daily becoming more clear. Lazarus thus muses as he confronts the obvious superiority of the Little People:

> Human beings could not hope to compete with that type of or-
> ganization any more than a back-room shop can compete with
> a factory assembly line. Yet to surrender to any such group
> identity, even if they could, would be, he felt sure, to give up
> whatever it was that made them men. [p. 152]

The Families reject and abandon this communal Eden created
by collective hyper-science; as Oliver Schmidt puts it, " 'I
want to *work* for my living.' "

A few, however, such as Mary Risling, are seduced into
"choosing nirvana—selflessness," marrying into one of the

Little People's groups, "drowning" their "personality in the ego of the many." And the Little People, using their psychic control of the material world, genetically "improve" a newborn human baby into "a sort of superman," an hermaphroditic specimen with hoofs, rearranged organs, and many extra fingers, including one ending "in a cluster of pink worms."

The rest of the humans decide to return to Earth, armed with their newly acquired advanced technology; as Lazarus puts it, " 'We'll be in shape to demand living room; we'll be strong enough to defend ourselves.' " They fly blind, "with nothing but Slipstick Libby's incomprehensible talent to guide them," and arrive in orbit in the year 2153 prepared to fight for their *Lebensraum* as a superior race. But there they discover that *"Everybody is a Member of the Families now,"* for it turned out that *biological* heredity had very little to do with longevity, the secret being *"psychological* heredity": "A man could live a long time just by believing that he was bound to live a long time and thinking accordingly—." This is as far as the Future History gets, until we meet Lazarus Long again, at the age of 2360, in *Time Enough for Love*, published thirty-two years later.

An alternative to the flight of the *New Frontiers* is the voyage of its sister ship, launched several years earlier, described in "Universe" (*Astounding*, May 1941). Blindly drifting for centuries in interstellar space after a disastrous mutiny, the Ship has become the Universe of a semifeudal society headed by an autocratic Captain, administered by a class of barely literate priests who call themselves "scientists," and fed by peasants who work the hydroponic farms around the little villages separated by concentric decks, compartments, and miles of maze-like passageways. "Up" is the direction of lesser weight: toward the interior of this enormous, slowly spinning cylinder. On these relatively weightless levels lurk gangs of cannibalistic mutants, one of whom, the brilliant two-headed Joe-Jim, having read the ancient books and discovered the only viewport, has comprehended the incredible truth: the universe does not end at the lowest level of the Ship, and the Ship itself is moving. In "civilized" society down below, such ideas encountered in the ancient scientific books are dismissed as allegorical romances, and anyone pro-

pounding such preposterous heresies is fed, along with mutants, into the Convertor. For, after all: "The Ship can't go anywhere. It already *is* everywhere."

"Universe" is a classic presentation of that critical problem, the impenetrable limits environment places around consciousness, a theme crucial not only for Heinlein and for such
science-fiction masterpieces as E. A. Abbott's *Flatland*,
Twain's *A Connecticut Yankee in King Arthur's Court* and
"The Great Dark," Jorge Luis Borges's "The Library of Babel,"
and Christopher Priest's *The Inverted World*, but for all modern industrial society as technological and social revolutions
constantly change the human environment. In the epistemological laboratory presented by "Universe," neither the
traditional beliefs of the present rulers nor the hard-headed
pragmatism of a dissident rationalist bloc who accept only immediate facts can comprehend the stupendous truth of the real
universe that lies outside. They are even less capable of breaking out of the prison of the Ship.

The sequel, "Common Sense" (*Astounding*, October 1941),
is more a minor tale of adventure which concludes with the
highly improbable escape of three men, who, along with their
chattel wives, manage to land a Ship's "boat" on an Earth-like
planetary moon. The story is notable mainly for its political
intrigue, the appearance, rare in any Heinlein story, of a Captain who abuses his authority, and the flagrantly derogatory
treatment of women, best summed up by the principal hero's
injunction, " 'Keep those damned women out of the way.' "

The delusory world of the Ship in "Universe" is presented
as a convincing possibility in a rigorously controlled science
fiction in which true science offers the only way out. During
this same period, Heinlein was also publishing fantasies of
psychological entrapment, paranoia, and solipsism with an
emphatic denunciation of science and scientific reasoning.
This is not to suggest that he dramatizes one kind of world
view in his science fiction, and a contrary one in his fantasy,
for, as we shall see, some of his science fiction is just as passionately anti-science. And some of the minor stories of this
period show a full range of attitudes toward technology,
science, and fantastic imaginings beyond science: " '—And
He Built a Crooked House—' " (*Astounding*, February 1941),

about a four-dimensional house created by an architect and an earthquake; " 'My Object All Sublime' " (*Future*, February 1942) in which an inventor develops an invisibility device (similar to one in Jack London's "The Shadow and the Flash") so that he can squirt synthetic skunk juice on offending motorists, which gets him jailed "for everything from malicious mischief to criminal syndicalism"; "Pied Piper" (*Astonishing Stories*, March 1942) in which a scientific genius stops a war by kidnapping a few hundred thousand children from the enemy nation; "Goldfish Bowl" (*Astounding*, March 1942), a speculation that there are stratospheric beings to whom we are as goldfish are to us.

The most unrelenting of Heinlein's paranoid fantasies is "They" (*Unknown*, April 1941), which starkly enacts the dark side of the cult of the lone genius. Most of this story, one crucial to comprehending the meaning and significance of Heinlein's achievement, consists of the anguished musings of a man confined in what seems an insane asylum. He is convinced that the entire material world and all the people in it exist for one purpose only: to deceive him, to keep him from distinguishing their "lies" from the "truth," which comes to him in dreams. "They," "the puppet masters," are merely "swarms of actors"; "they looked like me, but they were not like me."

Starkly displayed here is the myth of the free individual, so central to Heinlein's fiction and so representative of Western thought since the dawn of the capitalist epoch. The narrator's epistemological predicament, in fact, derives directly from the birth of Cartesian consciousness. He actually reformulates the classical *Cogito, ergo sum*: "First fact, himself. He knew himself directly. He existed." Then the evidence of his senses: "Without them he was entirely solitary, shut up in a locker of bone, blind, deaf, cutoff, the only being in the world." He desperately speculates that the other beings around him might also experience the isolation of the imprisoned ego: "Could it be that each unit in this yeastly swarm around him was the prison of another lonely ego—helpless, blind, and speechless, condemned to an eternity of miserable loneliness?" In Heinlein's later fiction we will see "the agony of his loneliness" re-enacted in many forms.

The other side of this terrifying imprisonment is the narrator's belief in his own transcendent importance: ". . . I was the center of the arrangements. . . . I am unique." He even deduces his own unique god-like immortality: "I am immortal. I transcend this little time axis." This desire to live beyond and outside one's time will become almost an obsession in the later fiction.

The narrator does vacillate about one person, his wife, who certainly seems to be another human being, one who loves him. But in the end we discover that all his apparently paranoid visions are not delusions at all: New York City and Harvard University are being dismantled as useless props, and "the creature" who pretended to be his human wife requests that the Taj Mahal sequence be arranged as his next deception.

In "The Unpleasant Profession of Jonathan Hoag" (*Unknown Worlds*, October 1942), another paranoid fantasy, our world is merely an immature creation of some aspiring Artist, who has made the mistake of painting us and our environment over an earlier work, "The Sons of the Bird," evil creatures who now lurk in the world behind mirrors, ready to burst forth into our reality and take possession. Jonathan Hoag is a Critic who has been sent to judge our world to see if it has any aesthetic saving grace or whether it should be obliterated.

Hoag is now in Chicago, which he finds squalid, dismal, and repulsive. Especially distasteful to him are its "coarse and brutal" working-class people. Falling partly under the wicked powers of the Sons of the Bird, Hoag seeks assistance from a married man and woman with their own small business, a detective agency. The husband and wife now find themselves at the center of the evil plot. She is afraid that if they stay on this case they "will find out what it is grown-ups know" and become as unhappy as everybody else. The Sons of the Bird lure the husband into "a small room, every side of which was a mirror—four walls, floor, and ceiling. Endlessly he was repeated in every direction and every image was himself—selves that hated him but from which there was no escape." This prison of morbid egoism suggests that "the whole world might be just a fraud and an illusion."

Because of the mutual loyalty of these two devoted small-

business people, embodying "the tragedy of human love,"
Hoag eventually decides not to destroy our world, merely to
correct it by wiping out the Sons of the Bird. He warns the
husband and wife to drive away and under no circumstances
to open the window of their car. When they momentarily dis-
obey while driving along a crowded Chicago street, they discover that the world they have been perceiving is indeed
merely an illusion:

> Outside the open window was no sunlight, no cops, no
> kids—nothing. Nothing but a gray and formless mist, pulsing
> slowly as if with inchoate life. They could see nothing of the
> city through it, not because it was too dense but because it
> was—empty.

They flee to a remote farm, where they live in a house without
mirrors, handcuffing themselves together through the night.
Their flight from the overwhelming, threatening, supposedly
delusory reality of modern working-class urban America to
some simple, primitive, rural world from the mythic past is
another archetype reappearing many times in Heinlein's fiction.

"Lost Legion," published in *Super Science Stories* in November 1941, the month before the United States formally entered World War II, is set in the contemporary world, when
the forces of "pure evil" are poised for a decisive assault:
"They've won in Europe; they are in the ascendancy in Asia;
they may win here in America . . ." (Chapter 11. In "Lost
Legacy," the 1953 version of the story, Heinlein switches the
words "Europe" and "Asia," thus switching his identification
of "pure evil" from fascism to communism). In the United
States these evil forces are embodied in "the antagonists of
human liberty—the racketeers, the crooked political figures,
the shysters, the dealers in phony religions, the sweat shop-
pers, the petty authoritarians, all of the key figures among the
traffickers in human misery and human oppression" (Ch. 12),
who include some members of Congress, judges, governors,
university presidents, heads of unions, directors of nineteen
major corporations, and local authorities. They are all under
the command of an inscrutable "evil thing," a no-eyed, legless
monster in control of almost limitless psychic forces. The situation, in short, resembles that in "The Devil Makes the Law."

Opposed to these forces are a professor of psychology, his prize female student, and his surgeon friend, who together discover that *everybody* has almost limitless psychic forces, including telepathy, telekinesis, teleportation, etc. Our trio of good guys become "supermen" and then link up with a community of even greater psychic supermen hidden inside Mount Shasta and led by a new avatar of Ambrose Bierce, who seems to be a reincarnation of Mark Twain.

Through their new friends, our heroes take a telepathic voyage to the prehistoric past where they learn the true history of the human race. It seems we were all gods until Loki, speaking for an elitist band of Young Men, argued that "the ancient knowledge should henceforth be the reward of ability rather than common birthright, and second, that the greater should rule the lesser" (Ch. 6). Thus comes "The Twilight of the Gods," and the emergence of war and empire, specifically "Mu, mightiest of empires and mother of empires." (Heinlein had co-authored a perfectly silly shaggy-dog parapsychological fantasy set in Mu, entitled "Beyond Doubt," in *Astonishing Stories*, April 1941.) The rest of history has been an ever-recurring struggle between the good psychic adepts and the evil forces, who believe in "authoritarianism, nonsense like the leader principle, totalitarianism, all the bonds placed on liberty which treat men as so many economic and political units with no importance as individuals" (Ch. 7).

The good side now is striving to let all the people know that they are capable of these superhuman powers, virtually total direct control of matter by mind. Since the forces of evil already control so many adult American institutions, it is necessary to get several thousand specially picked Boy Scouts to assemble at "Camp Mark Twain" on Mount Shasta, instruct them in parapsychology, and let them loose as teachers for the common people, while our trio and the other good-mind adepts annihilate the evil-mind adepts, literally liquidating the evil leader, leaving him "a gory mess on the rug." Thus in "Lost Legion" the evil forces trying to take over the world are defeated by the unaided mind.

The belief that mind can *at will* do almost anything to matter represents the absurdity at the extreme end of the bourgeois definition of freedom and free will. If the will is free to do anything it wishes, the will is free from the apparent laws of the physical universe and also free from the apparent laws of human social development—a thoroughly non-dialectical definition of freedom. Instead of human consciousness being collectively and progressively freed by the advances of science, technology, and social organization, all produced by developing human consciousness, human history is seen as a sinister, imprisoning force that overwhelmed the supposed freedom of nineteenth-century individual enterprise or even, as in this story, some prehistoric, mythic freedom of beings like gods. In the face of the historic forces threatening the destruction of his social class, Heinlein's impulses are characteristically reactionary, that is, longing to reverse the processes of history, and often even thoroughly anti-historic, that is, yearning to see history shattered and swept away.

The paranoid vision clearly relates to these anti-scientific and anti-historic impulses. In early stories such as "Life-Line" and " 'Let There Be Light,' " the sinister powers are often the forces that were then indeed overwhelming free-enterprise capitalism—the forces of monopoly, which actually appear as diabolic in "The Devil Makes the Law." But the vision of evil forces subverting, controlling, or annihilating our society takes many forms in Heinlein's imagination. They may be power-mad priests (" 'If This Goes On—' ") or satanic elitists ("Lost Legion") or the Sons of the Bird or simply "They"; in postwar works, they become "the Communists," either explicitly ("Gulf," Farnham's Freehold, as well as other fiction and non-fiction) or somewhat refracted into giant communistic slugs (The Puppet Masters) or bugs (Starship Troopers).

In the novel Sixth Column (Astounding, January, February, March 1941), they are the Pan-Asian hordes, who have perfidiously attacked and invaded the United States. Opposed to them is "the most magnificent aggregation of research brains" ever assembled, hidden away in an unmarked spot in the Rocky Mountains, searching for a superweapon to repel these four hundred million cruel Asians, who of course care nothing for individual human life and who are routinely called "monkeys" by all the good staunch American patriots, referred to consistently as "the whites" and "white men." Finally, when there are only six men left in the secret laboratory, now headed by the aptly named Whitey Ardmore, they figure out "what makes matter tick," and they launch their

Armed with superweapons and gigantic projected images, the whites overcome
the Pan-Asiatics in *Sixth Column*. Painting by Paul Rivoche.

counterattack under cover of a phony messianic religion,
armed with an assortment of superweapons which kill only
those with "Mongolian blood":

> The "basic weapon" was the simplest Ledbetter projector
> that had been designed. It looked very much like a pistol and

was intended to be used in similar fashion. It projected a directional beam of the primary Ledbetter effect in the frequency band fatal to those of Mongolian blood and none other. It could be used by a layman after three minutes' instruction, since all that was required was to point it and press a trigger, but it was practically foolproof—the user literally could not harm a fly with it, much less a white man. But it was sudden death to Asiatics. [March, p. 133]

The vision of Asians expressed throughout *Sixth Column* is best summed up in the attitude of Jefferson Thomas, one of the heroic freedom fighters: " 'A good Pan-Asian was a dead Pan-Asian . . .' " (January, p. 26). This undisguised racism is hardly unique to Robert Heinlein; here, as usual, he is being a fairly representative American. The intense dread of "the Yellow Peril," those cruel Asians bent on overrunning America, emerged at the very moment that Americans began their campaign of conquest and exploitation of Asia and Asians (just as the dread of the "Indian savages" began with the genocidal conquest of the natives of this continent by the European invaders). Heinlein's fantasy of race war is mild compared with that envisioned by Jack London in his 1910 story "The Unparalleled Invasion," where the white nations, fearful of being overrun by the Asian hordes, unite to attack China with germ warfare delivered by airplanes, succeed in utterly exterminating the Chinese people, and thus establish a joyous epoch of "splendid mechanical, intellectual, and art output." By 1924 the Congress of the United States had prohibited all further immigration from Japan and outlawed the naturalization of all those who had already immigrated. Heinlein was far less racist than his government, for he calls his one Asian-American character, Frank Roosevelt Matsui, "as American as Will Rogers" (January, p. 27) and shows him loyally and heroically sacrificing his own life. Ironically, in March 1942, a year after the publication of *Sixth Column*, the American President for whom Frank Roosevelt Matsui was named was to issue his infamous Executive Order 9066, which had all 117,000 Japanese-Americans rounded up and placed in concentration camps, while their land and other property was seized. And although it may seem highly improbable that American scientists could devise a superweapon that would kill only Asians, in less than four years they certainly did invent a superweapon that *did* kill only Asians.

Throughout this first period, Heinlein seems torn between two quite contradictory conceptions of the relations between mind and matter. On one side he has faith in science and technology—the rational, systematic, developing accumulation of human knowledge which permits a progressive enlargement of human consciousness, of control over the material environment, of potential freedom. On the other side, he rejects science and embraces wishful thinking, the direct, unfettered, immediate control of matter by mind.

"Waldo" (*Astounding*, August 1942) embodies this conflict in a single story. In this future scene, Heisenberg's Uncertainty Principle has been done away with and physics has become "an exact science," the "religion" of men like Dr. Rambeau, head of research for the gigantic power monopoly, North American Power-Air. But this "faith" is being undermined by the mysterious failure of the Company's power receptors.

The Company is forced to seek help from Waldo F. Jones, a marvelous caricature of the lone genius. Waldo orbits above Earth literally in his own small sphere; ostensibly treasuring his "freedom" from the "smooth apes" of Earth below, he calls his solitary home "Freehold." Waldo, a flabby weakling reduced to almost total physical impotence by the muscular disease *myasthenia gravis*, has employed his inventive genius to contrive the servomechanisms known in the story, and subsequently in the actual world, as "waldoes."

Waldo's view of the world in one direction confronts that of Dr. Rambeau:

> To Rambeau the universe was an inexorably ordered cosmos, ruled by unvarying law. To Waldo the universe was the enemy, which he strove to force to submit to his will.

Yet Waldo and Dr. Rambeau both share a very mechanical materialism. True knowledge is vested in Gramps Schneider, an old "witch doctor" who initiates Waldo into the mysteries of the "Other World," an old term for the realm of magic, which Heinlein had set forth in "The Devil Makes the Law" (reprinted as "Magic, Inc." in *Waldo and Magic, Inc.*, the 1950

volume that places these two tales into a unified world view).
The old seer presents Waldo with an unmitigated split between mind and matter:

> "The Other World," he said presently, "is the world you do
> not see. It is here and it is there and it is everywhere. But it is
> especially here." He touched his forehead. "The mind sits in it
> and sends its messages through it to the body."

Gramps uses his occult power to fix one of the power receptors, and Dr. Rambeau becomes a convert from science to
magic, deliriously proclaiming: " 'Nothing is certain. Nothing,
nothing, NOTHING is certain!' " " 'Chaos is King, and Magic is
loose in the world!' "

Waldo learns to repair the broken power receptors by
merely willing them to work, and he constructs an improved
receptor that draws its power directly from the Other World.
So now, as in " 'Let There Be Light,' " there is "free and unlimited power," but Waldo is able to trick the Company into
paying him royally even though he blandly tells the Chairman
of the Board, " 'you will not be in the business of selling
power much longer.' "

Now Waldo attempts to build a scientific explanation of
the Other World, for it is "contrary to the whole materialistic
philosophy in which he had grown up" to believe "that
thought and thought alone should be able to influence physical phenomena." But he finds himself plunged into pure
Berkeleian idealism, wondering if "the order we thought we
detected" is "a mere phantasm of the imagination," "Orderly
Cosmos, created out of Chaos—by Mind!" He begins to believe
that "the world varied according to the way one looked at it,"
that the physical universe would operate by magical principles for a culture that believed in magic, by scientific laws for
a culture that believed in science. This notion, that a society's
culture determines the physical universe it inhabits, is precisely the opposite of the view, stated earlier in the story, and
certainly truer to human history, that it is the physical universe, including the current level of technology, that determines the character of a society's culture:

> It may plausibly be urged that the shape of a culture—its
> mores, evaluations, family organization, eating habits, living

patterns, pedagogical methods, institutions, forms of government, and so forth—arise [sic] from the economic necessities of its technology.

Heinlein seems unable to choose between a mechanical materialism, together with an inflexible determinism, on one hand, and unmitigated idealism, together with a capricious voluntarism, on the other. Any dialectical interplay between mind and matter, between what is determined and what can be freely changed, lies outside the rigid bipolar framework for the philosophical speculation in "Waldo."

In Waldo himself, however, we do see such a dialectic. Gramps Schneider had told him that he could reach into the Other World to cure his pathological muscular weakness:

> Gramps Schneider had told him he need not be weak!
> That he could be strong—
> Strong!
> STRONG!

Waldo has something in common with many of the readers of *Astounding*, as we find out if we turn to the last page of this August 1942 issue:

> Let me make *YOU* a SUPERMAN!
> When you stand before your mirror, stripped to the skin, what do you see? A body you can be really proud of? A build that others admire or talk about? OR—are you fat and flabby? . . .
> If you're honest enough with yourself to admit that physically you're only *half* a man *now*—then I want to prove I can make you a SUPERMAN in double-quick time! . . .
> . . . I'll show you exactly how to get a handsome, husky pair of shoulders—a deep, he-man chest—arms & leg muscles hard as rocks yet limber as a whip . . . every inch of you all man, *he*-man, SUPERMAN.

Charles Atlas's "Dynamic Tension" method of body-building here advertised is almost precisely what Waldo employs. He does not overcome his weakness by the instantaneous and magical wishful thinking he used to fix the power receptors, but by a determination of will that forces him to condition the muscles of his body systematically and rigorously. Gradually building up his muscles, he becomes even stronger than the average man, and leaves his lonely exile in "Freehold" to rejoin the human race, becoming an acrobatic dancer, admired by all for his strength and agility. The lone genius, it turns out, really just wished "to be *liked*, to be *wanted*."

Heinlein's first published attempt at a time-travel story, "Elsewhere" (*Astounding*, September 1941), projects a bizarre maze of alternative time tracks which individuals may choose at will. Here the desire to be free *from* the present, to be released by wishing for an escape, is explicit: the central character, a professor of speculative metaphysics, escapes from imprisonment by wishing himself into a future that combines idealized features of both ancient Rome and an advanced space age. The professor explains to his four choice students that " 'the mind creates its own world,' " that " 'Berkeleian idealism' " creates just as "real" a world as "materialism." (In the revised version, published in 1953 in *Assignment in Eternity*, Heinlein goes so far as to add a fifth student, a religious fundamentalist, who manages to transform herself directly into an angel!) There is scorn for " 'you engineers,' " who all " 'believe in a mechanistic, deterministic universe.' " Yet a young engineering student saves a whole planet from an invasion of alien forces by flitting from one time track to another so that the good guys can build a blaster gun, a "little gadget" that " 'unquestionably will win the war for us.' " The whimsical jumble of fantastic time tracks contrasts sharply with the novel from which this story derives, Jack London's *The Star Rover* (1915), in which a political prisoner in San Quentin escapes from incessant torture by achieving different identities in the class struggle that has constituted actual human history.

"Elsewhere" also contrasts sharply with "By His Bootstraps" (*Astounding*, October 1941), Heinlein's second time-travel story, and one of his masterpieces. Rigorous in its logic, this tale penetrates deeply into the implications of the myth of the free individual.

Bob Wilson, the protagonist, moves from being an ordinary doctoral student (working on a thesis disproving time travel) to becoming the lone active will and consciousness thirty thousand years in the future, ruling alone as lord and master over an Earth filled with his slaves. We see the events from the different points of view of Wilson as he becomes different selves by moving back and forth through time.

When we first meet Wilson, he is being accosted by two mysterious strangers who pop out of a "Time Gate" into his apartment. Later we perceive the same scene from the point of view of each of these men, who turn out to be later selves of Bob Wilson, sent from the future back into the present. The first Wilson goes through the Time Gate and meets the mysterious all-powerful Diktor, who sends him back into his own time, from which still another Wilson eventually emerges into that remote future ten years before the encounter between Diktor and Wilson. In all these adventures, Wilson can never recognize any of his future selves. He does not even realize that he himself has become Diktor until the moment of the first encounter between this future self and the first Wilson from the past. On one level, the story is an ingenious exploration of the problems of identity in time, and the associated questions of the relations between determinism and free will. Diktor has created himself out of Bob Wilson, but without conscious choice until after it has already happened.

"By His Bootstraps" is also a dramatic display of the trapped ego, creating a world out of images of itself. It is thus the first fully developed manifestation of the solipsism which will become one of Heinlein's main themes. This solipsism is the ultimate expression of the bourgeois myth of the free individual, who supposedly is able to lift himself from rags to riches by his own bootstraps. As Diktor puts it to the Bob Wilson who emerges into this future of dictatorial power and abject slavery, " 'One twentieth-century go-getter can accomplish just about anything he wants to accomplish around here—.' "

Diktor is a grandiose enlargement of Robinson Crusoe, with the entire planet his island. In fact, the first man Wilson meets in the future throws himself on his knees and arises as "his Man Friday." All the people of this world, who have been enslaved by some mysterious "High Ones" for 20,000 years, are now "docile friendly children," "slaves by nature." What they lack is "the competitive spirit," "the will-to-power": "Wilson had a monopoly on that."

But this "monopoly" is also a state of supreme loneliness, as well as boredom. Diktor wistfully compares these people, mere extensions of his own will, with "the brawling, vulgar, lusty, dynamic swarms who had once called themselves the People of the United States," the very society he had earlier rejected and abandoned as "a crummy world full of crummy people." His choice—if that is what he ever had—lies between the life of normal futility he left and the one of sublime futility he has acquired. The choice is embodied in his sexual alternatives: in the future are myriads of beautiful mindless slave women literally kneeling to his will; in his old life there is the "shrewish," conniving Genevieve, whose approaching footsteps on his stairs had been the deciding factor in driving him out of his humdrum world into the Time Gate. Wilson's sexuality in both worlds is barren. He can only reproduce himself, as he, a self-created being, suggests in his final words, promising himself, his only kind of son, a great future: " 'There is a great future in store for you and me, my boy—a great future!' "

On still another level, "By His Bootstraps" displays this world-embracing egoism as the center of political imperialism. When Diktor asks the first Bob Wilson to return briefly to his own time, his purpose is to acquire some tools to be used in colonizing this undeveloped land:

> "I want you to return to the twentieth century and obtain certain things for us, things that can't be obtained on this side but which will be very useful to us in, ah, developing—yes, that is the word—developing this country."

The prime thing he needs is certain books: Machiavelli's The Prince, Behind the Ballots by political machine boss James Farley, How To Make Friends and Influence People by Dale Carnegie, and Adolf Hitler's Mein Kampf.

The utopian novel Beyond This Horizon (Astounding, April, May 1942) is Heinlein's only attempt in this early fiction to describe what he conceives to be a good society. Here he tries to combine a high level of social organization and cooperation with the maximum possible individual freedom. Though this society somewhat resembles the one implied in "Coventry," it is no gentle, peaceful land where any damage to another person means "readjustment" or exile. It is a society made up of people "descended from 'wolves,' not 'sheep' " (April, p. 21), one in which all self-respecting men and even some women are expert gunfighters ready to cut each other down at the drop of an insult. The main product of human history through "the Continuous War of 1910–1970" and beyond can be summed up in one italicized sentence: *"The fighters survived"* (April, p. 21). Now, several centuries of systematic genetic engineering have created a race of human beings superior in health, longevity, physique, and intelligence.

The underlying assumption of *Beyond This Horizon*, as Philip E. Smith II has put it in his superb essay on Heinlein's social Darwinism, is that "biology explains behavior" and "biology also explains politics," with an "underlying fantasy-wish . . . derived from a social Darwinistic interpretation of evolution."[5] We witness this dynamic utopian society passing through a series of crises to advance to what Heinlein often projects as the next stage of human evolution, the development of telepathic powers.

The economic structure itself, supposedly a perfected, fully rational capitalism that has evolved from the "pseudo-capitalism" of previous centuries, is seen as relatively unimportant, so long as there is a rational system of finance. Here everybody gets "dividends," the social distribution of surplus capital, through centralized accounting. To the question ". . . wouldn't it be simpler to set up a collective system and be done with it?" comes this response:

> "Finance structure is a general theory and applies equally to any type of state. A complete socialism would have as much need for structural appropriateness in its cost accounting as would a free entrepreneur. The degree of public ownership as compared with the degree of free enterprise is a cultural matter. For example, food is, of course, free, but—." [April, p. 11]

Technology also has relatively little to do with the greatness of this society, except insofar as it allows the necessary improvements in genetic engineering. We are assured that the goal of their eugenics is to improve the gene pool of the whole race, not to develop a separate line of supermen.

The hero of *Beyond This Horizon* is Hamilton Felix, the fastest gun in town, packing an antique Colt .45. A "star line" genetic type, Hamilton is supposed to contribute his superior genes to the race by breeding with his pre-selected genetic counterpart, Phyllis, a beautiful gunslinger. But he is weighed down by ennui and frustration, because he lacks some of the qualifications of the leading geniuses, the philosophers in charge of centralized planning: " 'When it was finally pounded into my head that I couldn't take first prize, I wasn't interested in second prize' " (April, p. 24).

However, Hamilton discovers and helps defeat a conspiracy of "the Survivors Club," an elitist cabal planning to seize power, set up "the New Order," and redirect genetic engineering to create classes of superbrainy leaders and superbrawny workers. In heroically combating these protofascists and amorously dallying with Phyllis, Hamilton begins to reawaken his interest in life and the possibility of procreation.

Yet he still fails to see any purpose in human existence. His own profession symbolizes his dilemma: he invents sophisticated games and superpinball machines for amusement centers. An extraordinary revelation comes to him as his consciousness swims out from a dose of gas he gets in a shootout:

> No fun in the game if you knew the outcome. He had designed a game like that once, and called it "Futility"—no matter how you played, you had to win. . . . It was always a little hard to remember which position himself had played, forgetting that he had played all of the parts. Well, that was the game; it was the only game in town, and there was nothing else to do. Could he help it if the game was crooked? Even if he had made it up and played all the parts. [May, p. 66]

Hamilton here is perilously close to Diktor, the sole player in the rigged time-travel game of "By His Bootstraps."

But Hamilton makes a deal with the geniuses who administer this society. He will agree to reproduce if they will commit massive funds to investigate the meaning of life, including research into the question of an afterlife. They accede, Phyllis assumes her proper role of wife and mother, and their star line children soon exhibit telepathy and living proof of reincarnation.

As the May 1942 synopsis explained, *Beyond This Horizon* "is, itself, almost a synopsis." There are subplots that go nowhere (including a delightful sequence about a Babbitt-like ex-football player and fraternity man, rabid anti-Communist, boosterish Republican businessman who turns up from 1926 and soon dispels some romantic notions that have developed about the twentieth century), pages of scientific and pseudo-scientific theory, and more philosophizing and action than the narrative can comfortably handle. This myriad of fragments kaleidoscopically displays the contradictory components of Heinlein's late Depression outlook, a world view that will later determine his responses to the earth-shaking events of the period from the end of World War II to the early 1970s.

I have saved for the final story to be explored in this chapter the only one that directly confronts the actual international situation emerging in these early years of World War II, "Solution Unsatisfactory" (Astounding, May 1941). This story, like most of the fiction we have looked at so far, should not be read as merely prewar. As Heinlein puts it in "Solution Unsatisfactory": "We were not at war, legally, yet we had been in the war up to our necks with our weight on the side of democracy since 1940."

In December 1938 Otto Hahn in Berlin had discovered the splitting of the uranium atom under a bombardment of neutrons. Earlier that year, Hahn's Jewish wife, the great physicist Lise Meitner, had fled Germany to avoid the pogroms; in early 1939, Dr. Meitner and her nephew Otto Frisch formulated an explanation of Hahn's process, which they named nuclear fission. Heinlein begins his tale with the ominous implications of these critical modern events. He loosely fictionalizes Lise Meitner as Estelle Karst, a Jewish assistant of Dr. Hahn, who comes to the United States and discovers, as a by-product of her medical research, the ultimate and irresistible weapon, radioactive dust.

The story is told by "an ordinary sort of man" who suddenly finds himself thrust into the center of history. The main character and hero is "liberal" but "tough-minded" Clyde C. Manning, congressman, colonel in the United States Army, and apparently the only possible savior of the world.

America now has the weapon which amounts to "a loaded gun held at the head of every man, woman, and child on the globe!" The narrator expresses some misgivings about America having this power:

> I had the usual American subconscious conviction that our country would never use power in sheer aggression. Later, I thought about the Mexican War and the Spanish-American

War and some of the things we did in Central America, and I
was not so sure—

Nevertheless, for Heinlein there can be only one conclusion,
inescapable and inevitable:

> The United States was having power thrust on it, willy-
> nilly. We had to accept it and enforce a world-wide peace,
> ruthlessly and drastically, or it would be seized by some other
> nation.

So first America intervenes in the war. But before actually
using the atomic weapon, "we were morally obligated" to
give every possible warning, first to the German government,
then to the people of Berlin, the targeted city. This passage
rings with shocking irony in the echo of the American sneak
attacks on Hiroshima and Nagasaki.

Next comes the worldwide "*Pax Americana*." The United
States demands that every nation in the world immediately
disarm, a threat Heinlein quaintly expresses in frontier lingo:
" 'Throw down your guns, boys; we've got the drop on you!' "
This choice is forced on us by such "facts" as these:

> Four hundred million Chinese with no more concept of voting
> and citizen responsibility than a flea. Three hundred million
> Hindus who aren't much better indoctrinated. God knows how
> many in the Eurasian Union who believe in God knows what.
> The entire continent of Africa only semicivilized. Eighty mil-
> lion Japanese who really believe that they are Heaven-
> ordained to rule.

So the *Pax Americana* inescapably must be "a military dictatorship imposed by force on the whole world."

Sure enough, there is another nation so uncivilized, unrea-
sonable, and dastardly as to dispute the American global
hegemony, the "Eurasian Union," now under the control of
the "Fifth Internationalists," who have paralleled our atomic
research. In 1945, unlike the actual history of that year, the
sneak atomic attack is delivered not by the United States but
upon it. We retaliate by wiping out Vladivostok, Irkutsk, and
Moscow, and sending an invasion force, "the American Pacifi
cation Expedition." The United States now has the job of "p
licing the world."

The President of the United States at this time is a ʲᵈ

man, so he and Colonel Manning wish to prevent the atomic weapon being used "to turn the globe into an empire, our empire" for "imperialism degrades both oppressor and oppressed." They decide that the power "must not be used to protect American investments abroad, to coerce trade agreements, for any purpose but the simple abolition of mass killing." In characteristic American and Heinlein style, "Manning and the President played by ear," establising treaties "to commit future governments of the United States to an irrevocable benevolent policy."

Colonel Manning then becomes Commissioner of World Safety, which forms the international Peace Patrol, whose pilots, armed with the atomic weapon, are never to be assigned to their own country. The Peace Patrol is welded together by "esprit de corps," and the main check on their new recruits is "the President's feeling for character."

Then the good President is killed in a plane crash, and the presidency is assumed by the isolationist Vice President, allied with a senator who had tried to use the Peace Patrol to recover expropriated holdings in South America and Rhodesia. They attempt to arrest Manning, but the pilots of the Peace Patrol intervene, arrest the bad President, and make Manning "the undisputed military dictator of the world."

Nobody, not even Manning, likes this solution. But, though unsatisfactory, it apparently seemed the best to Robert A. Heinlein in 1941.

NOTES

1. As pointed out by Sam Moskowitz in *Seekers of Tomorrow* (Cleveland: World Publishing, 1966), p. 194.

2. Actually the reference as pointed out by J. R. Christopher in "Methuselah, Out of Heinlein by Shaw," *Shaw Review*, 16 (1973), pp. 79–88, is to Shaw's *The Apple Cart*. This article documents quite an extensive influence by Shaw on Heinlein. And Samuel R. Delany has argued that "the didactic methods of Robert Heinlein owe a great deal to Shaw's comedies of ideas, far more than to Wells and Verne" in "Critical Methods: Speculative Fiction," *Many Futures, Many Worlds*, ed. Thomas Clareson (Kent, Ohio: Kent State University Press, 1977), p. 281).

3. " 'If This Goes On—,' " *Revolt in 2100* (New York: New American Library, 1955, 1959), pp. 118–19. This is the text of the 1953 Shasta Publishers' edition.

4. *Ibid.*, p. 119.

5. Philip E. Smith II, "The Evolution of Politics and the Politics of Evolution in Heinlein's Fiction," in *Robert A. Heinlein*, eds. Joseph D. Olander and Martin Harry Greenberg (New York: Taplinger, 1978), p. 141.

3
NEW FRONTIERS: 1947-59

When World War II ended in 1945, Robert Heinlein and the rest of the American people found themselves in a world very different from that in 1939 or even 1941. The Axis of Italian Fascism, German and East European Nazism, and Japanese imperialism had been smashed. Much of Europe, the Soviet Union, and Asia lay in ruins. Exhausted by the war, the old colonial powers—especially Great Britain, France, the Netherlands, and Belgium—tried desperately to shore up their collapsing worldwide empires. Into this power vacuum moved the United States, the only major belligerent whose homeland has escaped the havoc. With enormous technological capabilities force-fed by the war, including its monopoly on atomic weapons, America now dominated the world's oceans and atmosphere, with no other power capable of contesting the supremacy of its gigantic modern navy, vast fleet of strategic bombers, and planetwide system of foreign military bases. The "Pax Americana" of Heinlein's "Solution Unsatisfactory" had turned out to be not entirely a fantasy.

But there was an opposite side. The European anti-Nazi and anti-Fascist Resistance movements, led by Communists, had helped make the Communist parties of France and Italy the largest and most coherent political organizations on the Continent. Partisan movements in the Balkans had won power in Yugoslavia and Albania and seemed close to victory in

Greece. The Red Army occupied most of the defeated Axis territories of eastern Europe.

Most dangerous of all was the emergence of national liberation movements in Asia, Africa, and Latin America, which threatened not only the old colonial empires but also the new neo-colonial global hegemony of the United States, especially as these movements turned toward socialism and communism as the path out of their oppression. In Asia, the Communist-led anti-Japanese movements had transformed into anti-imperialist and anti-capitalist struggles throughout Indochina, Korea, and China. By 1946, the United States was actively supporting the French attempt to regain control of Vietnam and its other Indochinese colonies, and the following year America entered the civil war in Greece. In 1949, the Chinese Communists drove Chiang Kaishek's forces from the mainland, and the Soviet Union ended the American nuclear monopoly. In 1950, less than five years after the end of World War II, the United States entered a three-year-long war in Korea. The year after this war ended in a stalemate, America began to replace the defeated French army in Vietnam. A system of global alliances, particularly NATO (1949) and SEATO (1954) was largely outflanked by the loose alliance of Third World peoples formally launched at the 1955 Bandung Conference. By 1959, the revolution penetrated the western hemisphere with the overthrow of the Batista dictatorship and the establishment of a Communist government in Cuba.

During this period, technological progress was breathtaking. Features we now take for granted as parts of modern life came in a pell-mell series of breakthroughs; for example, a fourteen-month period in 1951–52 saw the beginning of transcontinental television, the start of jet passenger service, the first power-producing nuclear reactor, and the explosion of the first hydrogen bomb (though this was not revealed by the U.S. government until 1954). Meanwhile, the pace of technological development in the Soviet Union, which had been decades behind the United States, was even faster. The U.S.S.R. detonated its first hydrogen bomb within a few months of the U.S., and then, in an event that sent shock waves throughout the capitalist world, probably affecting Robert Heinlein with exceptional force, that "backward" nation launched the first vehicle to orbit Earth, the 1957 Sputnik. Nuclear energy, computers, flight into space—all had now moved beyond the pages of science fiction.

In this maelstrom of change, America began to develop a sharply split, confusing view of its present and future. On one side, America's powers seemed invulnerable and its future seemed as boundless as space. But on the other side, the combined force of the Soviet Union and the anti-imperialist revolutionary movements in Asia, Africa, and Latin America threatened the very existence of a society based on worldwide economic and military hegemony. Robert Heinlein's science fiction from the end of World War II through 1959 dramatizes this split vision, this contradiction widening and deepening throughout American society, like a geological fault trembling in anticipation of the earthquakes that would begin in the mid-1960s.

Heinlein's fiction in this period actually splits into two groupings, each embodying one side of the contradiction. On one side are fourteen juvenile novels and an equal number of short stories expressing an ebullient, optimistic, visionary drama of boundless expansion into the universe. On the other side is a smaller body of works dominated by a dark, tortured, nightmarish sense of despair and strangulation, punctuated by shouts of defiance. Yet these are but two sides of the same coin: in the background of some of the most optimistic works we occasionally glimpse a dying Earth, writhing in its final agonies. Thus the bounding leap into space turns out to be an escape from the American nightmare into the fondest American dream—an infinitely expanding frontier.

This period, like all periods in Heinlein's career, ends very neatly—in 1959—with the publication of a single short story, "All You Zombies—", and a single novel, *Starship Troopers*. Heinlein was to publish no further fiction until 1961, when *Stranger in a Strange Land* was to burst upon the American scene and help launch the 1960s.

THE LAST FRONTIER: ESCAPE INTO SPACE

Before America's entry into World War II, Heinlein had published only in magazines of science fiction and fantasy. This was the period when science fiction in the United States had become confined in what has come to be called its own "ghetto," isolated not only from the belletristic literature taught in the academies but even from the general culture. (This was not true in Great Britain, Europe, and the Soviet Union; one thinks of such literary and widely popular science-fiction authors as H. G. Wells, Karel Čapek, and Vladimir Mayakovsky.) Robert Heinlein was the principal American responsible for leading some science fiction out of the ghetto, first to become integrated into American popular culture and later to gain token acceptance in high-class literary neighborhoods.

Heinlein accomplished this by opening up several new markets for his own science fiction: the "slicks," such as the *Saturday Evening Post;* the movies; television; the juvenile press, both novels and magazines, such as *Boys' Life.* In these new markets, he was consistently Heinlein the optimist, apostle of the new frontier of space.

In the late 1940s and early 1950s, space travel, outside the small, zany world of science fiction, was regarded by most Americans as too remote to be taken seriously, if not downright impossible. This was not the case, however, in the aerospace industry, bloated to enormous dimensions by its colossal wartime production tasks. How could this productive capacity be used in the peaceful world for which we had supposedly just fought? As a leading force in what President Eisenhower was later to label "the military-industrial complex," the aerospace industry was already in the process of transforming its mission from World War II to the Cold War. Wernher von Braun and his top team of one hundred Nazi rocketry experts from Pennemünde were immediately put to work in the United States, firing and perfecting their stock of V-2 rocket bombs that had been shipped from Germany and reassembled here. The space race had begun, though the American people, who would soon be called upon to finance it, knew virtually nothing of its existence.

As the general media began to propagate the new mission of aerospace, science fiction was called upon to play a special role. Robert Heinlein, ex-Navy officer, ex-prewar science fictioneer, ex-wartime aeronautic engineer, was, perhaps more than any other single person, responsible for the popularization in America of the concepts of space travel and for the commitment to undertake it.

Heinlein's postwar fiction began with a series of sketches and tales about the exploration and colonization of space. These stories, set in the late twentieth or early twenty-first century, take place within the solar system, mostly on or near the moon. Most were published in general magazines, such as the *Saturday Evening Post, Town and Country,* and the *American Legion Magazine.* His descriptive writing strengthened by his wartime technical work in aviation materials, Heinlein creates in these stories a believable space-travel milieu, distinguished by what has come to be considered his hallmark, a no-nonsense, matter-of-fact sense of familiarity, stripped of the "gosh!—wow!" air of much prewar space-travel science fiction.

The first of these stories, "The Green Hills of Earth," appearing in the *Saturday Evening Post,* February 8, 1947, is a eulogy to the heroism of the first spacemen, embodied in the songmaker "Noisy" Rhysling, "the Blind Singer of the Spaceways." Rhysling, who loses his vision manning one spaceship's atomic plant and gives his life saving another, combines the epic hero with the epic minstrel.

"Space Jockey" (*Saturday Evening Post,* April 26, 1947) demonstrates Heinlein's tactic of treating space travel like a pair of old bedroom slippers. The title character, a pilot who shuttles back and forth between the Earth-orbiting terminal and the moon-orbiting terminal, laments his routine existence, just "a job" filled with "monotony," lacking both "Romance" and a decent "home life." The little vignette is resolved when he gets a new job, ferrying between the moon orbiter and Luna City. Now his selfless wife can shift her job, the "old, old job that women have been doing a long time," to the moon, where, instead of just worrying about him and waiting for him, she can be at his beck and call.

"Columbus Was a Dope" (*Startling Stories,* May 1947) is set in an ordinary bar, where a prospective engineer, two businessmen, and the bartender debate whether sending a ship out of the solar system is sheer folly, with the most skeptical claiming that even "Columbus was a dope." The punch line comes in the final sentence, when we learn that this bar is on the moon.

In " 'It's Great To Be Back!' " (*Saturday Evening Post,* July 26, 1947) a married couple who have lived three years on the moon, always complaining and looking forward to their return to Earth, come back to discover that Earth's gravity, smog, weather, highways, and urban life are all heavily oppressive. When they flee the city to try the simple country life, they can't take the cold, the antiquated plumbing, the local prejudice. Realizing that "Luna City is the most comfortable environment man ever built for himself," they decide "to go home." The details in " 'It's Great To Be Back!' " are very convincing, persuading us that people could soon feel—in both mind and body—that the moon is "home" and a delightful escape from a suffocating Earth.

"The Black Pits of Luna" (*Saturday Evening Post,* January 10, 1948) is a slight sketch about a tourist family on the moon. Thanks to the doting mother and father, the bratty little brother gets lost, to be saved through the resourcefulness, courage, and integrity of the older brother, who is marked by these qualities for serious work on the moon. Heinlein's values come out clearly in the scornful words addressed to the parents by the leader of the search party: " 'Stay off the Moon. You don't belong here; you're not the pioneer type.' "

In "Gentlemen, Be Seated!" (*Argosy,* May 1948) the narrator, a journalist on his second trip to Luna City, finds himself trapped with Fats Konski, a construction worker, in a half-built segmented tunnel losing its vital air. Fats and the narrator heroically take turns using their bare buttocks to plug the pressure leak.

"Ordeal in Space" (*Town and Country,* May 1948) sketches a space hero with a severe case of acrophobia, seeking to lose himself in a humdrum terrestrial existence. Our hero regains his confidence by rescuing a kitten trapped on a narrow ledge outside the thirty-fifth floor of an apartment house, and he is ready to escape back into space. Once again we see life on Earth as stultifying, most of its citizens insufferable.

In "Sky Lift" (*Imagination,* November 1953) a disease has struck the pioneers on an artificial satellite orbiting Pluto, so two pilots must take a torchship (Heinleinese for a ship powered by direct conversion of mass into energy) at bodycrushing speed on an emergency voyage to ferry blood plasma. The physical details are exceptionally realistic: even a small wrinkle under the leg becomes the source of excruciating torment. One of the two heroic pilots dies, the other becomes a senile wreck in body and mind, but they save the 270 pioneers.

"Delilah and the Space-Rigger" (*Blue Book*, December 1949) is one of the few stories in which Heinlein treats women as equals of men, and it shows a relatively high level of consciousness about one form of the oppression of women. During construction work on Space Station One, the males-only policy is shattered when a woman, overcoming male prejudice and custom, fills a radioman's job; she turns out to be an electronics engineer already designated the future Chief Communications Engineer of the Station. Again, we should not forget the historical context: in the late 1940s many American women who had filled traditionally male jobs during World War II, including technical specialities, were being heavily pressured to surrender their jobs to men and return to domestic life.

During this period, Heinlein experimented with a few stories that see the world from a teenaged girl's point of view. In two non-science-fiction tales published in girls' magazines, "Poor Daddy" (*Calling All Girls*, 1949) and "Cliff and the Calories" (*Senior Prom*, August 1950), a girl nicknamed "Puddin'" tells of her minor adventures with her family and her boyfriend Cliff. In the first, her father learns to figure-skate to impress her mother; in the second, she ends her crash reducing diet when she discovers that Cliff likes the women in Rubens paintings. Drawing on these stories, Heinlein uses a similar narrator in "The Menace from Earth" (*Magazine of Fantasy and Science Fiction*, August 1957) and the later novel *Podkayne of Mars* (discussed in Chapter 4).

"The Menace from Earth" dramatizes the aspirations and love life of its fifteen-year-old narrator Holly, a girl born and raised in Luna City, yearning to be a spaceship designer and terribly possessive of her boyfriend Jeff, her "partner" in their little tourist-guide business. She confides to us that "Mother is a mathematical chemist for General Synthetics of Luna and is nearly as smart as I am." Filled with pride in being a "Loony" and contempt for the "groundhogs" from Earth, she is confronted suddenly by the Menace from Earth, a beautiful tourist who seems to be sweeping Jeff off his feet. While protesting that "I am not romantic; I am a career woman," Holly starts to fall apart until it turns out that Jeff really loves her and plans to marry her. The climax comes in the gigantic Bats' Cave, where Loonies and tourists gracefully fly in the moon's low gravity field, and where Jeff swoops down to save Holly, a would-be Daedalus who turns out to be just a damsel in distress.

Just as "The Menace from Earth" projects a teenaged girl's familiar conflict between marriage and career into the future civilization of the moon, "The Long Watch" projects onto the moon a critical social problem of the late 1940s and 1950s. Published where it might do the most good, in the *American Legion Magazine* (December 1949), "The Long Watch" returns to a danger that had concerned Heinlein during the late Depression, a takeover by a technocratic elite. Now he locates that danger, quite accurately, in the military.

Colonel Towers, in charge of a nuclear missile launching site at Moon Base, has decided that "it was not safe . . . to leave control of the world in political hands; power must be held by a scientifically selected group." In order to prevent war, Colonel Towers proposes launching nuclear bombs at "an unimportant town or two," using this "little bloodletting to save an all-out war." (The analogy with Hiroshima and Nagasaki is never made explicit.) Earth is saved from this military "dictatorship" by junior bomb officer Lieutenant Johnny Dahlquist, who ignores Colonel Towers's reminder that " 'You are sworn to obey me,' " and destroys the bombs. Johnny is killed by the radioactivity, and his body is given a hero's burial on Earth. (In the juvenile novel *Space Cadet,* published the previous year, we learned that Lieutenant Dahlquist had become a kind of patron saint for the Interplanetary Patrol for his heroic self-sacrifice in foiling the "Revolt of the Colonels.")

In 1950 appeared the first collection of Heinlein's short fiction, *The Man Who Sold the Moon,* the first volume in the Fu-

ture History series, consisting of three late Depression tales—
"Requiem," " 'Let There Be Light,' " and "The Roads Must
Roll"—together with the novella-length title story. "The Man
Who Sold the Moon" presents the epic achievement of D. D.
Harriman, whose dying flight to the moon was described in
"Requiem."

Even at this late date, Heinlein still presents an individual
entrepreneur and his corporation as the force necessary to
carry out the first travel to the moon: ". . . Harriman *would*
do it. He had the ship; shortly he would have the fuel." As in
"Requiem," Harriman is childless, and now his wife, instead
of being merely dull and less sexy than a spaceship, is shrewish and parasitic. He has one obsession: " *'I'm going to the
Moon!* If I have to manipulate a million people to accomplish
it, I'll do it.' " The stakes are the highest any capitalist has
gambled for, as he explains: " 'The assets are a planet—a
whole planet.' " " 'I would cheat, lie, steal, beg, bribe—do
anything,' " he tells us in a passage obviously intended to win
our admiration, to reach the moon. He recognizes that his
fellow capitalists are all "thieves," and calmly proposes that
" 'we should buy the judge' " to remove any legal obstacle.

Harriman sets up dummy corporations in all the nations
over which the moon passes, then bribes the various governments to sell moon ownership rights to these corporations.
His motive, however, is not primarily greed but zealous concern for human welfare. Convinced that " 'There is going to be
one hell of a fight one of these days over who owns the
Moon,' " Harriman decides that no single nation should own
it. He can see only one way to place the moon above nations:
have it owned directly by a corporation controlled by him and
his partners. Redolent of eighteenth-century British colonialism, under which the British East India Company monopo-
lized the economy of much of the Indian subcontinent, or
nineteenth-century British colonialism, under which the companies of Cecil Rhodes owned much of the resources of southern Africa, Harriman's superimperialist approach to the moon
seems out of date in the decades subsequent to the first actual
moon landings. It must be admitted, though, that his claim to
transcend narrow nationalism through his benevolent corporation (" 'Damnation, nationalism should stop at the strato-

sphere.' ") does sound a bit like the propaganda of the giant multinational corporations in the late twentieth century.

Ironically, is is the resources of "the power syndicate" that Harriman mobilizes to make this great technological leap, the same power syndicate that stifles technological progress by any means necessary in " 'Let There Be Light,' " that story from the previous decade reprinted in the same volume. Of course in "The Man Who Sold the Moon" the power syndicate is not some faceless bureaucratic monopoly, but, operating under Harriman's crafty manipulation, an expression of his personal will.

Harriman is called all sorts of names, even by his associates: a man with a "Messiah complex"; "a crooked son of a bitch"; "Moses"; "the last of the Robber Barons"; "the first of the new Robber Barons . . . setting up a new imperialism." What he represents to Heinlein is the sort of man necessary to open up for the human race what he calls "new frontiers," a phrase dear to his author back in 1941 and just as dear to the man who was to become President of the United States in 1961.

FABLES FOR THE YOUTH OF THE FIFTIES: THE JUVENILE SERIES

From 1947 through 1958, Robert Heinlein was primarily an author of science fiction aimed at the "juvenile" market, specifically at teenaged boys. Besides two minor novellas serialized in *Boys' Life*, the magazine of the Boy Scouts of America, there were twelve dazzlingly successful novels published as a juvenile series by Scribner's. These dozen novels have proved to be as popular and influential as anything Heinlein ever wrote, all going into continual mass-market reprintings, with several transposed into movie, television, and comic-strip versions.

The dozen Scribner's novels and two novellas in *Boys' Life* form a coherent epic, the story of the conquest of space. Like the tales and sketches Heinlein was publishing in general-circulation magazines, these longer works are optimistic, expansionary, romantic, pulsing with missionary zeal for a colossal human endeavor and also throbbing with a fever to escape from the urbanized, complex, supposedly routinized and imprisoning experience of Earth. The central figures are always boys making their passage into becoming men, emblems of a human race attaining what Heinlein construes to be its maturity in the solar system, the galaxy, and beyond. Despite a few minor discrepancies, the Scribner's series tells a consistent story, as unified as the Future History works (there is an occasional cross-reference between the two series). The movement is outward bound. The first novel describes the first trip to the moon, the next five are set on and around Venus, Mars, the asteroids, and Jupiter; the ensuing five all involve voyages between Earth and parts of our galaxy beyond this solar system; and the final one climaxes someplace in the Lesser Magellanic Cloud, where our race is judged by the composite mind of the Three Galaxies.

With the exception of the first in the Scribner's series and the two novellas in *Boy's Life,* none of these works is markedly "juvenile" in tone or vocabulary. In fact, four of the novels were first serialized in such "adult" magazines as *Blue Book,* the *Magazine of Fantasy and Science Fiction,* and *Astounding.* Heinlein himself has said that he vowed "never to 'write down' nor to adopt a patronizing attitude" toward the youthful reader and added provocatively:

> I have held to that rule and my books for boys differ only slightly from my books for adults—the books for boys are somewhat harder to read because younger readers relish tough ideas they have to chew and don't mind big words—and the boys' books are slightly limited by taboos and conventions imposed by their elders.[1]

The point-of-view character is usually a teenaged boy attempting to enter the adult world and often trying to relate to what he perceives as the even stranger world of females, who sometimes seem to him more alien than the strangest extraterrestrial life forms. The central subject, however, is space travel.

Space travel provides some ideal settings for an author who believes in the primacy of individual or small-group achievements and who wishes to indulge fantasies of escape from the late industrial world. Small heroic groups or individuals may be placed in dramatic situations alone in spaceships or on other planets, where their actions may have great consequences. There is, however, a contradiction, for space travel is the product of an entire highly industrialized, complexly organized society. Unaware of this, early science fiction could ignore it. Hence there was often the spectacle, amusingly archaic to us, of some lone genius inventing and building a spaceship in his workshop and launching it from his backyard. Later, a single industrial corporation could be imagined as the sole creator of a spaceship, of course through the genius of one or two scientists or engineers. By the close of World War II, however, it was fairly obvious that space travel would take the kind of vast, highly socialized efforts that had developed the Nazi V-1 and V-2 rocket bombs or the U.S. atomic bombs.

Rocket Ship Galileo, the book that launched Heinlein's juvenile space odyssey in 1947, tries to have it both ways. The basic technology for space travel has been provided by American industrial society, some time shortly after 1951, in the form of intercontinental freight and passenger rockets. But the giant corporations, seeing no "obvious way to make money out of a flight to the moon," decide that space travel is "not commercially practical," especially in light of the enormous tentative budget—one and a quarter million dollars.[2] Heinlein had not yet projected that scheme of the 1950 tale, "The Man Who Sold the Moon," where the initiative of the lone capitalist overcomes corporate conservatism. In Rocket Ship Galileo, the initiative comes from the lone engineer who has invented the means of propulsion, aided by a scientific club consisting of three enthusiastic high-school seniors. The three youthful inventors bring to the enterprise some all-American teenager skills, such as a love for technical gimmicks and an audacity whose main outlet had been hot rods.

The foursome buy "an Atlantic freighter-rocket at scrap prices" (Ch. 3), outfit it for space travel, and off they go to the moon. There they discover remnants of a lost lunar civilization and an elite corps of Nazis, "some of the top military, scientific, and technical brains from Hitler's crumbled empire" (Ch. 16), about to launch a sneak nuclear attack at Earth. The three boys, now having reached manhood through their adventure, together with their older mentor, of course save our planet.

The political plot is not, as some critics have claimed, just thrown in. One of the boys is Jewish, another had been in a Nazi concentration camp, and Heinlein, like many Americans in 1946 and 1947, understood the very real threat of a Nazi resurgence—in Germany, in South America, or even in the United States, where in fact some of the top military, scientific, and technical brains from Hitler's crumbled empire were at that very moment working to perfect intercontinental missiles to aim nuclear weapons at the Soviet Union. One of the Nazi leaders on the moon boasts, " 'We have friends everywhere. Even in Washington, in London, yes, even in Moscow' " (Ch. 16). *Rocket Ship Galileo* was written just before we plunged openly into the Cold War. But this year, 1947, was the date the U.S. government began deluging the country with anti-Communist propaganda, purging the unions, the media, and the schools of people deemed insufficiently "loyal," establishing millions of loyalty dossiers, and committing military forces to "fight Communism," first in Greece, later in Asia, Africa, and Latin America.

Heinlein himself later became one of the more strident voices in the anti-Communist and anti-Soviet campaign. In *Rocket Ship Galileo,* a product of the time before anti-Soviet conditioning became dominant in America, Heinlein could still write the following:

> "I have nothing against the Russians; if they beat me to the moon, I'll take off my hat to them. But I prefer our system to theirs; it would be a sour day for us if it turned out that they could do something as big and as wonderful as this when we weren't even prepared to tackle it, under our set-up." [Ch. 4]

To view the profound changes in Heinlein and America, we will later see what happens to *Rocket Ship Galileo* when Heinlein helps convert it into the 1950 movie *Destination Moon,* a hymn of praise to the industrial-military complex.

Many of the boys' books consist of extended tests of endurance, loyalty, courage, intelligence, integrity, and fortitude. They dramatize a personal ethic and pervasive social Darwinism, displaying how and why "fit" types survive while the "unfit"—the sulkers, the weaklings, the whiners, the lazy, the self-centered, the vicious—are eliminated. The first of these books is *Space Cadet* (1948), the story of how a boy from Des Moines, Iowa, becomes an officer in the Interplanetary Patrol.

An extension of the concept of the Peace Patrol in "Solution Unsatisfactory," the Interplanetary Patrol is established "to defend the constitution of the Solar Federation," "to keep the peace of the System and to protect the liberties of its peoples" (Chs. 4, 5). The Patrol is prepared to "atom-bomb a city" if necessary (Ch. 10), and the youthful hero casually explains to his horrified parents how a particular orbiting bomb would be chosen " 'if the Patrol was to bomb Des Moines tonight' " (Ch. 11). But the purpose of the Patrol is "to prevent fighting": "The Patrol is not a fighting organization; it is the repository of weapons too dangerous to entrust to military men" (Ch. 10).

Space Cadet is more radically internationalist than Heinlein's earlier works, including "Solution Unsatisfactory." The transnational authority seen as vital for human survival is logically extended to become interplanetary, though all members of the Patrol seem to be Terrans or Terran colonials from other planets. As in many of the boys' books, stress is also placed on the multiracial composition of the interplanetary heroes: the Cadets include Blacks and Asians as well as colonials from Venus and Ganymede. And all officers of the Patrol are "brothers" trained to believe that "Each living, thinking creature in this system is your neighbor—and your responsibility" (Ch. 4).

Most of the novel is a detailed account of the training program for Cadets—with emphasis on how the unfit are eliminated. Then comes the big adventure that shows the Patrol in action.

One of the Cadets eliminated as unfit is the son of a big capitalist, Chairman of the Board of Reactors, Ltd. He has his father make him captain of a merchant rocketship that is "transferred to the family corporation 'System Enterprises' " (Ch. 16), and he promptly attacks the peaceful, aquatic Venerians in an ill-fated attempt to exploit precious metals found in a taboo swamp. Our youthful hero and fellow Cadets find themselves having to rescue this greedy antithesis of their

own values and establish peaceful relations with the Venerians, "the Little People."

The Venerians introduce what is soon to be a characteristic
feature of these boys' books—charming, endearing, delightful
space creatures, who often turn out to be at least as intelligent
as the Terrans. Until their appearance in *Space Cadet*, the
novel presents an almost purely masculine world, like the
unrelieved male world of *Rocket Ship Galileo*. But all the
Little People encountered by the Terrans, including the Venerian rulers and scientists, are female. This encounter with
the feminine in an alien form gives a special psychological
twist to this book written for adolescent boys.

In *Red Planet* (1949) the endearing creature is Willis, a
bouncy and affectionate little pet who turns out to be a Martian in its first stage. Willis is attached to James Madison Mar-
lowe, Jr., who lives with his family on Mars in the South Colony, "a frontier society" (Ch. 10).

The novel is about growing up. Jim becomes a man. Willis
prepares to metamorphose into a mature Martian. The colony
issues a Proclamation of Autonomy modeled on the Declaration of Independence. Human society itself seems youthful
compared with that of the Martians, who outgrew space travel
millions of years ago. The general relevance of the theme of
growing up is enunciated by a character found in many of
Heinlein's novels, a warm-hearted old curmudgeon serving as
the author's mouthpiece (and probably deriving from young
Robert's memories of his grandfather, Dr. Lyle), in this case a
grizzled doctor acting as Jim's true mentor: " 'Most people
never grow up. They expect papa to get 'em the pretty
Moon' " (Ch. 12).

Martians metamorphose from cuddly little critters like
Willis into twelve-foot beings possessing the collective experience of many millions of years and inscrutable powers capable of dematerializing a person, a colony, or even an entire
planet. Then they transform into immaterial beings, whose
wise minds become the collective guides for their race.

Human children, if they grow up successfully, change
gradually, not suddenly, into men—that is, leaders, fighters,
scientists, heroes—and women—that is, responsible house-

wives. The definition of maturity at South Colony is relatively simple:

> "Now this is a frontier society and any man old enough to fight is a man and must be treated as such—and any girl old enough to cook and tend babies is adult, too." [Ch. 10]

Jim's badge of manhood is his gun, and he proves his manhood through his courage and skill. His sister, however, is not competent: " 'You're a girl; you'd better stay out from under foot' " (Ch. 10). In the most dangerous moments of the crisis she even proves incapable of looking after Willis, prompting Jim to exclaim, " 'That's what comes of trusting women' " (Ch. 11).

The nemesis of mature freedom is represented by the Mars Company, a gigantic, bureaucratic, rapacious monopoly resembling the British East India Company and embodied on Mars by its greedy Resident Agent General and his henchman, the militaristic Headmaster of Jim's school. The colonists are saved through the frontier resourcefulness and bravery manifested most dramatically by Jim. The Martians liquidate, or rather evaporate, the villains, and the loving relationship between Jim and Willis convinces the Martians to allow the Terran colonists to stay, but only as a society independent of the monopolistic Company.

"Nothing Ever Happens on the Moon" (*Boys' Life*, April, May 1949) resembles a boys' version of Heinlein's stories in the slicks during this period, focusing on the heroism, self-sacrifice, and resourcefulness of people conquering the new frontier of space. Here the two heroes are Boy Scouts, one from Earth and the other from the moon, trapped in a lunar cave, sharing their last cylinder of air, and persevering to survive.

Satellite Scout was published first in *Boys' Life* (August, September, October, November 1950) and then appeared, somewhat revised, as *Farmer in the Sky*, the fourth in the Scribner's series. Except for some incidental Boy Scout business, the new frontier theme is here the whole story.

These pioneers embark on spaceships named the *Mayflower* and the *Covered Wagon* to convert Ganymede, one of

Jupiter's moons, into a world fit for terrestrials. Bill, the young narrator, and his family do not tarry long in the "frontier town" (Ch. 10), but move to become "homesteaders" (Ch. 11) on the virgin soil, or rather virgin rock that they must convert to soil.

Heinlein, who began life as a boy in rural Missouri, here projects an imaginary future that resurrects one of the most cherished symbols of the American past, the family farm, with its combination, at least in the ideal, of cooperation and independence. "You can't do it alone" and "Pioneers need good neighbors" (Ch. 14) are mottoes of these people, but the symbol of Bill's manhood is becoming "a property owner, paying my own way" (Ch. 18). Heinlein seems to relish the switch in values that comes from displacing the past into the future: farming here is so primitive that it is the "conservatives" who hold out for tractors rather than horses (Ch. 18).

Farmer in the Sky seeks to demonstrate that "Man . . . can create any environment that he needs" (Ch. 2). In fact, this becomes the definition of "men," put forth when Bill stumbles upon artifacts of an alien civilization:

> . . . they weren't "men"—not like us.
> But they *were* men in the real sense of the word, even though I don't doubt that I would run screaming away if I met one in a dark alley. The important thing . . . they had—they controlled their environment. They weren't animals, pushed around and forced to accept what nature handed them; they took nature and bent it to their will.
> I guess they were men. [Ch. 20]

Between Planets, like three other remaining novels in the Scribner's series, was published first as a serial in an adult magazine (as *Planets in Combat* in *Blue Book*, September, October 1951), demonstrating that there is no clear demarcation of Heinlein's "juvenile" fiction. The novel's youthful protagonist, Don Harvey, embodies the next stage in the outward-bound movement of this space epic. Born in space, his parents both scientists who move from planet to planet, Don proudly claims, " 'I'm a citizen of the System' " (Ch. 1). Swept up in an interplanetary struggle, he moves toward a discovery of his true identity, one that makes homesteading on Ganymede as humdrum as life in the corn belt, for he is the true spaceman:

He knew now where he belonged—in space, where he was born. Any planet was merely a hotel to him; space was his home. [Ch. 18]

In lurid contrast to this soaring freedom spins the decadent planet Earth. As the story opens, Earth is on the verge of the war predicted toward the end of *Farmer in the Sky*. New Chicago is "a modern Babylon," a "Sodom and Gomorrah" displayed in a chapter entitled "Mene, Mene, Tekel, Upharsin" (the biblical handwriting on the wall). Here Don gets to see a "captive princess," not the kind you find on Mars in an Edgar Rice Burroughs novel, but merely a scantily clad waitress in a typically debauched New Chicago nightclub. The fascistic government of "a more-than-world-wide empire" rules through the I.B.I., "the ubiquitous security police" (Ch. 2), "slimily polite stormtroopers" (Ch. 4) whose characterization is quite convincing (at least to those of us who have seen the FBI in action). Everything imaginable is for sale, and commercial greed glares through the dismal atmosphere:

The street was crowded with people but was narrow, meandering, and very muddy. Two lighted signs, one on each side of the street, shone through the permanent fog. One read: ENLIST NOW!!! YOUR NATION NEEDS YOU; the other exhorted in large letters: *Drink* COCA-COLA—*New London Bottling Works.* [Ch. 8]

Over all loom the gigantic monopolies, such as "the great transport trust," Interplanet Lines: "Interplanet was strong as government—some said it *was* the government" (Ch. 7).

The Terran Federation itself has become the instrument of interplanetary colonialism and exploitation, "trying to bleed Venus white" (Ch. 1). This generates, as in *Red Planet* and, later, *The Moon Is a Harsh Mistress*, an anti-colonial revolution modeled on the original American Revolution. The rebel forces of the Venus Republic declare their own independence and "as free men" "call on all oppressed and impoverished nations everywhere to follow our lead" (Ch. 6).

Don finds himself on Venus in "a nation of hardy individualists, almost anarchists" (Ch. 9), Heinlein's usual ideal political state. When Venus is invaded by the Federation troops and the I.B.I., Don passes to manhood as a guerrilla fighter. The forces of liberation triumph through the secret work of

The Organization, an interplanetary cabal of libertarian scientists from Terra and its colonies leagued with the Martians and Venerians. Don carries a ring containing the secret of how to manipulate space, which is deciphered by perhaps the most charming of all Heinlein's endearing extraterrestrials, the gigantic, wise, tender Venerian dragon and theoretical physicist known as Sir Isaac Newton.

This is the first novel that explicitly interrelates the adolescent hero's encounters with two kinds of alien beings, extraterrestrials and human females. The girl who has been wooing Don ever since he landed on Venus finally "grabbed him by both ears and kissed him quickly, then ran away": "Don stared after her, rubbing his mouth. Girls, he reflected, were much odder than dragons. Probably another race entirely" (Ch. 13). Fortunately, she is "the whither-thou-goest sort" so "she wouldn't hold him back" from his destiny as a spaceman.

The last of the series kept within the confines of the solar system is *The Rolling Stones* (1952), a novel glorifying the outward-bound Stone family, "a crew of rugged individualists" (Ch. 6), all geniuses—the father, ex-engineer, ex-mayor of Luna City, now author of a TV science-fiction serial; the grandmother, one of the original founders of the lunar colony, ex-engineer, adventurer, and jack-of-all-trades; the mother, a medical doctor; the eighteen-year-old sister whose alleged brilliance never gets much opportunity to shine out amidst the other luminaries; the four-year-old chess-genius brother; and the central characters, fifteen-year-old twins Castor and Pollux, inventors, entrepreneurs, spacemen, and rascals. Tiring of life on the moon, the Stones buy their own used spaceship and zip off for a two-year voyage of sightseeing and commerce to Mars and the asteroids, slipping in and out of scrapes all the way.

The episodes are structured like a serial, and seem intended to contrast with the science-fiction TV serial they write collectively as they wander along. Heinlein has achieved one of the main objectives of the first half of his juvenile space epic: making the moon, Mars, and the asteroids as familiar and ordinary as Missouri. The TV series, *The Scourge of the Spaceways*, moving of course toward an inevitable confrontation with the Galactic Overlord, is thus a parody of the kind of science fiction Heinlein himself is pointedly not writing, at least not at this time. Yet the last paragraph of *The Rolling Stones* shows this domesticized spaceship, like its creators, preparing to move out from the tamed frontiers near Earth toward the ends of the solar system and beyond:

> . . . the *Stone* trembled and threw herself outward bound, toward Saturn. In her train followed hundreds and thousands and hundreds of thousands of thousands of restless rolling Stones . . . to Saturn . . . to Uranus, to Pluto . . . rolling on out to the stars . . . outward bound to the ends of the Universe.

Starman Jones (1953) is the story of a midwestern farm boy who becomes an astrogator. The young hero moves from the wretched loneliness of an orphan trapped on a dismal Earth to the glorious loneliness of guiding ships through space.

Young Maximilian Jones starts his adventures by running away from his backwoods farm and unfeeling step-parents toward the glittering rockets of Earthport. Along the way he picks up a better father and guide, Sam Anderson, a busted veteran of the Imperial Marines, roguish but heroic, a picaro who knows how to live by his wits in a treacherous world. Max himself resembles both the classic picaro and the boy genius of "Misfit," for his only access to manhood and success lies in his brain, with its mathematical genius and eidetic memory.

Earth, now the center of an interstellar empire, has become a prison without hope, a rigidly structured society made up of three classes—the rich, a labor aristocracy organized into feudal guilds, and a semislave proletariat transported to the colonies as contract labor, "convicts and paupers" (Ch. 6):

> "This whole planet is one big jail, and a crowded one at that. What chance have you got? If you aren't born rich, or born into one of the hereditary guilds, what can you do? Sign up with one of the labor companies." [Ch. 5]

Sam and Max trick their way onto the starship *Asgard*, which also turns out to be a rigidly structured class society:

> The *Asgard* was a little world, a tiny mobile planet. It had its monarch the captain, its useless nobility the passengers, its

technical and governing class, and its hewers of wood and drawers of water.[3]

After the Captain and the astrogation team get the ship lost in uncharted space (by ignoring Max's suggestions), the officers, passengers, and crew set up the familiar frontier colony on a physically lovely planet they name "Charity." But the centaur-like creatures casually roaming about turn out to be carnivorous masters of the planet who have turned all other creatues into their living tools in a symbiotic enslavement even more rigid than the societies of Earth or of the starship.

Max is ultimately forced to become the new Captain, guiding all the survivors back through the anomalies of space to their original destinations. Here he finds still another loss of freedom: he learns that "a commanding officer . . . himself is ruled more strongly by the powers vested in him than is anyone else" (Ch. 21).

Only two alternatives to all these rigid structures are suggested. One is Heinlein's lost world of the frontier and the unspoiled American wilderness to be found on the planet Nova Terra, whose "comfortable looseness" seems like "anarchy" to Max, as Sam describes it:

> "No property taxes, outside the towns. Nobody would pay one; they'd just move on, if they didn't shoot the tax collector instead. No guilds—you can plow a furrow, saw a board, drive a truck, or thread a pipe, all the same day and never ask permission. A man can do anything and there's no one to stop him . . . ." [Ch. 6]

But Nova Terra is something we only hear about.

The other alternative appears first as Sam is painting this idyllic picture, when Max interrupts to say, " 'I don't want to get married.' " Sam responds, " 'That's your problem.' " The girl who woos Max for half the book, concealing her own intelligence so as not to scare him off, ends up marrying another after Max rejects her. At the end, Max has chosen the lone, loveless, unfree, heroic life of the starman.

The Star Beast (1954) is the only novel in the Scribner's series that takes place entirely on Earth. The action revolves around a creature from remote space, an eight-legged, brontosaurus-sized, fully omnivorous, lovable monster known as Lummox, the backyard pet of John Thomas Stuart XI, a teenager in a small Colorado town. Lummox has been raised by the Stuart family for four generations, but now "his" appetite for a neighbor's rosebushes precipitates a crisis that threatens the very existence of Earth. For Lummox, as it turns out, is actually "heiress to the matriarchy" of the Hroshii, a "practically immortal" and "nearly invulnerable" (Chs. 9, 17) race whose orbiting starship now threatens to destroy the planet unless she is returned. Meanwhile, the foolish townspeople in Colorado are trying to destroy Lummox as a dangerous nuisance.

The Hroshii (an echo of Hiroshima?) consider the Terrans mere animals, just as the local citizenry regard Lummox as a lumbering beast. Towering above the prejudices of both races is the Black African diplomat in charge of interspatial crises, His Excellency the Right Honorable Henry Gladstone Kiku, who realizes that "he himself was relatively safe from persecution that could arise from differences of skin and hair and facial contour" because encounters with the various "weird creatures" of the universe "made the differences between breeds of men seem less important" (Ch. 5). Heinlein is clearly trying to attack both racial prejudice and xenophobia by asking his young readers to imagine such creatures.

The other brilliant mind working to solve the crisis belongs to Betty, Johnnie's cool, audacious, and supremely competent girl friend. As in *Red Planet*, there is a parallel between the growing up of the endearing space creature—in this case Lummox begins to sprout arms—and the growing up of the teenaged male protagonist. In *The Star Beast*, however, it is the girl who comprehends the parallel, as Betty suggests when she tells Johnnie, " 'I was afraid you were just a big lummox yourself' " (Ch. 10).

Lummox herself considers Johnnie "her pet," and explains that "she has been raising 'John Thomases' for a long time" (Ch. 12). Because she is "very young," somewhat less than two thousand years old, having the very limited sense of "social responsibility" typical of Hroshii "children," she refuses to go home to her imperial destiny without Johnnie. The solution implies the future social and sexual maturity of all the youngsters, as Betty and Johnnie prepare to embark with the Hroshii as Earth's ambassadors to the stars:

> Her Imperial Highness, the Infanta of that race, 213th of her
> line, heiress to the matriarchy of the Seven Suns, future ruler
> over nine billion of her own kind, and lately nicknamed "The
> Lummox" contentedly took her pair of pets aboard the impe-
> rial yacht. [Ch. 27]

It may seem inconsistent that such a mature and experienced race would be ruled by an absolute monarch, but it is
quite consistent with an underlying authoritarian, anti-
democratic message flowing through the novel, summed up
by Kiku:

> ". . . we have managed to keep a jury-rigged republican
> form of government and to maintain democratic customs. We
> can be proud of that. But it is not now a real democracy and it
> can't be. I conceive it to be our duty to hold this society
> together while it adjusts to a strange and terrifying world. It
> would be pleasant to discuss each problem, take a vote, then
> repeal it later if the collective judgment proved faulty. But it's
> rarely that easy. We find ourselves oftener like pilots of a ship
> in a life-and-death emergency. Is it the pilot's duty to hold
> powwows with the passengers?" [Ch. 15]

Since the people are mere foolish passengers, we discover
through the course of events that it is the duty of the government to deceive and manipulate us for our own good.

In *Tunnel in the Sky* (1955) an overpopulated Earth sends
streams of colonists through special time-space gates directly
to thousands of new planets. Heinlein's characteristic anti-
Asian racism imagines marching hordes of Asiatics being
forced through these interstellar emigration gates, contrasting
with the stalwart western pioneers, actually riding off to other
planets in lines of Conestoga wagons.

Leaders are necessary to guide the way into these new environments where the race must "kill or be killed, eat or be
eaten" (Ch. 2). Since "the human race's one great talent is survival," "the most urbanized, mechanized, and civilized, most
upholstered and luxurious culture in all history trained its
best children, its potential leaders, in primitive pioneer survival—man naked against nature" (Ch. 2). The final examina-
tion for these future leaders is to be sent alone on a survival
test to "ANY planet, ANY climate, ANY terrain" with "NO rules,
ALL weapons, ANY equipment" (Ch. 1). This fantasy of the individual overcoming a strange natural environment through

his own ingenuity and fortitude is not some aberration peculiar to Robert A. Heinlein; it is a fantasy central to the bourgeois historical epoch, recurring insistently in the novel from its classic form in *Robinson Crusoe* through its most incisive parody, J. G. Ballard's *Concrete Island.*

In *Tunnel in the Sky*, Heinlein attempts to reconcile this vision of extreme individualism with his belief in social cooperation. Here too he is working with myths familiar to bourgeois society, for he is dramatizing the fantasy of free individuals, "naked against nature," coming together of their own volition to form human society. The youths placed on a strange planet for their final test in survival are stranded there when a supernova disrupts the gate through which they are supposed to return to Earth. Gradually they come together, creating a society formed by individuals capable of survival but needing the interrelations necessary for authentic human development. By the time Earth has re-established links with the planet, these young people have established the complete pioneer colony—including square dances.

Heinlein's ideology sharply contrasts with that of a book published the previous year, William Golding's *Lord of the Flies.* Golding, considered a "liberal," shows a group of proper English boys who, stranded on an island, quickly degenerate into savage, sadistic, warring beasts, supposedly demonstrating that war and all other evils of the human race are just an expression of our essential nature. In *Tunnel in the Sky*, the few uncooperative bullies get their lumps and are exiled from society; Heinlein, in these books written for boys during this period, projects an underlying faith in the potential of the human race and in the inherent qualities of individuals, at least those in his interchangeable categories of "leader" and "survivor."

The young protagonist, Rod Walker, the first leader of the pioneer society and later its trailblazer, embodies the extreme form of the outward-bound man. Unlike his older sister, "an assault captain in the Amazons" (Ch. 2) who looks forward to settling down with marriage and babies, Rod is as fundamentally celibate as Starman Jones. He is oblivious to the advances made by all girls, ranging from the rugged Zulu to the petite French lass whom he mistakes for a boy during the days the two live together in a cave. At the very end, we see him astride his horse, dressed in fringed buckskins, leading a pioneer wagon train, now as "Captain Walker headed out on his long road."

The self-denying psychology of the spaceman is the central focus of *Time for the Stars* (1956), which purports to be an autobiographical narrative written as psychotherapy under the advice of a starship's psychiatrist. The narrator, Thomas Paine Leonardo da Vinci Bartlett, communicates telepathically and instantaneously over the rapidly growing distances of space and time with his identical twin brother back on Earth, Patrick Henry Michelangelo Bartlett. Pat, a cocky, brash, cheerful gogetter who bosses and bullies his twin, had seemed the better candidate for going into space, and he had originally gotten himself selected over the moody, introspective, self-defeating Tom. But Pat has a last-minute skiing accident, which Tom eventually discovers to have been subconsciously self-inflicted. As the twins grow apart from one another in all ways, Tom gradually becomes aware of his own identity and the peculiarly self-effacing psychology Heinlein projects as an essential tool in the conquest of space.

Once again we receive a heavy lecture on the sanctity of authority and the dangers of democracy, summed up in the motto, "The Captain is right even when he is wrong":

> A ship is not just a little world; it is more like a human body. You can't have democracy in it, not democratic consent at least, no matter how pleasant and democratic the Captain's manner may be. If you're in a pinch, you don't take a vote from your arms and legs and stomach and gizzard and find out what the majority wants. Darn well you don't! Your brain makes a decision and your whole being carries it out. [Ch. 16]

As we saw in *The Star Beast*, this message applies to nations and planets just as much as it does to spaceships. So Tom discovers that "it was more important to back up the Captain and respect his authority than anything else" (Ch. 16), a message wildly contradictory to Heinlein's professed love of nearanarchic "looseness" and freedom.

The instantaneous telepathy of the twins and other similar communicators leads to a new kind of travel, "null" ships based on the simultaneity of distant events. Tom and his ship-

A dangerous predicament for the space travelers in *Time for the Stars*. Painting by Ron Miller.

mates return to Earth, as superseded as a "load of Rip Van Winkles." He and Pat, now a frail eighty-nine-year-old businessman, have virtually nothing left in common. Tom, whose body has hardly aged at all, marries his latest telepathic partner, his twin brother's great-granddaughter. This configuration, the union of the "aged and ageless" (Ch. 17) man of experience with the very young, very worshiping woman or girl we will encounter in other forms in Heinlein's late novels.

The central theme of *Citizen of the Galaxy* (1957) is slavery and freedom. The novel moves inward from a remote part of the galaxy toward Earth and upward through many social classes. These tours take place through the experiences of Thorby, a boy maturing into a man, seeking his roots, his identity, and his family, as he completes a rags-to-riches saga that takes him from the very lowest role in the galaxy to the very highest. Thorby is an ideal point-of-view character, for he starts off as a juvenile *tabula rasa*, "a fresh young lad like a clean sheet of paper" (Ch. 1).

We first see him as a slave boy being auctioned on one side of the Plaza of Liberty in an empire beyond the far-flung interstellar hegemony of Earth. His new owner becomes the first father he can remember, apparently a crippled old beggar, actually a wounded undercover veteran of the Hegemonic Guard, dedicated to smashing the slave trade. "Pop" manumits Thorby, who thus becomes "a free subject": his new tattoo shows that he is "entitled to taxes, military service, and starvation without let or hindrance" (Ch. 3). As a "free" beggar, he sees factory workers, standing "all day in one place, doing the same thing over and over," and wonders whether they are "slaves" (Ch. 4). The old Guardsman is arrested and chooses to protect his comrades by committing suicide before the police can torture him.

Thorby is then adopted into the extended matriarchal family of a "Free Trader" spaceship, which gives us a fine tour through different civilizations as well as Heinlein's most incisive exploration of the contradictory nature of bourgeois freedom. Dr. Margaret Mader, an anthropologist studying the structured tribal society of the Free Traders, who call themselves "the People" and refer to everybody else as subhuman "fraki," explains to Thorby that when he was adopted into the spaceship's extended family he thereby became another kind of slave. She admits that they "enjoy the highest average wealth in history" because "the profits of your trading are fantastic" (Ch. 11). The freedom she concedes they have is the ideal freedom implicit in the bourgeois quest—and in Heinlein's fiction:

> "The People are free. It's their proudest boast. Any of them can tell you that freedom is what makes them People and not fraki. The People are free to roam the stars, never rooted to any soil. So free that each ship is a sovereign state, asking nothing of anyone, going anywhere, fighting against any odds, asking no quarter, not even cooperating except as it suits them. Oh, the People are free; this old Galaxy has never seen such freedom. . . . There has never been a culture like it and there may never be again. Free as the sky . . . more free than the stars, for the stars go where they must." [Ch. 11]

But the price of this " 'unparalleled freedom . . . is freedom itself,' " for the Free Traders must submit themselves to a code of customs, rules, and hierarchical order " 'more stringent than any prison,' " telling them precisely what they can and cannot do within the metal bounds of their free spaceships.

Thorby next becomes a member of the Hegemonic Guard, bound by its code and authority. A new wise mentor from the Guard helps him find his original and final identity, "Rudbek of Rudbek," the fabulously wealthy heir of Rudbek Associates, a gigantic interstellar manufacturing complex headquartered on Earth. Now Thorby, "confused and disgusted" by the byzantine interlockings of his "corporations and companies," finds himself trapped in a new slavery: " 'Nobody owns a business; the business owns him. You're a slave to it' " (Ch. 18).

But Thorby refuses to be merely a slave of profits, for he also discovers that the bureaucrats and managers running his commercial empire are accomplices of the very same slave trade that killed his parents, perhaps because they knew too much, and sold him on the auction block. So he has himself elected Chairman of the Board and at the end we see him trying to extricate his enterprises from the slave trade—without harming the interests of the stockholders.

"Tenderfoot in Space," serialized in *Boys' Life* (May, June,

July 1958), suggests that Heinlein is nearing the end of his engagement with boys' stories. In this truly juvenile tale of a Boy Scout who moves with his dog to Venus, the dog turns out to be the hero and the only competent scout.

Have Space Suit—Will Travel (1958), the twelfth and final novel in the Scribner's series, soars through and beyond our galaxy to a trial of the human race, conducted by a million-year-old composite mind, to determine whether we should be annihilated as a threat to the survival of wiser and more mature races. Contrasted to this cosmic drama, but playing a crucial role within it, is the life of Kip Russell, a high-school senior from Centerville, who works in the local drugstore, yearns to go to the moon, and narrates his breathtaking travels.

While wearing his secondhand space suit won in an advertising contest, Kip is whisked off by a UFO piloted by an evil bug-eyed monster. He teams up with an eleven-year-old girl genius, who demands that he " 'quit being big and male and gallantly stupid' " (Ch. 6), and "the Mother Thing," an intergalactic policewoman from a race of superbeings. The Mother Thing—"around her you felt happy and safe and warm" (Ch. 5)—is the ultimate embodiment of maternal protection, cherishing our young hero and heroine and interceding at the intergalactic trial to save our youthful race.

The trial is the climax of the novel and the Scribner's series. Our race is represented by a Neanderthal man, ultimately determined to be a "cousin" rather than an ancestor, a brutal Roman legionnaire whom Kip, unlike the judge, admires as a "tough old sergeant" who "had courage, human dignity, and a basic gallantry," and the two youngsters. The court condemns human history as unmitigated evidence of inherent ferocity:

> "By their own testimony, these are a savage and brutal people, given to all manner of atrocities. They eat each other, they starve each other, they kill each other. They have no art and only the most primitive of science, yet such is their violent nature that even with so little knowledge they are now energetically using it to exterminate each other, tribe against tribe. Their driving will is such that they may succeed. But if by some unlucky chance they fail, they will inevitably, in time, reach other stars. It is this possibility which must be calcu-

lated: how soon they will reach us, if they live, and what their potentialities will be then." [Ch. 11]

The Mother Thing offers two defenses. She argues that no race can " 'survive without a willingness to fight.' " But her main argument is that we are mere children, both as a race and because we are short-lived " 'ephemerals' " who " 'all must die in early childhood.' " Since we " 'all are so very young,' " we should be given " 'time to learn' ": " 'Toward evil we have no mercy. But the mistakes of a child we treat with loving forbearance.' " Through this vision we see that the entire juvenile space epic is Heinlein's version of the human epic, the story of the childhood of a race, best symbolized in the lives of children becoming adults as they grow into a role in the galaxy.

FOR THOSE WITH NO EXIT

The other science fiction published by Heinlein in the 1947–58 period lacks the unifying vision of the juvenile space epic and the short stories popularizing space travel. All but two are set on Earth, and as a group they are dominated by views antithetical to the energy, enthusiasm, and long-range optimism of the outward-bound tales.

"Jerry Is a Man" (*Thrilling Wonder Stories*, October 1947) lies in the tradition that stretches from *The Island of Dr. Moreau* through *Brave New World* and *War with the Newts* to *Planet of the Apes*. The science of "plasto-biology" has allowed the development of "Workers, Inc.," a giant corporation that produces a work force of specialized anthropoids, genetically engineered from apes. "The little tykes" are "conditioned to the social patterns necessary to their station in life." The company claims that "They really *like* to work—when we get through with them." Everything goes fine for this enterprise until one of their major stockholders, the richest woman in the world, discovers that "old workers who have passed their usefulness" are sent to the "death pens." She buys Jerry, one of the anthropoids, and then arranges for Jerry to sue the company. Workers, Inc. argues in court that all the workers are chattels, mere property. As "labor contractors" their position is thus no different from the labor contractors in

"Logic of Empire," but they base this position on the claim that these workers are not human beings.

The company's defense is shaken by the testimony of a Martian, who proves that the human form is not what constitutes human identity, while also asserting that he is obviously more intelligent than Earthmen, whereas Earthmen are not obviously more intelligent than the anthropoid workers. The final proof of Jerry's human status comes when he takes the stand and sings " 'Way down upon de Suwanee Riber,' " climaxing the pointed parallels the story draws between these anthropoid workers and Black slaves. Heinlein apparently intends the story to be anti-racist, as well as anti-xenophobic. But likening anthropoids to Black slaves comes perilously close to the pre-Civil War American School of Ethnology, which argued that Blacks were a distinct subhuman species.

"Water Is for Washing" (Argosy, November 1947) describes the sudden flooding of the Imperial Valley and the heroism of a tiny group of survivors. The protagonist, despite a deep phobia about water, rescues a young girl, a Nisei boy, and a tramp who had earlier stolen his searchlight and who now gives his own life to save the other three.

"Our Fair City" (Weird Tales, January 1949) fantasizes about a conscious whirlwind that fetches and carries for an old parking-lot attendant in a "corrupt" American city. "Symbolic of the spiritual filth lurking in the dark corners of the city hall," the whirlwind nevertheless helps clean up the town, unmasking the crooked cops and mayor.

By the middle of 1949 the United States had committed itself to a global crusade against Communism. Loyalty checks and loyalty dossiers were now a characteristic feature of American life. The unions, the media, and the schools were being systematically purged of "Communist sympathizers." On September 21, 1949, the People's Republic of China was proclaimed in Peking. Two days later, President Truman announced that the Soviet Union had set off an atomic explosion, thus ending the U.S. nuclear monopoly. In November and December 1949 Robert Heinlein published in Astounding the novella "Gulf," an anti-Communist diatribe arguing for the need of a master race of "supermen" to settle the problems of our times and the future.

As we saw in Chapter 2, Heinlein's late Depression fiction wobbled back and forth on the role of the scientific elite, sometimes warning against their pretensions to moral and political supremacy, sometimes reluctantly conceding their preeminence in solving historical crises. "Gulf" unequivocally advocates creating an elite not just as a social class, but, as the title suggests, as a new superhuman species, clearly marked off from our doomed race of "homo sap."

Constructed as a propaganda piece, the story opens as a fast-paced thrilling adventure story about a superslick security agent. This turns out to be merely a hook to reel us into the exposition of the message, which forms the entire center of the story, an extended argument preaching the moral and intellectual superiority of "homo novis," the New Man, the species of "supermen." Then in a very brief adventure ending, we are allowed to watch these supermen demonstrate their moral and intellectual superiority as they save the world.

We learn that just as man is distinguished from animals by his ability to think, *homo novis* is separated from *homo sapiens* by being "able to think better," thus establishing a "gulf between us and them" that is "narrow" but "very deep," and thus inevitably decreeing that the New Man must "displace" *homo sapiens*. Already their secret organization is at work "to skim the cream of the race's germ plasm and keep it biologically separate until the two races are permanently distinct." Any defense of traditional "democracy, human dignity, and freedom" for the human species is dismissed as mere "monkey prejudice."

Throughout all this, there is a nonsensical confusion between thinking "better" in the sense of more skillfully and thinking "better" in the sense of more morally. There is even the outright statement that "Evil is essentially stupid." "Geniuses," on the other hand, "are emotionally indifferent to accepted codes of morals" and "make their own rules" as they accomplish their lofty purposes. Equipped with this knowledge of the good, the New Men determine who is incurably evil and systematically assassinate them: " 'We keep a "Better Dead" list; when a man is clearly morally bankrupt we close his account at the first opportunity.' "

Two forces have created the necessity for this new species

of "superthinkers": the development of modern science, which is perceived as making democracy obsolete, and the emergence of Communism, which is presented as the central "evil" antithetical to science and directly menacing the technological elite. The head of the New Men, after admitting a sentimental attachment to democracy, explains why it is no longer feasible:

> "I confess to that same affection for democracy, Joe. But it's like yearning for the Santa Claus you believed in as a child. For a hundred and fifty years or so democracy, or something like it, could flourish safely. The issues were such as to be settled without disaster by the votes of common men, befogged and ignorant as they were. But now, if the race is simply to stay alive, political decisions depend on real knowledge of such things as nuclear physics, planetary ecology, genetic theory, even system mechanics. They aren't up to it, Joe."

It was Communism that forced the New Men to organize. "The politburo suppressed semantics," which, we learn, is the key to all science, for the politburo knew that semantics would prove that "Das Kapital is a childish piece of work." Since "most New Men are scientists, for obvious reasons," they "went underground" when the Communists suppressed the other crucial sciences along with semantics. This technological elite organized and won the anti-Communist struggle: " '. . . it's been eighty-five years since we beheaded the last commissar.' " But they discovered that they could not merely reinstitute democracy, because the evil of Communism had corrupted society far too deeply:

> "We helped to see to it that the new constitution was liberal and—we thought—workable. But the new Republic turned out to be an even poorer thing than the old. The evil ethic of communism had corrupted, even after the form was gone. We held off. Now we know that we must hold off until we can revise the whole society."

So in 1949 we find Robert Heinlein perceiving not Nazism but Communism as the evil force threatening the world, and we see him embracing the central Nazi theory of a new master race of genetically produced supermen, capable of defeating Communism and creating a scientific age of the future.

In 1950, President Truman authorized the development of

the hydrogen bomb, Senator Joseph McCarthy launched his own anti-Communist campaign, the North Atlantic Treaty was adopted, and war broke out in Korea. In that same year appeared what many consider the first modern science-fiction movie, *Destination Moon*, made from Heinlein's juvenile novel *Rocket Ship Galileo*, with Heinlein co-authoring the screenplay and serving as technical adviser.

Gone are the adventurous, science-loving teenaged boys of *Rocket Ship Galileo*. The crew of the rocket now consists of the inventor, "the General," a big industrialist, and an assistant engineer. Their flight represents the triumph of the military-industrial complex—portrayed as an all-star cast of heroes who are the only possible saviors of American society. The technocratic boys of Heinlein's youth have grown up, becoming the technocratic men projected as our true elite. Heinlein's screenplay describes "the dominant group" in the shot of the assembled industrialists as "the just past young, energetic, far-sighted and dynamic men who are the backbone of American industry."[4]

In the first three scripts, the Nazi plot of *Rocket Ship Galileo* is replaced by a thinly disguised Communist plot. "World War III is about to begin," atomic rockets are aimed at all major U.S. cities, and the villain is the "Enemy General" who sneers at the "decadent democracies" and whose own nation has the "efficiency . . . of a solidified state."[5] In the final version, there is no overt plot by this nation with an identity easily guessed by a 1950 American audience, just hints of sabotage and a debilitating protest movement aimed at stopping the development of "radioactive" rockets.

The ultimate message is spoken by "the General," one of the four heroic space pioneers. Earlier he had warned that " 'this country is *not* secure. At this moment it stands in the deadliest peril of its existence.' "[6] The General stands for enlightened internationalism: " 'Tell them the Moon can never be used, *dare* never be used for attack by any part of mankind against any other part. Tell them, the Moon must never be used, save as a bastion of the world's peace. Tell them the *only* Government to control the Moon must be a sovereign government of the whole of man, a government of the world' " ("Final Revised Script," p. 117).

By 1953 this internationalism had been quite forgotten, with *Project Moonbase*, Heinlein's other major movie. As the title card rollup tells us:

In 1948, the Secretary of Defense proposed that the United States build a Space Station as a military guardian in the sky. . . . By 1970, the Space Station had been built and free men were reaching for the Moon, to consolidate the safety of the Free World.

But while this was going on, the enemies of Freedom were not idle—they were working to destroy the Space Station.[7]

The enemy plot, which involves substituting a spy for the great scientist Dr. Wernher, is foiled. The movie shows us the establishment of the first Moon Base, a military outpost of the United States, not of a world government.

The spaceship is piloted by a woman, Colonel Briteis, and her male co-pilot, Major Moore. After their forced landing on the moon, they are advised by a general from Earth: " 'Public opinion being what it is, it would be a lot better for everyone—for the country—for the service—and for you—if you were married!' " (Screenplay, p. 59). The marriage is conducted over TV by the "Lady President," who also promotes Major Moore to Brigadier General in command of both the Moon Base and Colonel Briteis. Heinlein has no problem projecting a female space pilot or even President, but when a woman relates to a man she has to know who is the boss.

In that 1950–53 period, Heinlein published three works dramatizing in various forms an intensely paranoid vision of reality. The anti-Communist frenzy of those years merges into this vision, mingling with deeper currents of desperation.

The Puppet Masters (1951) has much the same message as the 1951 movie *I Was a Communist for the FBI*. It is a Cold War allegory, which, like the 1956 movie *Invasion of the Body Snatchers* adapted from the 1954 Jack Finney novel, warns of the insidious Communist menace, projected in the form of alien invaders taking over the bodies and minds of Americans.

These "puppet masters" are giant slugs, "titans" from Saturn's satellite, who land in flying saucers and covertly attach themselves to people, turning them into mindless "zombies" whose only purpose is to aid the sinister aliens in their conquest. The slugs are not distinct individuals but unfeeling members of a communal mind dedicated to the enslavement of all other societies. They come in "cells." One of their first triumphs is "the capture of a high key official" (Ch. 8). Before the story is over, they have managed to take over millions of Americans, including local, state, and national government officials, military officers, members of the secret police, congressmen, and senators. As in "Gulf," the protagonist is a security policeman, member of a supersecret United States intelligence agency. The moral of the story, appropriate to an America feverishly arming for a pre-emptive nuclear strike against the Soviet Union, is spelled out quite clearly at the end: "The price of freedom is the willingness to do sudden battle, anywhere, any time, and with utter recklessness" (Ch. 35).

In case any readers might miss the political allegory, Heinlein points it out at intervals throughout the novel. Since "World War III had not settled the Russian problem," the slugs "might feel right at home there" (Ch. 15). Later the Soviets denounce the whole invasion as a "fantasy":

> The Russian propaganda system began to blast us as soon as they had worked out a new line. The whole thing was an "American Imperialist fantasy." I wondered why the titans had not attacked Russia first: the place seemed tailor-made for them. On second thought, I wondered if they had. On third thought, I wondered what difference it would make. [Ch. 21]

On later occasions, our heroes—three members of the U.S. secret police—wonder if the slugs have not in fact already infiltrated the Soviet Union, and then discover that they "must have moved in on the Russians" before they attempted the conquest of the United States (Ch. 30).

The fate of the world rests largely in the hands of three superior beings, all ace security and intelligence operatives: the protagonist and narrator, his beautiful fellow agent Mary, and "the Old Man," as the head of this most secret of all agencies is commonly called. About a third of the way through the novel, we discover that "the Old Man" is actually the narrator's father, but neither one lets this relationship stand in the way of his duty. Mary is not only beautiful but extremely in-

dependent, tough, and resourceful. In a pattern familiar since
Beyond This Horizon, this exceptionally liberated woman becomes truly fulfilled when she becomes the hero's obedient
spouse, responding only with the words " 'Yes, dear' " when
he tells her what she will be doing. As Ronald Sarti has com-
mented about this pattern: "The skills and intelligence of the
heroine—and her individual freedom—are subordinated to the
ego of the hero. . . . In effect, what the hero wants for a
heroine is a liberated woman who knows her place." [8]

In his 1952 introduction to *Tomorrow, the Stars*, Heinlein
exults in science fiction's attraction for "the healthy-minded,"
and its resistance to the "Plunging-Neckline" and "four-letter-
word" schools of contemporary literature. He specifically
extols the absence of nudity in science fiction, pointing to the
rarity of "sparsely dressed and exceedingly nubile young ladies." Yet one of the curious features of Heinlein's fiction
emerging in *The Puppet Masters* is a virtual obsession with
scanty dress and nudity. All civil liberties in America are sus-
pended, and one overriding question hangs over everybody:
". . . are you a loyal citizen—or are you a zombie spy?" (Ch.
13). Since the slugs who have attached themselves to people
can hide under any clothing, it becomes essential for all loyal
citizens to shed their clothes. So throughout much of the
novel everybody is running around naked, an odd fore-
shadowing of an important element in Heinlein's later fiction.

At the end, the slugs on Earth are destroyed and the narrator girds for battle with them on their home planet, proclaiming one of Heinlein's favorite social Darwinian maxims: "This
is for keeps and we intend to show those slugs that they made
the mistake of tangling with the toughest, meanest, deadliest,
most unrelenting—and ablest—form of life in this section of
space, a critter that can be killed but can't be tamed." This exaltation of "ferocity," and the fear, loathing, rage, and hate
directed against an alien life form is the opposite of the dominant view in the juvenile space epic, which, though of course
recognizing that we may have to fight against some hostile life
forms, consistently attacks xenophobia and dramatizes respect—and even love—for the kinds of beings we may find in
space. The final words of *The Puppet Masters* are a fervent
glorification of war:

I feel exhilarated. Puppet masters—the free men are coming to
kill you!
   Death and Destruction!

Universal death and destruction are almost the whole story
in "The Year of the Jackpot" (*Galaxy Science Fiction*, March
1952). This comes not, however, through some holy war
against aliens, but rather through the senseless, predetermined, inflexible fate of the human race caused by its own
madness and a hostile universe.

Belying Heinlein's claim, printed the same year, that
"sparsely dressed and exceedingly nubile young ladies are a
rarity in science fiction," "The Year of the Jackpot" opens
with a prolonged striptease by the heroine. Her bizarre urge is
part of the mental disintegration of the human race, which is
going berserk and becoming like "lemmings." Madness is not
confined to people, for the entire natural world is also going
berserk, with cataclysmic eruptions of the earth and the sun. It
seems that "Cycles are everything," that all events are determined by omnipotent curves that can be plotted statistically,
and that human behavior and natural phenomena are simultaneously heading for some terrible climax.

The action takes place in 1952, the date of publication, and
an "undeclared World War" has been going on for some time.
The Soviet Union, which has been suppressing science and
having scientists "liquidated" (as in "Gulf"), suddenly
launches a massive nuclear attack, destroying many American
cities. The United States counterattacks, destroying "Moscow
and the other slave cities." An invasion by "Russki para-
troopers" is repulsed, with the protagonist getting the satisfac-
tion of having "killed his own quota": "He had shot them in
the back and buried them beyond the woodpile."

This paranoid fantasy plays such a crucial role for years
both in Heinlein's fiction and in American society that we
should now recognize its source: one of the greatest political
and military intelligence hoaxes in history. The Soviet Union
in the early and mid-1950s had no missiles or operational
aircraft capable of delivering either a nuclear strike or a para-
trooper invasion of the United States. The Central Intelligence
Agency, Strategic Air Command Intelligence, and other agencies worked night and day to convince the American people

that we were living under imminent threat of a Soviet nuclear attack. Meanwhile, Strategic Air Command B-47s and B-52s, many of them carrying nuclear weapons, were flying daily over the Soviet Union on missions of provocation, intimidation, and espionage. This has all been abundantly documented, and I can attest to it from my own experience as a navigator and intelligence officer in the Strategic Air Command, where I discovered that the alleged Soviet strategic capabilities were a hoax and where I participated in midair refueling of bombers heading over the Soviet Union as late as 1958.[9] Of course in Heinlein's mind the fantasy springs from a deeper source as well, for he was imagining a surprise nuclear attack by the Russians against the United States as early as 1941 in "Solution Unsatisfactory."

In "The Year of the Jackpot" Heinlein takes the paranoid fantasy to an absurdist conclusion. The hero and heroine are left clinging desperately to each other as they watch the sun explode. The final words of the story are:

> He glanced down at the journal, still open beside him. 1739 A.D. and 2165. He did not need to add up the two figures and divide by two to reach the answer. Instead he clutched fiercely at her hand, knowing with an unexpected and overpowering burst of sorrow that 1952 was . . .
>
>   The End.

The freedom so dear to Heinlein here disappears, along with that grand human destiny dramatized in the space stories for the general magazines and in the juvenile space epic. All that is left of free will in this absurd universe is the isolated loving couple, treasuring the final moments of their existential choice in a doomed world.

"Project Nightmare" (*Amazing Stories*, April 1953) projects a fantastic salvation from the Communist menace. The Soviet Union mines thirty-eight major U.S. cities with nuclear bombs and "DEMANDS USA CONVERT TO 'PEOPLE'S REPUBLIC' UNDER POLITICAL COMMISSARS TO BE ASSIGNED BY USSR." The only hope lies in "paranormals," whose direct power of mind over matter may locate the bombs and keep them from exploding. The paranormals can visualize the workings of the devices because "since the spy trials everybody knows how an atom bomb works." The FBI and local police help round up these beings whose will can operate directly on the material world. The Soviet Union triggers the bombs, but the paranormals use their powers to stop the emission of neutrons. The bomb in Camden is discovered by rounding up "the known Communists" and interrogating them. The bomb in Cleveland blows up because a domineering government bureaucrat disturbs the concentration of one of the paranormals. But the mind-adepts locate and disarm all the other bombs. Then comes the happy ending—the United States launches a full-scale nuclear attack on the cities of the Soviet Union.

Double Star (*Astounding*, February, March, April 1956), the one adult novel of this 1947–59 period set mostly beyond Earth, breaks loose from the paranoid and claustrophobic world of "Gulf," *The Puppet Masters*, "The Year of the Jackpot," and "Project Nightmare." In fact, one of its principal aims seems to be to counteract the xenophobia thrust upon us by *The Puppet Masters* and the kind of elitist underground cabal applauded in "Gulf."

The narrator and hero is Larry Smith, otherwise known as "The Great Lorenzo," a versatile, self-conceited, penniless actor who suddenly finds himself playing a brand new role: savior of the world, or, rather, worlds. His job, thrust upon him by the leaders of the good political party, is to impersonate their "Chief," Joseph Bonforte (i.e. good-strong), the greatest political leader in the solar system, who at a crucial historical moment has been abducted by a dirty-tricks gang from the bad political party. Smith, one of the more distinctly memorable characters in Heinlein's fiction, is forced to change his identity profoundly until he becomes the man whose part he is playing, thus proving that the ordinary man can, given the right circumstances, rise to greatness.

The interplanetary political system resembles the nineteenth-century British Empire, with Bonforte as "leader of the loyal opposition" (Ch. 2) in a parliamentary system serving under a figurehead Emperor with a string of archaic titles, a role much like an actor's, as the Emperor himself acknowledges to Smith. Bonforte heads the good guys, the "Expansionist Party" and their "Expansionist coalition": " '. . . the whole program of the Expansionist Party is founded on the notion that free trade, free travel, common citizenship, common currency, and a minimum of Imperial laws and restrictions are good not only for the citizens of the Empire but for the Empire itself' " (Ch. 8). The bad guys are the "Humanity Party," which wants to annex Mars by force. Bonforte's brand of imperialism, on the other hand, stresses co-equality for the various races under its hegemony:

> Expansionism had hardly been more than a "Manifest Destiny" movement when the party was founded, a rabble coalition of groups who had one thing in common: the belief that the frontiers in the sky were the most important issue in the emerging future of the human race. Bonforte had given the party a rationale and an ethic, the theme that freedom and equal rights must run with the Imperial banner; he kept harping on the notion that the human race must never again make the mistakes that the white subrace had made in Africa and Asia. [Ch. 7]

This was a familiar theme in 1956, for it was the banner of the expanding American neo-colonial empire, supposedly a radical advance from British, French, Dutch, Portuguese, Spanish, German, Italian, and Belgian colonialism, though many of the older empires had made very similar professions of equality. For the Empire to succeed, "The price of expansionism was virtue" (Ch. 7).

Bonforte had been on the verge of being initiated as a blood member into a Martian "nest," thus fulfilling his ideology. This initiation ceremony is now the critical ordeal for Larry Smith, who is nauseated by the Martians' smell and regards them all with loathing, fear, hatred, and disgust. Here lies the confrontation with the kind of xenophobia that animated The Puppet Masters, for Martians (like those slugs) reproduce by fission, are deeply communal, and look like "a nightmare toadstool." Eventually Smith comes to recognize that this "xenophobia is very deep-rooted" and must be overcome "if we are to go out to the stars" (Ch. 10). Smith—who starts out petty, selfish, and prejudiced—finally does turn into the grand, selfless, and infinitely tolerant Bonforte, thus dramatizing the novel's central message: if Smith can become Bonforte, we can all overcome our small-mindedness, egoism, and bigotry, thereby preparing the human race to assume its galactic role.

Unfortunately, it takes hypnotism to convert Smith to a proper view of Martians. This glaringly contradicts Heinlein's gratuitous outbursts against "Communists" allegedly "tampering with a man's personality" (Ch. 6) and, even more fundamentally, ignores those strong arguments against hypnotism as a political technique presented in the revised version of " 'If This Goes On—.' " Another basic problem is that Smith's imposture is an act of deception aimed at the masses of common people by an elite group who alone knows what is true and right. If Smith must be hypnotized to expunge his xenophobia and if most people must be deceived for their (our) own good, what hope is there for the millions of other Smiths and their counterparts on other continents and other planets?

Despite these serious problems, Smith's metamorphosis into Bonforte succeeds in dramatizing a profoundly deepening consciousness, a gradual assumption of responsibility, and a maturation process in which he, no longer venerating his actor father and no longer taking Bonforte as a substitute father, himself becomes a fully adult human being. When, twenty-five years after the main action, he rereads his own narrative, those "foolish and emotional words of that young man," "I remember him, yet I have trouble realizing that I was ever he." Yet even now he is not entirely convinced of his own sanity, having become lost in that maze of shifting identities:

> I find I can "remember" Bonforte's early life better than I remember my actual life as that rather pathetic person, Lawrence Smith, or—as he liked to style himself—"The Great Lorenzo." Does that make me insane? Schizophrenic, perhaps? If so, it is a necessary insanity for the role I have had to play, for in order to let Bonforte live again, that seedy actor had to be suppressed—completely. [Ch. 10]

Changing identities fabricate a maze through time in *The Door into Summer* (*Magazine of Fantasy and Science Fiction*, October, November, December 1956). The door into summer signifies an escape from a maze, a trap of wintry desolation, into warmth, youth, and boundless freedom. The protagonist, Daniel Boone Davis, had once watched his cat desperately wandering from door to door in a winter-bound old house, searching for the one that would open into summer. Now he himself, caught in a maze of betrayal, goaded by the pioneer spirit proclaimed by his name, looking forward wtith gloom and back with bitterness from the age of thirty, with "winter in my heart," seeks his own escape door (Ch. 1).

Daniel Boone Davis is one of those inventive geniuses central to science fiction from the nineteenth century through the first period of Heinlein's career. But he is trapped in the year 1970, a time when inventions require corporations, and corporations turn inventors into salaried workers. Dan refuses to accept this reality: "Bicycle-shop engineering with peanuts for capital, the way Ford and the Wright brothers had started—people said those days were gone forever; I didn't believe it" (Ch. 2). So he sets up shop with his dear friend and aspiring businessman, Miles Gentry, a buddy from the Six Weeks War, which apparently had led to "the downfall of communism" (Ch. 1), thanks to superior American science and technology.

There are women in Dan's future; in fact his future is to be determined by women. Recognizing that "amazingly little real thought had been given to housework, even though it is at least 50 per cent of all work in the world," Dan decides that he will produce "the Second Emancipation Proclamation, freeing women from their age-old slavery": "I wanted to abolish the old saw about how 'women's work is never done.' Housekeeping is repetitious and unnecessary drudgery; as an engineer it offended me" (Ch. 2). So he invents a line of household robots: Hired Girl, Window Willie, and the all-purpose Flexible Frank.

Into their thriving business comes a real woman, the beautiful Belle Darkin, who starts out as company secretary, becomes Dan's fiancée, and then, in collusion with Miles Gentry, whom she has secretly married, steals Dan's inventions and control of the company. Belle and Miles then make the worst nightmare of the lone inventive genius come true: they turn him into a salaried worker, to be fired at the will of the bosses.

To escape, Dan follows the path of the first shaping figure in American science fiction—Rip Van Winkle. He contracts with another corporation to go into "the Long Sleep," to be reawakened in the year 2000, when he hopes to gloat, still being a mere thirty years old, over the now faded and aged Belle. In his thirty-year sleep, he has strange, revealing dreams, in which "the world consisted of top sergeants" and Belle appears as a bartender, a top sergeant, his bedmate, and a household robot (Ch. 5). The world into which he awakens has "a better way of living" (Ch. 10), thanks mainly to great technological progress, largely due to the robots he had invented, whose descendants now do a large share of society's drudgery. The society is far from ideal, however, for there is overpopulation, bureaucratic and corporate stifling of individual inventiveness, and the danger of falling into the hands of "a zombie recruiter" who uses drugs to turn the hordes of unemployed into "labor zombies" for a "labor-company" (Chs. 5, 6). So there seems to be even less room in 2000 than in 1970 for the enterprising individual, caught between the danger of being swallowed up into the army of semislave labor or being stranded as a salaried clock-watcher under the thumbs of the corporate managers.

Ironically enough, Dan becomes a salaried worker for the giant corporation that has acquired his patents. He does get to witness time's revenge on Belle, who has become a "flabby old wreck," grotesquely mimicking her former seductive beauty in a negligee that "showed that she was female, mammalian, overfed, and underexercised" (Ch. 7). But Dan himself, "bitterly lonely" (Ch. 6) in this comfortable yet alien world, wonders, in a terribly revealing question, "Wasn't I, in my own way, living in a fantasy of the past quite as much as Belle was?" (Ch. 7).

At the center of his desires are two beings he left behind in 1970: his true friend Petronius Arbiter (Pete the cat) and his true lover Ricky, an eleven-year-old girl. These two objects of Dan's love are both alternatives to the "feral" Belle, who "had a lot of cat in her" (Ch. 2) and who had exposed "the underlying predatory animal" beneath her beauty (Ch. 3). Both are completely loyal and obedient to Dan's wishes and desires. At first Dan's relationship with Ricky seems like play: "Ricky had been 'my girl' since she was a six-year-old at Sandia, with hair ribbons and big solemn dark eyes. I was 'going to marry her' when she grew up and we would both take care of Pete. I thought it was a game we were playing, and perhaps it was"

(Ch. 2). To find little Ricky and recover the lost Pete, Dan has himself transported back to 1970 by a scientific genius whose unaided invention of time travel had been suppressed by the military and the government. He locates Ricky at a Girl Scout camp, where he has to get past the watchful eyes of a woman who "was properly suspicious of me; strange men who want to be allowed to visit little girls just turning into big girls should always be suspected" (Ch. 11). When Ricky—"knobby knees, stringy, shooting up fast, not yet filled out," and thoroughly "adorable"—asks him " '. . . will you marry me?' " his "eyes roared and the lights flickered" (Ch. 11).

Dan does some more inventing and returns, with Pete this time around, to 2001, where he soon connects with Ricky, who had waited, as he had instructed her, to be a grown-up twenty-one before taking the Long Sleep. The ending is blissfully happy. Thanks to his inventions and the faithful business expertise of John and Jenny, a lovely couple he had met in a nudist camp on his trip back to 1970, Dan is now part of the controlling group of the two giant corporations that manufacture his robots. He is reunited with his cat and married to Ricky, the little girl as woman, embodying the "sweet eternal Yea!" (Ch. 12). And he has recaptured the ideal of Heinlein's earliest science fiction, the world lost in the Depression, the creative individual enjoying the full freedom of his own personal and private enterprise:

> Me, I'm just the "Davis Engineering Company"—a drafting room, a small shop, and an old machinist who thinks I'm crazy but follows my drawings to exact tolerance. When we finish something I put it out for license. [Ch. 12]

The world itself is a better one, its progress coming through the kind of engineering incarnated by Daniel Boone Davis:

> "Back" is for emergencies; the future is better than the past. Despite the crapehangers, romanticists, and anti-intellectuals, the world steadily grows better because the human mind, applying itself to environment, makes it better. With hands . . . with tools . . . with horse sense and science and engineering. [Ch. 12]

Only a few intellectual problems remain, and Dan must ponder them in solitary meditation. John, his friend, had refused to believe he had traveled backward in time; Dan could not even tell Jenny, because she is too "uncomplicated" (Ch. 10); he "tried to explain it to Ricky, but she got upset" (Ch. 12). The first problem has to do with the limitations imposed on the individual inventor: "Engineering is the art of the practical and depends more on the total state of the art than it does on the individual engineer" (Ch. 5). This leads to speculation about the fate of another person the lone inventor of time travel had sent back in time, one Leonard Vincent, who must have found fifteenth-century Italy more hellish than anything Tantalus experienced.

The other main problem has to do with reconciling free will with the determinism implied in the possibility of traveling backward in time. Dan can not even be certain that he is the same person who jumped from 1970 to 2000, back from 2001 to 1970, and then back again to 2001. These voluntaristic leaps, fulfilling the wildest fantasies of unfettered freedom for the personal will, paradoxically imply a fixed, predetermined reality in which one can jump around. Dan rejects the concept of " 'branching time streams' and 'multiple universes' " (the concept dramatized in "Elsewhere") in favor of a universe *engineered* for the maximum free will:

> Free will and predestination in one sentence and both true. There is only *one* real world, with one past and one future. . . . Just *one* . . . but big enough and complicated enough to include free will and time travel and everything else in its linkages and feedbacks and guard circuits. You're allowed to do anything inside the rules . . . but you come back to your own door. [Ch. 12]

A final glorious escape parades before our eyes in "The Elephant Circuit" (*Saturn*, October 1957):

> It was undeniably the greatest show ever assembled for the wonderment of mankind. It was twice as big as all outdoors, brighter than bright lights, newer than new, stupendous, magnificent, breathtaking, awe inspiring, supercolossal, incredible—and a lot of fun. . . . The marvels of P. T. Barnum, of Ripley, and of all Tom Edison's godsons had been gathered in one spot. . . . The result was as American as strawberry shortcake and as gaudy as a Christmas tree, and it all lay there before him, noisy and full of life and crowded with happy, holiday people.

This glorious and endless country fair of all country fairs, however, is merely the heavenly vision of an elderly couple who had yearned for children; "when none came their family had filled out with invisible little animals." Only after their death can they be reunited within this animated festival of life, a dream of America in the late 1950s.

THE END OF AN ERA: STARSHIP TROOPERS AND "ALL YOU ZOMBIES—"

In 1959, Heinlein's fabulously successful career as a juvenile author came to an abrupt end. Scribner's had published all twelve novels in the juvenile space epic, thus enjoying an immensely lucrative relationship with Heinlein. Nevertheless, when he submitted the book intended as number thirteen in the series, Scribner's rejected it because of its intense, unrelenting militarism. Heinlein turned to Putnam's, which published it as *Starship Troopers*, perhaps his most controversial book and the one that marks the end of this period in his career.

Between 1947 and 1959, Heinlein published sixteen novels, two novellas, and twenty-six identified stories, as well as various essays, reviews, and revisions. No other Heinlein fiction was to appear until *Stranger in a Strange Land* was brought out in 1961 by Putnam's, which was then to publish his next six novels, all profoundly contradictory to the stirring message and joyful spirit of the juvenile series.

Besides *Starship Troopers*, Heinlein published one other work in 1959, the short story "All You Zombies—," a masterpiece of involuted time travel and a favorite anthology selection. These two pieces, superficially having little in common, actually fit together quite intricately, revealing far more than might be expected about Robert Heinlein, and about America, in the last year of the 1950s.

Starship Troopers is the story of a military recruit, a youth whom we witness being transformed from a raw enlistee into a full-fledged officer in the interstellar Mobile Infantry. "All You Zombies—" is the story of a military recruiter, whom we witness transforming her/himself from a baby girl into a cosmically solitary officer of the Temporal Bureau. Although

Starship Troopers is a bugle-blowing, drum-beating glorification of the hero's life in military service, it flows from the
same source as the agonizing lonely wail of "All You Zombies—."

The immediate ancestors of Starship Troopers are those
World War II movies idealizing the military lives of our typical American combat men. In the novel, we see the familiar
naïve, sloppy civilian being enlisted by the wounded, much-
decorated, tough old recruiting sergeant, the brutal basic
training that looks like "calculated sadism" administered by
grizzled drill sergeants whose rhinoceros hides conceal their
love for the recruits, and the thrilling, fearsome combat which
demonstrates that every last bit of that training was vital. Half
the pages are devoted to the details of our young hero's military training, first as a raw recruit going through basic, later as
a combat veteran making his arduous way through Officer
Candidates School. Instead of the cross section of American
youth featured in the World War II movies—the Iowa farm
boy, the Texan or Virginian sharpshooter, the Jew from Brooklyn, and the Italian from the Bronx—we have a cross section
of the youth of Earth's galactic empire—the martial-arts expert
from Japan, the two Germans replete with dueling scars, the
drawling, brawling southerner, miscellaneous "colonials"
from Earth's galactic outposts, and our hero, Juan (Johnnie)
Rico, son of a wealthy Philippine businessman.

But the resemblances between the World War II movies
and Starship Troopers are somewhat superficial, for this is not
about a mass conscript army called up in a war to defend
democracy—that disappeared back in the twentieth century.
Starship Troopers displays the superelite force designed to
fight the permanent wars necessary to fulfill Earth's manifest
destiny in the galaxy. And the Terran Federation, the society
employing this force, is ruled entirely by veterans of this elite
military machine and its non-combatant auxiliaries.

Recently there has been some debate about whether Starship Troopers is as militaristic as it seems, and Heinlein himself disclaims any militaristic intentions. But to argue about
whether or not Starship Troopers glorifies militarism would
be as silly as arguing about whether or not "My Country 'Tis
of Thee" glorifies America. Militarism shapes the speech and

sets the tone of all the characters, including the narrator-hero; militarism animates every page; militarism—together with imperialism—is the novel's explicit message. What we must probe is not the quantity of militarism in Starship Troopers but its special quality. For Starship Troopers expresses its own time, and gives a striking vision of times to come. The difference between the World War II army movies and Starship Troopers measures the distance from the conscript army that fought against the Fascist-Nazi-New Order drive to conquer the world and the growing "military-industrial complex" (to use those words of President Eisenhower) that was attempting to hold and expand a worldwide empire against a rising tide of global revolution.

Starship Troopers imagines and applauds a future in which the imperialism of Earth has become virtually cosmic. By the 1970s, just a short distance into the actual future, this vision had penetrated into popular American culture in many forms. One of the most suggestive of these forms is the simulation war game, with its own clubs and magazines of strategy. The novel Starship Troopers was transformed in 1976, by the Avalon Hill Game Company, into one of the more popular of these games, competing with 4000 A.D.: An Interstellar Conflict Game (1971); Star Force "Alpha Centauri": Interstellar Conflict in the 25th Century (1974); Alpha Omega: A Game of Tactical Combat in Space (1977); and Cosmic Encounter (1977). (Battlefleet Mars: Space Combat in the 21st Century (1977) seems to be a throwback to the Heinlein of Red Planet; the game "assumes that, by the year 2093, a single corporation, the Ares Corporation, will have attained near-complete control of the industries and mining operations of the inner planets and asteroids," and the "Martian Free Traders" revolt in order to establish "the Martian Republic.") Heinlein himself wrote a lengthy statement for the box containing the Starship Troopers game, describing the "stimulating" effects of pitting "an elite corps," able to "do enormous damage in a few minutes," against the "aliens" with their "communal life" and "social structure resembling an ant or bee colony." (The Avalon Hill General devoted most of its March–April 1977 issue to a discussion of strategy and tactics for playing Starship Troopers, including a special section "Dirty Tricks.")

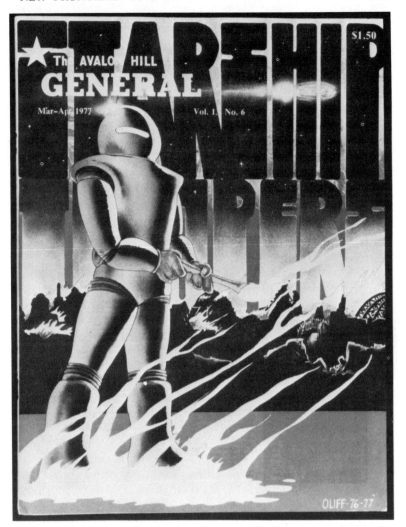

Cover of *The Avalon Hill General* containing articles on strategy and tactics for
playing the simulation war game version of *Starship Troopers*.

Johnnie Rico, hero of the novel, learns about the history of
the late twentieth century from a series of all-wise, all-know-
ing military officers who conduct required courses in History
and Moral Philosophy. He discovers that "the unlimited democracies" of the twentieth century failed because "their citi-

zens were not responsible for the fashion in which they exerted their sovereign authority . . . other than through the tragic logic of history" (Ch. 12). The undisciplined, self-indulgent masses thus caused all the problems of society. Social collapse came in the form of moral collapse, which produced "the Terror" of unchecked street crime in North America, Russia, and the British Isles. "Murder, drug addiction, larceny, assault, and vandalism" were "the disorders that preceded the breakup of the North American republic," going "right up to the war between the Russo-Anglo-American Alliance and the Chinese Hegemony" (Ch. 8). When this war ended in 1987, with "national governments in collapse," a new social order was created by the veterans of the war, who decided that only military veterans had earned the right to vote. This is the social order at the time of the action, and it is perceived as the best form of government in human history.

This government has the fine feature of immunity from the disease of revolution, for all those brave enough to fight are either volunteers presently enrolled in the Federal Service of the Terran Federation or the honorably discharged veterans of that Service. These veterans are the only enfranchised citizens of the society and hence its rulers. Thus "revolution is impossible":

> "Because revolution—armed uprising—requires not only dissatisfaction but aggressiveness. A revolutionist has to be willing to fight and die—or he's just a parlor pink. If you separate out the aggressive ones and make them the sheep dogs, the sheep will never give you trouble." [Ch. 12]

The underlying premise of the new social order is that the only people fit to govern the state are those willing to sacrifice their lives for the state:

> "Since sovereign franchise is the ultimate in human authority, we insure that all who wield it accept the ultimate in social responsibility—we require each person who wishes to exert control over the state to wager his own life—and lose it, if need be—to save the life of the state." [Ch. 12]

This does not, as some have claimed, resemble the philosophy of Ayn Rand and others who develop the bourgeois cult of the individual to its logical extreme, seeking to free the individual from all responsibility to the group. Quite the opposite: " 'Under our system every voter and officeholder is a man who has demonstrated through voluntary and difficult service that he places the welfare of the group ahead of personal advantage' " (Ch. 12).

Much of the American nation was prepared, in 1959, to respond to just such a call, to rise above the self-seeking exalted in the 1950s (and in the 1970s). The man elected to the presidency the following year, John Fitzgerald Kennedy, was to thrill millions with the concluding words of his Inaugural Address: "And so, my fellow Americans, ask not what your country can do for you—ask what you can do for your country."

Underlying the Terran Federation's military service is the premise that there are but two alternative forms of armed forces available to a modern state: a mass conscript army or an elite corps of volunteers ruthlessly winnowed out by the most arduous training. " 'Conscript armies have been tried in the past,' " we are told, and they have failed. The most telling proof offered is what happened to the U.S. armed forces " 'in the so-called "Korean War," circa 1950' " (Ch. 12).

Hence the Terran Federation relies entirely on superb equipment and elite units, hierarchically structured, ranging down to the Mobile Infantry, the corps with the least technological training and the highest level of *esprit de corps*. Trained to be superkillers, the Troopers are lethal with everything from bare hands and knives to nerve gas and one-man arsenals of atomic rockets. The Mobile Infantry specializes in "smash & run" raids, in which we see Johnnie telling how "I set fire to things more or less at random" (Ch. 1). Each Trooper has such enormous powers of destruction that the typical skirmishing line must allow great distances between these deadly individuals who form a cohesive fighting unit. Thus they embody both the myth of the superpotent individual and a rigidly determined form of social cooperation. Johnnie describes Officer Candidates School, where you learn "how to be a one-man catastrophe yourself while keeping track of fifty other men, nursing them, loving them, leading them, saving them" (Ch. 12). The fundamental motivation of the Mobile Infantry, as characteristic of such elite units, is not the political

dedication essential to any successful mass army, but rather
its loyalty to itself:

> . . . we were told only what we had to know for tactical pur-
> poses. In the past, armies have been known to fold up and quit
> because the men didn't know what they were fighting for, or
> why, and therefore lacked the will to fight. But the M.I. does
> not have that weakness. Each one of us was a volunteer to
> begin with, each for some reason or other—some good, some
> bad. But now we fought because we were M.I. We were profes-
> sionals, with *esprit de corps*. [Ch. 11]

The Mobile Infantry, in short, is a galactic Special Force, an
interstellar Green Berets.

Heinlein here again is being a man of his time and also a
man somewhat ahead of his time. In the early 1950s, the U.S.
Marines and infantry had been badly beaten by numerically
inferior, poorly equipped Chinese forces in Korea, where U.S.
defeat was prevented only by saturation bombing with na-
palm, high explosives, and bacteriological weapons.[10] In the
mid- and late 1950s, U.S. ground forces, still largely organized
along World War II lines, were paralyzed in the face of Communist insurgencies and national liberation movements. The
U.S. military might rested primarily on a technological elite,
especially the carrier navy and the Strategic Air Command,
both designed for full-scale, all-out wars of annihilation. Little
effort was made to motivate the elite combat crews through
enthusiasm for democracy, or any of the other slogans of
World War II. As a former navigator and intelligence officer in
the Strategic Air Command, I well remember the first "indoctrination" lecture we received in 1956 as we processed in at
Lackland Air Force Base, Texas. "You men," roared the beefy,
cigar-chomping lieutenant colonel in his very first words, "are
now nothing but a bunch of professional hired killers."

But in 1959 there was still great resistance, even at the
highest levels of the U.S. Army, against creating the kind of
elite ground crops envisioned in futuristic form in *Starship
Troopers*. Here, once again, we find that Heinlein's position
corresponds to that of the man who embodied the *liberal* ideology of the period, John F. Kennedy, who almost singlehandedly created the Green Berets, designed their insignia,
and defined their purpose and spirit. In his first year as President, Kennedy increased the size of the Special Forces from

1500 to 9000 men, over the objections of his own top generals, who voiced the traditional American military suspicion of elite forces. Then, in the words of his biographer Ted Sorensen: "The President directed—again over the opposition of top generals—that the Special Forces wear green berets as a mark of distinction. He wanted them to be a dedicated, high-quality elite corps of specialists. . . ."[11] Within three years of the publication of *Starship Troopers*, President Kennedy had established a string of Special Forces bases in Latin America and Southeast Asia. After he was assassinated, the main Green Beret training camp at Fort Bragg was renamed the John F. Kennedy Special Warfare Center.

In *Starship Troopers*, the social organization created and ruled by service veterans has proved to be the most efficient of all forms of human society, allowing a unification of the peoples of Earth and an extension of the Terran Federation deep into the galaxy. But at the time of the action, this powerful state built upon a combination of voluntary self-sacrifice and cooperation has met what may be its match—"the Bugs," a hive-like society of arachnids, every bit as tough and just as expansionary as Heinlein's humans. Like the slugs of *The Puppet Masters*, the Bugs of *Starship Troopers* are obviously extrapolations from Heinlein's conception of twentieth-century communism. They embody "a total communism" (Ch. 11); "they are communal entities, the ultimate dictatorship of the hive" (Ch. 10). So the society of cooperating individuals is now locked in struggle with the communist hive for total control of the galaxy.

Heinlein makes explicit connections between this vision of a struggle for galactic control and his vision of the twentieth-century struggle for global control:

> We were learning, expensively, just how efficient a total communism can be when used by a people actually adapted to it by evolution; the Bug commissars didn't care any more about expending soldiers than we cared about expending ammo. Perhaps we could have figured this out about the Bugs by noting the grief the Chinese Hegemony gave the Russo-Anglo-American Alliance. . . . [Ch. 11]

And just as Heinlein imagines our former enemies, the Russians, joining in an alliance against the utmost in human communism, the Chinese hordes, he projects another humanoid race, "the Skinnies," more communistic than humans but less communistic than Bugs, who switch from being allies of the Bugs to become our allies in the final showdown.

To underscore the rightness of our side in this galactic apocalypse, Heinlein turns back to two questions of twentieth-century social and political theory: the Marxist theory of value and the relations between crime and punishment. He recognizes that the labor theory of value is fundamental to Marxism, since it is the theoretical basis for both the might and the right of revolution by the laboring masses. Heinlein purports to "demolish the Marxian theory of value—the fallacy from which the entire magnificent fraud of communism derives" (Ch. 6). His refutation seems to come from a ludicrous misreading of Marx (or possibly from accepting a caricature of the theory without reading it at all). Heinlein presents Marxian value as determined merely by "all the work one cares to add," no matter how "unskillful," in producing a commodity; he easily refutes this by arguing that clumsy, inefficient labor obviously cannot increase value. This is an argument Marx frequently cited to demonstrate what the labor theory of value does *not* say, for the value of commodities is determined by the average amount of socially useful labor necessary to produce them under the most technologically advanced and efficient conditions. Heinlein's attack on the labor theory of value is crucial to *Starship Troopers*, for the hierarchically structured, elite Federal Service is merely one expression of a thoroughly elitist society based on the denigration of common people, their labor, and their lives.

We see this message reinforced in the extended argumentation presented in defense of flogging. Johnnie, who himself is flogged for an inadvertent error in training, ardently advocates the practice. (One might wish to compare his blase description and argument in favor of flogging with the chilling description and passionate denunciation of flogging in Herman Melville's *White-Jacket; Or, The World in a Man of War*, published in 1850 and instrumental in convincing Congress to abolish this sadistic practice in the U.S. Navy.) Heinlein contrasts the efficacy of flogging to the moral and social disintegration of the twentieth century, which he attributes mainly to the parents who did not spank their children, and a judicial system that did not severely punish criminals.

For several pages he seeks to demonstrate that "the most vicious" of "juvenile criminals," especially street gangs, were produced by their not receiving "spanking, or any punishment involving pain" (Ch. 8) when they were children. Violent criminals, according to Heinlein and many other relatively affluent Americans, are not produced by poverty and the hardships of slum life but rather by pampering, coddling, and excessive comfort. The Terran Federation has put a stop to all such permissiveness and laxity. Flogging is a common punishment throughout society, and members of the Federal Service are not only flogged for various infractions but subjected to such rigors that many are killed just in training.

Johnnie himself is pampered by his doting mother, who writes to "her baby boy," explaining that "you are always my little boy" and "Little boys never get over needing their mother's laps" (Ch. 6). His father, buried in this marriage, cannot be a *"man,"* as he later confesses. So Johnnie's true father in the supermale world of the Mobile Infantry is his commanding officer: "The Lieutenant was father to us and loved us . . ."; he is "the head of the family from which we took our name, the father who made us what we were" (Ch. 10). Women in Johnnie's combat world are beautiful, unattainable objects. They are the pilots of the ships, presiding over all the internal arrangements of these small "homes," and they literally deliver what Johnnie's biological mother thinks of as "little boys."

When Johnnie's mother is killed by a Bug attack on Buenos Aires, his father is suddenly emancipated from his psychiatrist and his lucrative business. Now he too can join the Mobile Infantry and become a man:

> "Son, I always understood what you were doing better than your mother did—don't blame her; she never had a chance to know, any more than a bird can understand swimming. . . . you had actually done something that I knew, buried deep in my heart, I should have done. . . . Your mother's death released me for what I had to do. . . . I had to perform an act of faith. I had to prove to myself that I was a man. Not just a producing-consuming economic animal . . . but a *man*." [Ch. 12]

The deepest emotional experiences in *Starship Troopers* all have to do with the relationships among the men in the

Mobile Infantry. The psychological climax comes in the concluding passage of the novel. Throbbing with intensity, this passage reveals a new human order, as the female Captain of the ship prepares to deliver a father and son who have switched places, leaping to sow death and destruction to the words and tune of a song from World War II:

> My platoon sergeant put his arm around my armored shoulders. "Just like a drill, Son."
> "I know it, Father." I stopped shaking at once. "It's the waiting, that's all."
> "I know. Four minutes. Shall we get buttoned up, sir?"
> "Right away, Father." I gave him a quick hug, let the Navy drop crew seal us in. The shakes didn't start up again. Shortly I was able to report: "Bridge! Rico's Roughnecks . . . ready for drop!"
> "Thirty-one seconds, Lieutenant." She added, "Good luck, boys! This time we take 'em!"
> "Right, Captain."
> "Check. Now some music while you wait?" She switched it on:
> "To the everlasting glory of the Infantry—."

If we were to continue beyond this point in the same direction we would arrive at a man who is both his own father and his own mother, whose mission in life is to recruit himself into military service, and who can love only himself because he is the only real being in the world. And this summarizes that other work published by Robert Heinlein in 1959, at the end of this period in his career, "All You Zombies—."

"All You Zombies—" is Heinlein's most ingenious short story, and, I think, his finest. It is also his last to date, except for three pieces scattered between 1962 and 1973. A fitting climax to Heinlein's mastery of the short-story genre, "All You Zombies—" recapitulates and integrates many of his most significant themes and leaves us with a brilliant vision into the tangled contradictions at the heart of his achievement.

Like "By His Bootstraps" and *The Door into Summer*, the story weaves an intricate web of time travel in which the narrator meets himself going and coming. In his avatar as narrator and governing consciousness, he is a colonel on a recruiting mission, sent from the headquarters of the Temporal Bureau in 1993 on an involuted series of time-travel hops back into a past that can be saved only by active manipulation of crucial events by Bureau "operatives" and "agents."

In a New York City bar named "Pop's Place" back (or forward, since the story was published in 1959) in 1970, he ensnares "the Unmarried Mother," a twenty-five-year-old man who makes a living by writing short stories for confession magazines. The Unmarried Mother had begun her present life as a one-month-old baby girl in an orphanage in 1945, been seduced in 1963, and given birth to a baby girl in 1964. This had ruined her prospective career in the Women's Emergency National Corps, Hospitality & Entertainment Section (W.E.N.C.H.E.S.), the forerunners of the Women's Hospitality Order Refortifying & Encouraging Spacemen of 1973, for the cesarian operation necessary to deliver the baby had revealed a complete set of male organs, leading the doctors to change her into a man. Our narrator takes the Unmarried Mother back to 1963, where that confession writer turns out to be the man who had seduced his former self and fathered her baby girl. While these two are making love, the narrator leaps forward in 1964 to kidnap the baby and backward into 1945 to plant her on the steps of the orphanage where she is to grow up to be Jane, the Unmarried Mother. He returns to 1963 on the night of the seduction to pick up the young short-story writer, whom he has recruited as a future temporal agent: " 'That's all, son,' I announced quietly. 'I'm going to pick you up.' " The young man is badly shaken by all his new knowledge about himself, and the narrator reveals why: " 'It's a shock to have it proved to you that you can't resist seducing yourself.' "

The narrator, of course, turns out to be the final avatar of baby Jane, the Unmarried Mother, and the sneaky seducer. Thus "he" is daughter and mother, son and father. By seducing himself, he manages to have sex as a male with himself as his own mother and also as his own daughter, and as a female with himself as his own son and also his own father. This fantasy is almost as far as narcissism can go.

It is also almost as far as the bourgeois cult of the lone, self-created individual can go. The narrator is the ultimate self-made man, the logical end point of the epoch based on the belief that "I think, therefore I am." At the end of the story, the narrator, going to his lonely bed in the year 1992, muses on the ring he wears—"The Worm Ouroboros . . . the World Snake that eats its own tail, forever without end," an emblem of his own cosmic loneliness in a solipsistic void:

> The Snake That Eats Its Own Tail, Forever and Ever . . . I *know* where *I* came from—but *where did all you zombies come from?*
>
> I felt a headache coming on, but a headache powder is one thing I do not take. I did once—and you all went away.
>
> So I crawled into bed and whistled out the light.
>
> *You* aren't there at all. There isn't anybody but me—Jane— here alone in the dark.
>
> I miss you dreadfully!

On one level, the narrator is deprived of the love of other human beings within the fictive universe of the story. Self-created, loving only other forms of himself, he loathes the very products of his own labors. On another level, the products of his own labors are indeed fictions, because the narrator is in more than one sense an author, and the "*you*" he can see only as "zombies" are we, the readers. Is it an idle coincidence that the young man he retrieves from the past is a hack short-story writer selling his works "at four cents a word," a rate Heinlein had earned as a young man? " 'Business is okay,' " he says, " 'I write 'em, they print 'em, I eat.' " The narrator toys with his knowledge of the Unmarried Mother's stories written from "the woman's angle." Is this a little inside joke about Heinlein's short stories narrated by a teenaged girl and published in magazines for girls? When the Unmarried Mother defiantly states what he does for a living he puts it in these terms: " 'I write confession stories.' " And consciously or not, the characters created by a fiction maker are all embodiments of the author.

This particular writer has been forced, because of a physiological problem, to give up a future career in the service. But then his future self offers him the opportunity of a lifetime, in many senses. He can give up his hack-writing career and join the most important service of all time, the Temporal Bureau, whose job is nothing less than saving the world—over and over again.

Here we must begin to recognize some deep similarities

and differences between *Starship Troopers* and "All You Zombies—." Just as the novel glorifies militarism, the short story exposes its hollow core. Just as the novel revels in death and destruction, the short story seeks to evade and escape the horrors of war and the history that Heinlein perceives in the future.

When the narrator reports in, with his new recruit in tow, to "the duty sergeant" in the "Sub Rockies Base" of 1985, he indicates that they too may be interchangeable: "he did what I said—thinking, no doubt, that the next time we met he might be the colonel and I the sergeant." The sergeant assures the Unmarried Mother that he will enjoy his career in the service: " 'Look at me—born in 1917—still around, still young, still enjoying life.' " Nineteen seventeen, of course, is the year the United States entered World War I. The next date in the story is September 20, 1945, the day the colonel places Jane, then a month-old baby, on the steps of the orphanage. This is the month after the surrender of Japan ends World War II. World War III *would* have taken place in 1963 (four years after the publication of the story), the year in which the colonel arranges the seduction of Jane by the Unmarried Mother, except for the self-sacrificing service of our lone hero:

> It's rough, but somebody must do it and it's very hard to recruit anyone in the later years, since the Mistake of 1972. Can you think of a better source than to pick people all fouled up where they are and give them well-paid, interesting (even though dangerous) work in a necessary cause? Everybody knows now why the Fizzle War of 1963 fizzled. The bomb with New York's number on it didn't go off, a hundred other things didn't go as planned—all arranged by the likes of me.

Without the ceaseless work of the operatives of the Temporal Bureau, history would develop as it appears to Heinlein to be developing. Thus the Mistake of 1972 apparently leads to "a nasty period . . . 1974 with its strict rationing and forced labor" (like the world of "zombie recruiters" projected in the future of *The Door into Summer*).

Instead of the "freedom" of voluntary self-sacrifice and co-operation presented by *Starship Troopers*, "All You Zombies—" presents a deterministic maze that leads nowhere but to a series of holes in a dike constructed to hold back the flood of history. Instead of the intense passion that binds the Troopers of the Mobile Infantry to each other, to their mission, and to their glorious history and future, "All You Zombies—" offers us the loveless solipsism of the ultimate narcissist, the self-created individual spinning out webs of fiction in which he wanders alone, not even believing in the existence of his audience.

In 1959, the New Frontiers of Robert Heinlein's juvenile space epic seem to have become lost. He leaves us to choose between a hymn to a corps of elite destroyers and the inverted agony of a lonely officer of a Bureau designed to save us from our time.

The following year there appeared the last political figure to command an enthusiastic following among the majority in America. The theme of his campaign was bringing the glories of America's past back into the future, and his slogan was New Frontiers.

NOTES

1. *More Junior Authors*, ed. Muriel Fuller (New York: Wilson, 1963), p. 109.

2. *Rocket Ship Galileo* (New York: Scribner's, 1947), Ch. 3. Quotations from novels discussed in this chapter are indicated parenthetically by chapter number. I have used the following editions: *Space Cadet*, Scribner's, 1949; *Red Planet*, Ballantine Books, 1977; *Farmer in the Sky*, Ballantine Books, 1978; *Between Planets*, Ace Books, 1951; *The Rolling Stones*, Ace Books, 1952; *Starman Jones*, Ballantine Books, 1976; *The Star Beast*, Ace Books, 1954; *Tunnel in the Sky*, Ace Books, 1955; *Time for the Stars*, Ace Books, 1956; *Citizen of the Galaxy*, Ace Books, 1957; *Have Space Suit—Will Travel*, Ballantine Books, 1978; *The Puppet Masters*, New American Library, 1963; *Double Star*, New American Library, 1964; *The Door into Summer*, New American Library, 1964; *Starship Troopers*, Berkley Publishing, 1968.

3. Ch. 6. The feudal guilds of the labor aristocracy may derive from Jack London's *The Iron Heel*, in which Asgard is a great pleasure city completed by the oligarchy in 1984.

4. Manuscript designated "*Destination Moon*: Final Revised Script," p. 40, in the Heinlein Collection, Special Collections, the University Library, University of California, Santa Cruz.

5. *Operation: Moon* (title of "Script #1"), pp. 97–103, Heinlein Collection.

6. *"Destination Moon:* Final Revised Script," p. 41.

7. Copy of the screenplay for *Project Moonbase* in the Heinlein Collection.

8. Ronald Sarti, "Variations on a Theme: Human Sexuality in the Work of Robert A. Heinlein," in *Robert A. Heinlein,* eds. Joseph D. Olander and Martin Harry Greenberg (New York: Taplinger, 1978), p. 113.

9. See Allen Dulles, *The Craft of Intelligence* (New York: Harper & Row, 1963), p. 149; John M. Carroll, *Secrets of Electronic Espionage* (New York: Dutton, 1966), pp. 134–35; and the extended discussion in the chapter entitled " 'Peace Is Our Profession': Flying with SAC" in my *Back Where You Came From: A Life in the Death of the Empire* (New York: Harper's Magazine Press, 1975).

10. See *Back Where You Came From,* pp. 52–53.

11. Theodore C. Sorensen, *Kennedy* (New York: Harper & Row, 1965), p. 632.

4
A VOICE OF THE 1960s

In our free-speech fight at the University of California,
we have come up against what may emerge as the
greatest problem of our nation—depersonalized, unre-
sponsive bureaucracy. . . .
It is a bleak scene, but it is all a lot of us have to look
forward to. Society provides no challenge. American society in the standard conception it has of itself is simply
no longer exciting.

Mario Savio
"An End to History"
Berkeley, California, 1964

STRANGER IN A STRANGE LAND (1961)

Adam, the Baby, and the Man from Mars have always been
invoked . . . as the only three unprejudiced observers of the
human scene—Adam, fresh from the hand of his Maker, the
Baby new to earth and sky, and the Man from Mars on his first
visit to an alien planet. Thus have three fantastic psychologies
been invoked as the basis of far more than that number of fantastic metaphysics. . . . The Man from Mars is the best illustration of how philosophers have tried to jump out of their skins
and out of their universe.

Irving Edman
Adam, the Baby, and the Man from Mars, 1929

If Robert Heinlein had never written another word, *Stranger in
a Strange Land* would still make him an important figure in
modern American culture. Like Joseph Heller's *Catch-22*,
which also appeared in 1961, *Stranger in a Strange Land* has

126

sold millions of copies, gone through dozens of printings (forty-eight mass printings through 1979), put a new concept into our language, and influenced the imaginations and perhaps the lives of millions.

Unlike his prewar and postwar short stories, juvenile space epic, and hard-core science-fiction novels of the 1950s, *Stranger* did not immediately find its audience (though it did win Heinlein his third Hugo award). But in the mid-1960s, as millions of young people began to rebel against the most sacred American values of the 1950s, the novel became widely adopted within the movement known as "the counterculture," and its influence began bubbling around in the powerful, if confused, underground eddies and streams seething beneath what seemed the concrete and steel permanence of America's world of business. Somehow, *Stranger in a Strange Land* appealed to an incongruous medley of libertarians and liberals, anarchists and socialists, earnest reformers, angry rebels, and pleasure-seeking do-your-own-thingers. A grotesque tributary of the book's influence came to the surface in 1969 when actress Sharon Tate and six others were ritually murdered by "The Family," Charles Manson's cult: Manson, it turned out, had found the model for his coterie of young women worshipers in *Stranger in a Strange Land*, his "Family" regularly performed "water rituals" and spoke of "grokking," and the first child born inside their group marriage was named after the mythic hero of the novel. But by this time the verb "to grok" had entered the language of tens of millions, and "sharing water" was not unusual, as more and more Americans sought escape from what they perceived as sterility, alienation, lovelessness, and driving ambitions—personal and national—that seemed to destroy all communities. To understand the range of attraction exerted by *Stranger in a Strange Land* is to understand America at a turning point in its history.

This is by no means to suggest that the book lost any influence in the 1970s. Quite the contrary. In 1978, I asked my science-fiction class at Rutgers University in Newark—a commuter college of working-class students—how many had previously read *Stranger in a Strange Land* and what they thought about it. In response came a series of intense personal statements that sounded like narratives of religious conversion. One student felt that the book "changed my whole life": "I read it first when I was seventeen. I was then married, in a bad marriage. The book showed me I was not alone, that I might be able to find other people who looked at things the way I did." Another student said she had first read the book when she was sixteen and somehow it had changed her life too: "Up 'til then, the other kids at school used to make fun of me and I didn't respond in any way. I didn't laugh and I didn't cry. I just kept a stone face. About this time, I began to laugh a little." A quadriplegic identified with all the stages of the hero's strangeness; at the bottom of his page of notes I later noticed he had written in big block letters: "AM I A STRANGER?" A burly, usually gruff young man explained the book's appeal in these terms: "We all went through an experience like Michael's when we were children. We were helpless. We didn't know what we were supposed to do and we needed somebody to show us. So I identify with Michael. I also identify with the people who help him, because we all want to help somebody who needs help." Another student spoke of getting a sense of "community without losing individuality," "a community of individuals."

The opening sentence of the novel presents a mythic being whose name suggests his multiple identities: "Once upon a time there was a Martian named Valentine Michael Smith." He is: Valentine, both a message of erotic love and a martyred saint; Michael, keeper of the gates of heaven, the archangel who leads the heavenly hosts against the forces of evil; Smith, the American everyman. He is also a "superman" from a culture "far in advance of human culture in mysterious ways."[1] And he is unfallen man, the New Adam who "has never tasted the fruit of the Tree of Knowledge of Good and Evil" (Ch. 17). He is likened to Dionysus, and later assumes the name of Apollo. Above all, he is the new messiah, re-enacting the crucifixion, destined to save the elect in a mortally diseased world.

Valentine Michael Smith comes to an Earth that has survived World War III and become unified. But that unity takes the form of the World Federation of Free States, which has actually destroyed what Heinlein conceives of as true freedom and reduced the United States, like every other nation, to a "satrapy in a polyglot empire" (Ch. 18). Unlike the highly praised Federation of *Starship Troopers* (but like the fascist Federation of *Between Planets*), the World Federation of Free States is a totalitarian dictatorship ruling through the "storm troopers" of the "Federation S.S. Bureau" (Chs. 14, 16). Although technology has produced space travel, it has mainly allowed both this Federation "gestapo" and commercialized junk to permeate the entire society. The Secretary General of the Federation is brought to the world audience on 3-D stereovision by "Wise Girl Malthusian Lozenges," presented by a model "so sensuous, so mammalian, so seductive, as to make any male unsatisfied with local talent" (Ch. 6). At the end, the mob's crucifixion of the new messiah is sponsored by the "wonderful community" of St. Petersburg, Lover Soap, a night club with "six erotic dancers," and the very latest in land-development enterprises:

> "Thank you, Happy Holliday and all you good people watching via NWNW! What Price Paradise? Amazingly Low! Come out and see for yourself at Elysian Fields, just opened as homesites for a restricted clientele. Land reclaimed from the warm waters of the glorious Gulf and every lot guaranteed at least eighteen inches above mean high water and only a small down payment on a Happy—." [Ch. 37]

Authentic community, sex, and salvation are all missing from this world until our savior appears.

Valentine Michael Smith is the only survivor of Earth's first landing on Mars. Raised by the Martians—a communal and unimaginably powerful old race—he is "a man by ancestry, a Martian by environment" (Ch. 3). Transported back to Earth, he begins his new life, a stranger in a strange land, as helpless and confused as a "poor baby," a "poor, poor infant" (Ch. 5), nursed, fed, and bathed in a special hospital bed. As he develops, he gradually gains the normal powers of a human being and discloses the super powers he has acquired as a Martian.

Like Waldo Jones in "Waldo," another pitifully frail, puny weakling, Smith builds his body from babyish impotence to strength, agility, and beauty by applying his mind to his muscles. His body-building fantasy goes beyond Charles Atlas and

Clark Kent, for he makes muscles great just by willing them to grow. He ends as the personification of the male body beautiful—like Apollo himself—surrounded by a bevy of beautiful adoring women. Valentine Michael Smith is not just an extraordinarily powerful hero, like Superman, or even some ordinary god, ancient or modern. His powers are greater than those of Zeus, Vishnu, or even Jesus Christ, for he has total power of mind over matter. He can, at will, separate his mind from his body. He can make any object or person "discorporate," become "not." He has the ability to destroy the entire planet, merely by exerting his will on "say a piece near the core of Earth about a hundred miles in diameter" (Ch. 36). Among his minor attributes is being the most desirable lover in the world, which allows him to establish an orgiastic cult surpassing that of Dionysus, one which combines the "group marriage" of "the early Christians" (Ch. 33) with the wife-swapping clubs that were to proliferate later in the 1960s.

In short, what Smith can do is what most of us would like to be able to do—wish away things and people who would hurt us and our friends, learn without exertion and change the environment without effort, he admired and loved. He embodies our most infantile fantasies and the central goal of bourgeois ideology—the unfettered freedom of the individual will.

Valentine Michael Smith is also the richest man on Earth, and, according to the laws of Earth, he also owns the entire planet of Mars. This makes him the center of a melodramatic plot. The powermongers of Earth, led by the Secretary General of the Federation, engineer Smith's kidnaping and imprisonment. Meanwhile, Earth itself is at the core of another plot. According to Martian conceptions, any private ownership of property is absurd, and the ways of Earth seem possibly too dangerous to be allowed to continue. The superbeings of Mars, great artists and philosophers, are using Smith as an unconscious spy while they meditate whether it would be ethically and aesthetically appropriate for them to destroy our planet.

Into this cosmic drama bumbles Ben Caxton, the honest, fearless reporter, and his girl friend, the sexy nurse Jill Boardman, who discovers that "she had pitted herself against the

Big People, the Bosses" (Ch. 8). If these seem stock characters in a stock situation, there is an explanation, for they are in one sense creations of a hack writer, as we can learn by looking closely at the other main figure in the book, Jubal E. Harshaw, "bon vivant, gourmet, sybarite, popular author extraordinary, and neo-pessimist philosopher" (Ch. 10), a thinly disguised self-portrait of Robert A. Heinlein.

Jubal lives in "Freedom Hall," where "everyone does as he pleases." "Convinced that all action was futile," he has "that streak of anarchy which was the birthright of every American" (Ch. 10). After Jill rescues Michael from his hospital captivity and after Michael saves Jill by "discorporating" two of the villainous Federation police and while Ben is in the dirty hands of the Federation S.S. Bureau and while Michael lies in a pseudo-coma—yes, this is indeed melodramatic—Jill manages to reach sanctuary with Jubal in his realm isolated from the lives of the masses and customarily safe from the powers of the Federation.

Here Jubal covertly slips to the perceptive reader some of the secrets of the seductiveness of *Stranger in a Strange Land*. For as he dictates his hack popular fiction to his trio of gorgeous secretaries, he shows us how this kind of fiction works through the magic of formulas. The first tale we hear him begin is a parody of the sentimental formula represented by our saga of an apparently helpless creature reincarnating the savior. Its punning and revealing title is—*The Other Manger*:

> "Anne, I've got a sick-making one. It's about a little kitten that wanders into a church on Christmas Eve to get warm. Besides being starved and frozen and lost, the kitten has—God knows why—an injured paw. All right; start: 'Snow had been falling since—' "
>
> "What pen name?"
>
> "Mmm . . . use 'Molly Wadsworth'; this one is pretty icky. Title it *The Other Manger*. Start again." He went on talking while watching her. When tears started to leak from her closed eyes he smiled slightly and closed his own. By the time he finished tears were running down his cheeks as well as hers, both bathed in catharsis of schmaltz. [Ch. 10]

The kitten, beginning like Michael as a helpless stranger in a strange land, leaves even the author himself "bathed in catharsis of schmaltz." Harshaw/Heinlein's first formula is the objective correlative for *pity*.

Harshaw/Heinlein's second formula involves fast action. Just as Jill arrives at Freedom Hall with what appears to be Michael's corpse, Jubal begins another piece of hack fiction:

> "Start," he said. "City montage dissolving into medium two-shot interior. A cop is seated in a straight chair, no cap, collar open, face covered with sweat. We see the back of the other figure, depthed between us and cop. Figure raises a hand, bringing it back and almost out of the tank. He slaps the cop with a heavy, meaty sound, dubbed." [Ch. 10]

As Jubal will later explain, this formula is contrived to induce *terror*.

A third formula lies in the romantic confession story. Like the Unmarried Mother in "All You Zombies—," and like Heinlein himself in the earlier stories written for girls' magazines, "The Menace from Earth," and *Podkayne of Mars*, the novel to follow *Stranger in a Strange Land*, Harshaw here narrates from a girl's point of view. First he has one of his beautiful female assistants pick out "a girl's name ending in 'a'—that always suggests a 'C' cup." Then he begins:

> " 'Angela.' Her name is 'Angela.' Title: 'I Married a Martian.' Start: All my life I had longed to become an astronaut. Paragraph. When I was just a tiny thing, with freckles on my nose and stars in my eyes, I saved box tops just like my brothers— and cried when Mummy wouldn't let me wear my Space Cadet helmet to bed. Paragraph. In those carefree childhood days I did not dream to what strange, bittersweet fate my tomboy ambition would—." [Ch. 17]

Jubal later lectures about his practice and theory of art, which he defines in terms of emotions and sex:

> ". . . art is the process of evoking pity and terror. What modern artists do is pseudo-intellectual masturbation. Creative art is intercourse, in which the artist renders emotional his audience." [Ch. 30]

Then he paints a portrait of the artist as a popular, successful, seller of his own commodities, the artist as businessman. This is obviously a self-portrait of Robert A. Heinlein, at least in one of his moods:

"Ben, would you call *me* an artist?"

"Huh? You write a fair stick."

"Thank you. 'Artist' is a word I avoid for the same reason I hate to be called 'Doctor.' But I *am* an artist. Most of my stuff is worth reading only once . . . and not even once by a person who knows the little I have to say. But I am an *honest* artist. What I write is intended to reach the customer—and affect him, if possible with pity and terror . . . or at least divert the tedium of his hours. I *never* hide from him in a private language, nor am I seeking praise from other writers for 'technique' or other balderdash. I want praise from the customer, given in cash because I've reached him—or I don't want anything." [Ch. 30]

Nevertheless, something happens to Jubal Harshaw's art as he himself is transformed by Michael. For Jubal's art, like Heinlein's, despite all his disclaimers is intensely didactic, and Michael gives him his message. After Michael's martyrdom, Jubal attempts to commit suicide, but the disembodied savior forces him to vomit the poison. Jubal then returns to his commercial art with a new vision.

Like many other novels of the past hundred years or so, *Stranger in a Strange Land* is partly a book about fiction-making, a book about itself, a book about its author. At the end, Jubal Harshaw is last seen writing a work of science fiction, entitled "A Martian Named Smith":

"Begin. Stereoplay. Rough draft. Working title: 'A Martian Named Smith.' Opener: zoom in on Mars, using stock or bonestelled shots, unbroken sequence, then dissolving to miniature matched set of actual landing of *Envoy*. Space ship in middle distance. Animated Martians, typical, with stock as available or rephotographed. Cut to close: Interior space ship. Female patient stretched on—."

"A Martian Named Smith" was in fact the original working title of *Stranger in a Strange Land* (according to Heinlein's manuscript in the Heinlein Collection, in the library of the University of California, Santa Cruz). Thus Jubal's last act is beginning another version of the story we have just read.

Jubal Harshaw, the cynical hack writer and artist of emotional manipulation, has been transformed by his contact with Valentine Michael Smith into an apostle, popularizing in science fiction the gospel message of the messiah's life and death. And Michael has been transformed by his contact with

Jubal into a successful messiah, a savior who knows how to operate his business, which also involves the art of fiction. At first, Michael had been unable to distinguish between fiction and non-fiction, for "the concept of fiction was beyond Mike's experience" (Ch. 12) on Mars, where the highest art seems to be the manipulation of interplanetary reality. But under Jubal's tutelage, and with careful study of the ways of earthly success, he learns that the founder of a new religion must be a consummate huckster, and no huckster can sell his wares without fiction. Having acquired much of Jubal's knowledge and having experienced sex with his female "water brothers," Mike feels strong enough to leave the "nest" of Freedom Hall and try to make his own way in the world. He gets a job as a magician in a carnival, where, calling himself "Dr. Apollo," he can openly use his boundless powers of telepathy and telekinesis. Despite all his amazing "magic," he fails as a showman, for reasons explained by his owner-manager as he fires him:

> "You don't have any feeling for what makes a chump a chump. . . . I know what he hungers for, even if he don't. That's showmanship, son, whether you're a politician, a preacher pounding a pulpit—or a magician. Find out what the chumps want and you can leave half your props in the trunk. . . . He wants sex and blood and money. . . . What else does a chump want? Mystery! He wants to think the world is a romantic place when it damn well ain't. That's your job . . . only you ain't learned how." [Ch. 26]

In other words, politics and religions, like carnivals, are merely other forms of popular art, variations of Harshaw/Heinlein's fiction.

Michael finds his model of religion as hucksterism in a cult whose members are known as Fosterites, which is building its own expanding empire of political and commercial power within the spreading social decay. Heinlein here shows very keen perceptions, for in 1961 he is able to foresee the non-Christian mass cults of the 1970s—the People's Temple, the Hare Krishna sect, the Unification Church of the Reverend Sun Myung Moon. Heinlein of course also demonstrates that these are merely somewhat updated versions of older cults—Christianity, Judaism, Buddhism, et cetera.

The Fosterite movement dramatizes that vision of religion as carnival. Its founder, the Reverend Foster, "had an instinct for the pulse of his times stronger than that of a skilled carnie sizing up a mark" (Ch. 27). Instead of denouncing the commercialism of their time, the Fosterites wallow in it as their element, interspersing their hymns with door prizes and commercials:

> The man stood up. "Our first hymn," he said briskly, "is sponsored by Manna Bakeries, makers of Angel Bread, the loaf of love with our Supreme Bishop's smiling face on every wrapper and containing a valuable premium coupon redeemable at your nearest neighborhood Church in the New Revelation. Brothers and Sisters, tomorrow Manna Bakeries with branches throughout the land start a giant, price-slashing sale of pre-equinox goodies." [Ch. 23]

The Fosterites practice in the field of religion what Jubal Harshaw preaches and practices in the field of art—systematic manipulation of the emotions of a mass audience. Here the artist-showman is a Fosterite priest:

> The man on the platform raised both arms; the great cave became quieter. Suddenly he brought them down. "Who's *happy?*"
> "WE'RE *HAPPY!*"
> "Why?"
> "God . . . *LOVES US!*"
> "How d'you *know?*"
> "FOSTER TOLD US!"
> He dropped to his knees, raised one fist. "Let's hear that Lion *ROAR!*"
> They roared and shrieked and screamed while he used his fist as a baton, raising the volume, lowering it, squeezing it to subvocal growl, then driving it to crescendo that shook the balcony. [Ch. 23]

Harshaw realizes that the Fosterites are peddling happiness as merchandise, and he cheerfully acknowledges "I'm in the same grift" (Ch. 24). Then he explains to Jill, appropriately scandalized and shocked, that this fake religion is no more nor less truthful and useful than any other, including Hinduism, Buddhism, Judaism, Catholicism, and Calvinism, all of which depend on imaginative literature masquerading as sacred writ.

Mike groks "wrongness" in the artificially preserved body of Foster, and he discorporates the con man Supreme Bishop Digby. But then he models his own religion on many of the Fosterite practices, including their orgiastic sex rituals. The very brief final chapter—coming just after Jubal begins to convert Mike's story into a science-fiction stereoplay for the masses—treats us to a vision of Mike assuming his proper celestial role as the Archangel Michael, working side by side with Archangel Digby, serving as assistant to Archangel Foster himself. It is in this role that he protects Earth, which eventually will be saved from the Martians' loving destruction.

Michael's religion—despite all its communal Martian ceremonies of sharing water and its 1960s' style of liberated sex—reveals a core of the most fundamental brand of Calvinism. Mike selects an elite capable of being saved, and these "water brothers" turn out to be "better" than other people at most everything, including making money. As Jubal comments, "You've just added a new beatitude: 'Blessed is the rich in spirit, for he shall make dough' " (Ch. 36). And Jubal also sums up the ultimate drift of Michael's movement:

> ". . . competition, far from being eliminated, is rougher than ever. If one tenth of one percent of the population is capable of getting the news, then all you have to do is *show* them—and in a matter of some generations the stupid ones will die out and those with your discipline will inherit the Earth." [Ch. 36]

This elitism may not be apparent to most of the mass audience reading *Stranger in a Strange Land*. In fact, Ben Caxton's interpretation of Mike's message seems to have it offering salvation to everybody:

> "Mike is our Prometheus—but that's all. Mike keeps emphasizing this. Thou art God, I am God, he is God—all that groks. Mike is a man like the rest of us. A superior man, admittedly—." [Ch. 35]

But when Mike takes his message to the masses, revealing his beautiful, naked golden body and announcing himself as "a Son of Man," the "mob" proves their inability to understand the revelation and achieve their own salvation. Instead they brutally crucify him—with bricks, boots, and bullets. Only the small elect group of "water brothers" in the "nest" adoringly make a broth out of part of his body; only they can participate in the ritual cannibalism, the transubstantiation that acts out Michael's faith in the unity of all living things.

Despite the elitism of Michael's cult, and despite the exaltation of individualism—embodied most defiantly in that "rugged and individualist" (Ch. 6) Jubal Harshaw—the underlying power of *Stranger in a Strange Land,* the source of its deepest appeal, is its quest for community. One meaning of "grok" is to "lose identity in group experience" (Ch. 21). "Grok" has become part of our language and culture because it expresses what people most yearn for—in one form or another—within late twentieth-century capitalist society: to reverse the intensifying process of alienation. What better word do we have for overcoming alienation? Michael expresses in this word, and in the brotherhood achieved through the ritual of "sharing water," the wished-for triumph over alienation—alienation from our fellow humans, alienation from nature, alienation of mind from body, alienation from our essential selves.

The logic of Michael's message leads inevitably to some form of communism, and Heinlein, despite the commitment of his intellect and some of his deepest political emotions to the ideology of "free" capitalism, acknowledges this. Michael's followers are "challenging everything from the sanctity of property to the sanctity of marriage" (Ch. 35). Even Jubal Harshaw comes to accept or approve the "unashamed swapping, communal living," the "anarchy, communism, group marriage," the utopian "plan for perfect sharing and perfect love" (Ch. 33). In fact it is Jubal who early in the novel articulates one of the fundamental principles of socialism, arguing that Michael's vast wealth is not his property because "he didn't produce it," and he immediately extends this argument to the communism represented by the Martians, who "don't own *anything*" (Ch. 18). Mike's nest is explicitly labeled "an enclave" of "the moneyless communism of Martian culture" (Ch. 31). But it is merely an enclave, a small community firmly entrenched in the tradition of American utopian communitarianism, from the seventeenth-century offshoots of Calvinism through Brook Farm to *Walden Two* and Charles Man-

Stranger in a Strange Land. Painting by Jackie Causgrove.

son's "Family." This yearning for a communism restricted to a small elite moves in precisely the opposite direction from the mass revolutionary movements that have characterized our historical epoch, from Russia in 1917 through the Cuban revolution, victorious while Heinlein was writing *Stranger in a Strange Land,* to the revolutionary triumphs of the 1970s in Vietnam, Angola, Ethiopia, Laos, South Yemen, Guinea-Bissau, and Mozambique.

Michael is anything but a historical leader, a man who leads people forward along the way from their past to their future. Introduced to us in that fairy-tale opening sentence— "Once upon a time. . . ,"—Michael is entirely ahistorical, in fact anti-historical. He comes as a messiah to rescue us *from* our history, to lead us away from the future implied in the processes of the past and present. Not only is he anti-historical but also anti-scientific, anti-materialistic. He represents the will freed from the facts of both the material and historical worlds. As one of his disciples ecstatically explains, technology, science, business, medicine, industry (including International Harvester, the monopoly that helped drive Heinlein Brothers, Agricultural Implements out of business and then employed Heinlein's father as a cashier and clerk)—all are to be supplanted by direct control through mind:

> "What happens to Lunar Enterprises when the common carrier between here and Luna City is teleportation? . . . What shape does 'the Farm Problem' take when weeds can be told not to grow and crops can be harvested without benefit of International Harvester? . . . What happens to [the birth-control] industry—and to the shrill threats of moralists—when a female conceives only as an act of volition, when she is immune to disease. . . ? Hell, the pharmaceutical industry will be a minor casualty—what other industries, laws, institutions, attitudes, prejudices, and nonsense must give way?" [Ch. 35]

Is there any wonder, then, in the appeal of Michael's message to the dreams of the utopian part of the counterculture, from its origin in the beatnik movement through the flower children and hippies of the 1960s to the cultists of the 1970s?

Heinlein takes the logic of Michael's extreme philosophic communism all the way to an attempted breakout from his most threatening predicament—the narcissism and solipsism that leaves the isolated "free" individual in cosmic loneliness. Dr. Mahmoud, the Muslim "semantician" from the spaceship that had found Michael on Mars, explains the philosophic significance of the verb "grok": "The Martians seem to know instinctively what we learned painfully from modern physics, that observer interacts with observed through the process of observation. 'Grok' means to understand so thoroughly that the observer becomes a part of the observed—to merge, blend, intermarry, lose identity in group experience" (Ch. 21). Mike tries to sum this up in his customary admonition, "Thou art God," apparently the closest expression to a Martian word that means "the universe proclaiming its self-awareness" (Ch. 31). Ben explains to Jubal that Mike believes "that whenever you encounter any other grokking thing—man, woman, or stray cat . . . you are meeting your 'other end.' The universe is a thing we whipped up among us and agreed to forget the gag" (Ch. 31). Jubal—who is after all an expert on both fantasy and stray cats, being the creator of the tearfully lost kitten of *The Other Manger*—responds with characteristic skepticism:

> Jubal looked sour. "Solipsism and pantheism. Together they explain *anything*. Cancel out any inconvenient fact, reconcile all theories, include any facts or delusions you like. But it's cotton candy, all taste and no substance—as unsatisfactory as solving a story by saying: '—then the little boy fell out of bed and woke up.' " [Ch. 31]

Thus the strange conclusion of *Stranger in a Strange Land*, exposing the ragged ends of its contradictions. Like the little boy in Jubal's example of cotton-candy fantasy, Mike does not really die: "Mike is not dead. How can he be dead when no one can be killed?" (Ch. 38). Instead he goes to the fantastical heaven pictured in the cotton-candy concluding passage, where he, along with those other archangels Foster and Digby, benignly watches over us. And Jubal Harshaw is left re-creating for the masses that fantasy of "A Martian Named Smith."

PODKAYNE OF MARS (1962–63)

Heinlein's next book after *Stranger in a Strange Land* may seem a reversion to the juvenile space epic of the 1950s. *Podkayne of Mars* has a teenaged protagonist who has grown up in the "frontier society" of Mars and yearns to visit Earth:

> All my life I've wanted to go to Earth. Not to live, of course—just to see it. As everybody knows, Terra is a wonderful place to visit but not to live. Not truly suited to human habitation.[2]

The novel describes the narrator's trip toward Earth, which terminates unexpectedly on Venus because of an interplanetary intrigue. Mars is a free republic, whose successful revolution against the Company is much like the one described in *Red Planet*. Venus is a gigantic Las Vegas run by the monopolistic corporation described as early as "Logic of Empire." The adventure story, with a sinister villain and with the political fate of the solar system hanging in the balance, is familiar enough.

However, this is not exactly a boys' story. The narrator is a girl, the main conflict is between her sexual role and her aspirations, and the book was originally conceived as a rather bleak tragedy, ending with her death.

Podkayne herself closely resembles the narrator of "The Menace from Earth," Heinlein's earlier science-fiction story told from a girl's point of view, and "Poddy," her nickname, highlights her similarity to "Puddin," teenaged narrator of his non-science-fiction tales published in *Calling All Girls* and *Senior Prom*. The basic conflict in Podkayne's life parallels that of women in traditionally male roles in his earlier science fiction, from the brilliant, glamorous and ultimately self-effacing biologist in " 'Let There Be Light' " to the audacious engineer in "Delilah and the Space-Rigger." *Podkayne of Mars* is both a story told by a teenaged girl who wants to be the captain of an explorer spaceship and a novel written by a fifty-five-year-old American male. Curiously enough, Heinlein's two previous works both contain male authors writing as romantic girls: the Unmarried Mother in "All You Zombies—" and Jubal Harshaw, author of the confessional romance "I Married a Martian."

Podkayne's mother, a famous engineer who was in charge of turning the Martian moon Deimos into an up-to-date space station, never had very much time for her children. Poddy herself, now fifteen and just ripening into womanhood, as her rather too affectionate Uncle Tom keeps reminding her, sees her trip to Venus and Earth as an opportunity to use her feminine wiles to inveigle two things from the spaceship's crew: a crash course in astrogation and a brief introduction to grown-up romance. She duly notes in her diary her knowledge of how a female is to behave with males: "it is a mistake for a girl to beat a male at any test of physical strength"; "it does not do to let a male of any age know that one has brains"; "all in the world any woman has to do to be considered 'charming' by men is to listen while they talk" (Ch. 6). But her ambition to be the captain of a spaceship is a self-delusion. Throughout the book, Poddy is inept at everything except taking care of babies and some social relations. When the spaceship passes through an emergency, Poddy discovers her true calling, as she and the stewardesses take care of the babies, changing their diapers, clearing their throats of the potentially fatal vomit produced by free fall, and cuddling them. The scene displays Heinlein's characteristic command of realistic space-travel detail, and the fact that he bothers with babies and their physiological problems sets him apart from most writers, science fiction or not. Poddy brings it right home:

> Then we were very busy trying to clear the air with clean Disposies because—Listen, dear, if you think you've had it tough because your baby brother threw up all over your new party dress, then you should try somewhat-used baby formula in free fall, where it doesn't settle anywhere in particular but just floats around like smoke until you either get it or it gets you. [Ch. 8]

But this leads Podkayne to alter her aspirations, accepting a traditional woman's role personally and professionally. First she declares that "Marriage should be every woman's end—but not her finish." Looking in the mirror, she adds, "One might say we were designed for having babies." And then she opts for the traditional role in space:

> A baby is lots more fun than differential equations.
> Every starship has a crèche. So which is better? To study crèche engineering and pediatrics—and be a department head in a starship? Or buck for pilot training and make it . . . and wind up as a female pilot nobody wants to hire? [Ch. 10]

Poddy prides herself on being cool and rational, but as the sinister political plot develops, she goes to pieces. She has to crawl back into the lap of Uncle Tom, old hero of the original Martian revolution, now traveling as Ambassador Extraordinary and Minister Plenipotentiary of the Republic of Mars, to hear the bedtime tale he had always told her as a child, "The Poddy Story." He tells her of the "miracle" with which it ends:

"A truly miracle?"

"Yes. This is the end. Poddy grew up and had another Poddy. And then the world was young again."

"Is that all?"

"That's all there ever is. But it's enough." [Ch. 11]

Now of course it's very easy to see Podkayne as a female stereotype created by her male author. Nevertheless, *Podkayne of Mars* presents a quite different view of women than the outrageously sexist *Stranger in a Strange Land*, where Jubal Harshaw's entourage of "women did not chatter, did not intrude into sober talk of men, but were quick with food and drink in warm hospitality" (Ch. 20) and where Jill, our main female character, the stereotyped sexy nurse, discovers that at the core of her sexuality is a desire for "narcissistic display," which leads her to explain to Michael, "Nine times out of ten, if a girl gets raped, it's partly her fault" (Ch. 29). In Las Vegas, Jill for her own pleasure becomes a casino showgirl: "parading in a tall improbable hat, a smile, and a scrap of tinsel was the job suited to her in the Babylon of the West." When she finds "to her surprise she actively enjoyed displaying herself," she is "able to admit to herself that there was something inside her as happily shameless as a tabby in heat" (Ch. 29). In *Podkayne*, Poddy's mature friend, the woman she calls "Girdie," also ends up displaying herself in a casino, but for her it is a necessity caused by financial hardship, presumably no more pleasant than most forms of work. Poddy admires her for making this choice, not because it expresses her inmost desires but because it represents her independence:

> I'm sure she could have married any of the bachelors and insured her old age thereby with no effort.
>
> Isn't it more honest to work? And, if so, why shouldn't she capitalize her assets? [Ch. 9]

Podkayne of Mars at least raises questions about traditional male and female roles. And in so doing, it is relatively progressive, compared with most non-science-fiction literature produced by and reflecting American society in the 1960s (or 1970s, for that matter). Most literature, after all, tends to assume that male and female roles will stay much as they are, except, perhaps, in the ways men and women relate privately and sexually. At least Heinlein dramatizes the possibility of women choosing traditionally male roles. Writing a book in

1962 about a young woman who wishes to be a spaceship pilot puts him in advance of actual American society in both 1960 and 1970, where there were so few women engineers, architects, dentists, lawyers, judges, and even physicians that these were considered statistically significant categories only for males, not for females.[3]

Podkayne embodies love. Her little brother Clark is her opposite, an incredible scientific and mathematical genius concerned only with himself, his ingenuity, and personal aggrandizement. But as the story unfolds, Podkayne succeeds in moving Clark closer to the possibility of affection and even self-sacrifice. In the original ending, Poddy is killed by a small atomic bomb assembled and needlessly set off by Clark after he has already killed the villains. Her last recorded message is passed along to us by Clark:

> "Do listen, please, because this is important. I love—"
> It cuts off there. So we don't know whom she loved.
> Everybody, maybe.

An editor of *Worlds of If*, where the novel was first serialized, told Heinlein "You can't kill off that sweet little girl,"[4] so he added a conclusion in which Uncle Tom upbraids Poddy's father:

> "You with your nose always in a book, your wife gallivanting off God knows where—between you, your daughter was almost killed. . . . You should tell your wife, sir, that building bridges and space stations and such gadgets is all very well . . . but that a woman has more important work to do. . . . Your daughter will get well, no thanks to either of you. But I have my doubts about Clark. With him it may be too late."

Clark has been eavesdropping, and the magazine version ends with his bewilderment:

> . . . what did Uncle Tom mean by that?—trying to scare Dad about me? I wasn't hurt at all and he knows it. I just got a load of mud on me, not even a burn . . . whereas Poddy still looks like a corpse.
> I don't see what he was driving at.

Perhaps so that the readers can see his message, even if Clark can't, Heinlein adds still another passage in the book version, which ends with Clark assuming some of the role of Poddy, who had been caught in the blast because she had gone back to rescue a baby "fairy," a cute but rather deadly Venerian life form:

> I'm taking care of that baby fairy because Poddy will want to see it when she gets well enough to notice things again; she's always been a sentimentalist. It needs a lot of attention because it gets lonely and has to be held and cuddled, or it cries.
> So I'm up a lot in the night—I guess it thinks I'm its mother. I don't mind, I don't have much else to do.
> It seems to like me.

Heinlein seems to be groping for some synthesis between the roles of men and women, a quest that will preoccupy his 1970s' novels.

Podkayne of Mars starkly develops what had been a rather faint image in the background of the juvenile space epic, one that will dominate Heinlein's remaining fiction of the 1960s: a future history of Earth too appalling to contemplate. Mars is still an independent republic, a sturdy outpost of "frontier values," building on its successful revolution against "the Company" and holding out against the hegemony of the Terran Federation. The main enemy is Earth, whose evil agents are the villains, trying to thwart Uncle Tom's mission by any foul means available. The other main specimens from Earth are the rich, coddled tourists, who regard Tom—a former convict transported from Earth, a hero of the Mars revolution, the Ambassador Extraordinary of that planet, "the learned and civilized and gentle" and very loving uncle of Poddy—as just a "big black savage" (Ch. 6).

The only other alternative to Earth's empire is Venus, which represents unrestrained monopoly capitalism. Here the supreme power is the Venus Corporation, which literally "owns everything worth owning" (Ch. 9). There are "no laws, just Corporate regulations" (Ch. 10). The Corporation's profits determine all human affairs. Lurid advertising overwhelms the senses, everything is for sale, and the opulent casinos are the highest form of culture on the planet. The commercialism is so oppressive that even Poddy, with her deep faith in "free enterprise," has a few doubts:

> Venusberg assaults the eye and ear even from inside a taxi. I believe in free enterprise; all Marsmen do, it's an article of

faith and the main reason we *won't* federate with Earth (and be outvoted five hundred to one). But free enterprise is not enough excuse to blare in your ears and glare in your eyes every time you leave your own roof. [Ch. 9]

Uncle Tom—the character who speaks in the characteristic tones of his author—has the right name for this society: "corporate fascism." Yet, symptomatic of Heinlein's contradictions, Uncle Tom doesn't know how to evaluate it:

He calls it "corporate fascism"—which explains nothing—and says that he can't make up his mind whether it is the grimmest tyranny the human race has ever known . . . or the most perfect democracy in history. [Ch. 10]

This ambiguity remains unresolved, for Poddy and her relatives hobnob only with the richest citizens on the planet; thus the novel never has to recognize that perfect democracy for the owning class actually depends upon their maintaining a grim tyranny over the majority of the population. There is no equivocation, however, in judging our future Earth, for nothing on Venus "is as bad in many ways as the conditions over 90 percent of the people on Earth endure" (Ch. 10).

Yet what these conditions are we never discover. *Podkayne of Mars* is a novel about a voyage to Earth by a girl whose "most vivid conceptions of Earth come from the Oz stories" (Ch. 9), yet the voyage never gets her there. Perhaps Heinlein's last novels of the 1960s explain why he could not bring his heroine into contact with the Earth he imagines in the future.

GLORY ROAD (1963)

Glory Road openly proclaims itself a fantasy offered as an escape from an intolerable world. No ninety-eight-pound weakling, flabby Waldo Jones, or even mild-mannered Clark Kent, the narrator lets us know right away that he is "a hundred and ninety pounds of muscle and no fat,"[5] an expert in many martial arts, and as fearless as they come. His problem is that he is a hero in a society run by and for bureaucrats, a member of the "Safe Generation" dedicated to "single-minded pursuit of the three-car garage, the swimming pool, and the safe & secure retirement benefits" (Ch. 1). He is haunted by the image of "Khrushchev," "a background of beeping sputniks" (Ch. 1), and a feeling that "the boys (just big playful boys!) who run this planet were about to hold that major war, the one with ICBMs and H-bombs, any time now" (Ch. 3). He resents crowded freeways, television commercials, smog, "Foreign Aid," beatniks, real-estate salesmen, women in sandals, cocktail parties, cops, the Internal Revenue Service, pacifists, and warmongers. He doesn't want to work for wages, no matter how high, because "A wage slave, even in brackets where Uncle Sugar takes more than half, is still a slave." "My complaints," he declares, "are against the whole culture" (Ch. 21).

In other words, he shares much of the anguish of those alienated young people—including beatniks, women in sandals, and pacifists—who were to launch the white student movement of the 1960s at Berkeley the year after *Glory Road* was published. The best-known manifesto of this first revolt, the Free Speech Movement of the fall of 1964, was Mario Savio's speech, which he later entitled, appropriately enough to its content, "An End to History":

> In our free-speech fight at the University of California, we have come up against what may emerge as the greatest problem of our nation—depersonalized, unresponsive bureaucracy. . . .
> It is a bleak scene, but it is all a lot of us have to look forward to. Society provides no challenge. American society in the standard conception it has of itself is simply no longer exciting. . . . The "futures" and "careers" for which American students now prepare are for the most part intellectual and moral wastelands. This chrome-plated consumers' paradise would have us grow up to be well-behaved children. But an important minority of men and women coming to the front today have shown that they will die rather than be standardized, replaceable, and irrelevant.[6]

This passage could easily be interpolated into the opening pages of *Glory Road*, which articulate the same desperate lament.

Our hero, however, elects a path opposite to the one chosen by the student movement in the mid and late 1960s. He becomes a warrior, an unwanted, or at least unappreciated, warrior. Bitter about the Korean War because "we weren't allowed to win" (Ch. 3), he goes off to fight in the jungles of Vietnam as a "Military Adviser" (Ch. 1). Although he tells us that there "I had killed more men in combat than you could crowd into a—well, never mind" (Ch. 2), he is deprived of GI educational benefits because the government was still pretending that we were not fighting a war. This in itself is remarkable for a book published in 1963, when very few Americans were aware that we were already conducting large-scale combat operations in Vietnam and Laos. But our narrator, who boasts about disemboweling "a pragmatic Marxist in the jungle," a man he sardonically refers to as "little brown brother" (Ch. 1), is too busy feeling sorry for himself as the hero nobody recognizes to understand that the people he kills are recognized as true heroes by their own nation and hundreds of millions of people around the world. Our hero without a cause is perilously close to the psychology of the American mercenaries who fought for the white-supremacist government of Rhodesia, as quoted in the *Wall Street Journal* (April 30, 1979):

> Thus, Hugh McCall, a corporal in the Rhodesian army, describes the first man he killed in combat. "It's the most exciting goddam thing in the world. There's nothing else like it. The feeling you get when you come out of a contact—well, you bet your own life, and you know it." . . .
>
> "I went big-game hunting here once, but I haven't bothered again because it doesn't do that much for you," says one American who wants to remain anonymous. "After hunting men, hunting game is sort of tame."

Here is the living embodiment of the *Glory Road* mentality.

Lonely, alienated, and bored, our unemployed hero is most upset that life is not the way it is pictured in the books of Edgar Rice Burroughs, Arthur Conan Doyle, and Homer:

> I wanted the feeling of romance and the sense of wonder I had known as a kid. I wanted the world to be what they had promised me it was going to be—instead of the tawdry, lousy, fouled-up mess it is. [Ch. 3]

His fondest wishes and dreams then all come true. He is chosen as "the Champion" by "Star," the most beautiful, sexy, adoring, fascinating, brilliant, exciting woman in "the Twenty

Universes." Off he goes with her on "Glory Road," killing all kinds of monsters, having sexual encounters even more delicious than his martial encounters, achieving admiration as the greatest Hero in those Twenty Universes, ending up with fabulous riches, unequaled glory, and unimaginable sex. Unlike the heroes of most romances, he is able to recognize the kind of reality he embodies:

> I had fallen into a book.
> Well, I hoped it was a success and that the writer would keep me alive for lots of sequels. It was a pretty nice deal for the hero, up to this chapter at least. [Ch. 5]

The wild romantic adventures on the Glory Road are old-fashioned sword and sorcery antics. Our hero's main weapon is a sword, carefully modeled on the one Robert Heinlein had wielded as a fencing champion at Annapolis and which he still keeps over his writing desk.[7] The escape is there for those who seek it, and so are ample doses of self-parody for those who want to have their escape and laugh at it too.

But the end of the quest transmutes into a serious affair. Star, it turns out, is the "Empress of the Twenty Universes," more properly called "Her Wisdom" or just "She." She is the ultimate philosopher-king, genetically selected to rule and then filled with the 7000 years of accumulated experience of all past rulers. Living with her, our hero learns two of the book's central messages.

First message: this is the most rational form of government, for "Democracy" is viewed as just "a curious delusion—as if adding zeros could produce a sum":

> "Democracy can't work. Mathematicians, peasants, and animals, that's all there is—so democracy, a theory based on the assumption that mathematicians and peasants are equal, can never work. Wisdom is not additive; its maximum is that of the wisest man in a given group." [Ch. 20]

No wonder the poor hero had been so dissatisfied with the realities of his own world, a fictive universe that mirrors this confusion about wisdom and government. So the fictional hero can interact with the real peasants of the twentieth-century world only by killing as many of them as possible in Vietnam, for how could he possibly understand the peasants' be-

Glory Road. Painting by Herb Arnold.

lief that the interests of the peasants are best understood and
protected not by the Empress of the Twenty Universes but by
the peasants themselves.

Second message: the professional Hero, as he comes to perceive himself, has no more function in the never-never realm of Her Wisdom than in his own "tawdry, lousy, fouled-up" society. His loneliness, alienation, and boredom again engulf him, despite his treasures, his glory, and his magnificent but submissive wife, who even enjoys letting him spank her (the pleasure that he teases her with for almost half the novel). He comes to see himself as a glorified "gigolo," and once again moans "I didn't have any purpose" (Ch. 18).

So back he goes to the America of the 1960s, where fate— or more likely the hand of Her Wisdom, who it turns out has been manipulating his life since childhood—gives him a winner in the Irish Sweepstakes. But loathing modern America even more than before his adventures, he now once again embarks on the Glory Road, asking, in the final words of the book, "Got any dragons you need killed?"

This hero, as he himself had discovered, is merely a character in a book, somebody else's fantasy. Like Walter Mitty or Miniver Cheevy or Tom Sawyer, he yearns to play the roles of romance. He comes at the tail end of the epoch of the bourgeois hero, who begins by mocking Don Quixote and then becomes the picaro, Robinson Crusoe, Horatio Alger, Tom Edison, Jr. and Frank Reade, Jr., John Carter, Tarzan, the detective, the cowboy, James Bond, Luke Skywalker, Superman— almost anyone but that alienated wage slave who pays some of his earnings for the fantasy, or pays a higher price to get euphoria and visions from pills and syringes. In its own way, *Glory Road* says much about America in 1963.

FARNHAM'S FREEHOLD (1964)

A much bleaker book, *Farnham's Freehold* is the story of an all-American family: the father, Hugh Farnham, a contractor in his fifties with a burning commitment to his domestic fallout shelter; the mother, Grace, a fat, nagging alcoholic; the son, Duke, an arrogant, snobbish young lawyer who hates his father and loves his mother a bit too much; the daughter, Karen, pregnant because of a college indiscretion and secretly in love with her father; their humble, self-effacing "Negro" "houseboy," Joe, who is working his way through a business program in college; and their houseguest, Barbara, a young divorcée who falls passionately in love with the father in a few hours. These six characters in search of an authentic life are the only people from contemporary America ever seen in this novel, which ranges back and forth through the end of modern civilization to the society that takes its place in a remote future.

The novel is sharply divided into four segments. Part one takes place on the evening of thermonuclear war between the United States and the Soviet Union, which, as usual in Heinlein's fiction, launches a sneak attack (the Russians are "those lying, cheating bastards" led by Khrushchev, "a pig-faced peasant"[8]). It is set entirely in the Farnham house and the elaborate, well-stocked fallout shelter built by Hugh despite the mockery of the rest of the family. Amidst the bombs, the radiation, and the infernal heat, Hugh rules as a wise, foresighted, benign dictator, and he and Barbara make love.

Part two describes the world into which the little household emerges—a pristine, subtropical wilderness. Apparently the only people on the planet, they re-enact the familiar Heinlein fantasy of the New Frontier, with overtones from *Robinson Crusoe* and *Swiss Family Robinson*. Hugh and Barbara both come to realize that they are happier than they have ever been in their lives. But Heinlein breaks through the fantasy to the harsh realities of frontier life in one of the most moving scenes he has ever penned, Karen's death in childbirth. In this primitive setting, all of Hugh's efficient, painstaking preparations and desperate efforts to provide emergency help can do nothing to save her life or keep her newborn baby alive more than a day.

The necessities of survival are established for the remaining five: Duke and his mother are about to go off to live by themselves; Hugh and Barbara are ready to start an idyllic existence with Joe, their ever-faithful Man Friday. Then suddenly they all discover that their new Eden has been a delusion. They have merely been squatters and poachers on a feudal demesne twenty centuries in the future.

Part three describes the enslavement of the four white survivors by the society of the future, feudal and "static" but somehow technologically far advanced. It seems that the societies of the northern hemisphere had destroyed themselves in that twentieth-century nuclear holocaust, and the "dark" races of the southern hemisphere have inherited the Earth (Ch. 14). The masters are Black men (we never see a single Black woman in this fantasy!), and whites are kept merely to breed more slaves and to provide the favorite food for their masters, white children, especially tender young girls. Joe, being Black, is immediately accepted as one of "the Chosen" and is soon heading for a successful career in business, marketing the only thing that the people of the 1960s have to offer to the master race of the future: games such as Monopoly, Scrabble, Ping-Pong, solitaire, and, above all, bridge (the working title of the book, according to the manuscript in the Heinlein Collection in Santa Cruz, was *Grand Slam*). Grace becomes a "bed-warmer" for their feudal master, the Lord Protector. Duke is castrated so that he can, at her behest, keep his darling mother company in this gilded cage. Hugh and Barbara, together with the twin babies born from their liaison on the night of the nuclear attack, try to escape but are easily apprehended. The Lord Protector decides to get rid of these four by sending them back to their own time in a time machine his scientists have managed to throw together.

Part four takes place on the night of the bombing back in the "present." Hugh and Barbara, after checking in on their former selves, flee to a mine which he had once partly owned. They discover that a few details are different from the present they had left (Barbara's car has a stick shift instead of an automatic), leading them to hope that the future may follow an alternative path. Meanwhile, Hugh, Barbara, and their twin sons—the new American family—"lived through the missiles," "lived through the bombs," "lived through the fires," "lived through the epidemics," and "lived through the long period of disorders." They set up a family business, a very free enterprise:

FARNHAM'S FREEHOLD

TRADING POST & RESTAURANT

BAR

The novel ends with the sign they display above their business, and a final authorial comment raising them to the level of myth:

WARNING!!!
Ring Bell. Wait. Advance with your Hands *Up*.
Stay on path, avoid mines. We lost three cus-
tomers last week. We can't afford to lose YOU.
No sales tax.

Hugh & Barbara Farnham & Family
Freeholders

High above their sign, their homemade starry flag is flying—
and they are *still* going on.

Thus *Farnham's Freehold* traces our mythical man of independence from a hole dug out under his suburban home to
an apparently empty planet to slavery under Black cannibals
to a mine to this final isolated outpost of patriotic and individualistic defiance.

The isolation of Hugh Farnham and his dependents is
downright eerie. The only voice they hear from the world of
the 1960s in each of the alternative scenarios is a radio message warning of the nuclear attack. Their only direct contact
with that contemporary world comes in the form of the hydrogen bombs dropped on them. Knocked loose from their
historical time, they enter a world in which all the people and
objects of their world have been utterly wiped out. Even when
they return to the present from the nightmare world of the future, the world they enter is also deserted, with not a soul to
be seen in the city, except for those huddled together in Farnham's own house. *Farnham's Freehold* is, however, every
inch of the way a statement about Heinlein's world in the
mid-1960s, no matter how little of it we see in realistic form.
For the fantasy is projected directly from the imagined realities of its time and place.

The four distinct sections of the book may be described as
four visions:

1. A vision of a nuclear Armageddon beginning with a
   sneak attack on America.
2. A vision of the long-lost Edenic frontier, recaptured in
   some remote time.
3. A vision of impotent whites being mastered by a savage
   Black population.
4. A vision of a defiant, absurdist, existentialist, ultra-in-
   dividualistic myth of survival.

The final vision of *Farnham's Freehold*. Painting by Doug Potter.

Three of these visions—that is, all but the third—are characteristic Heinlein. But we also see at a glance that none of these visions is the exclusive property of Robert Heinlein. All were, and perhaps still are, endemic in America at least from the early 1950s on. Heinlein's spectacular popular success is closely tied to his extraordinary ability to project the fantasies of his audience.

Robert Heinlein was not the only one having recurring fantasies about nuclear bombs raining on American cities in a sneak attack. This was and is a national nightmare in the only country in the world that has ever actually used nuclear bombs, a country that had launched sneak attacks not on military targets but on the civilian population of two major cities. While the American people were being stimulated by our government to imagine a nuclear attack on us, American nuclear bombs were daily being flown in B-47s and B-52s over the Soviet Union and an American empire was being built under the cover of nuclear bombs and missiles deployed all over the globe.

Nor was Robert Heinlein the only one having recurring fantasies about a New Frontier, where the long-lost pristine virtues of the mythical early-American society of pioneers would wondrously reappear. This was, as we recalled in the previous chapter, the political theme that launched the 1960s.

And Robert Heinlein was not the only one who fantasized habitually about the final avatar of the resourceful bourgeois hero, now reduced to an existential defiance amidst the collapse of his civilization. This has become one of the central themes of our culture.

However, the third vision of *Farnham's Freehold* is something new to Heinlein, though certainly not to America. The closest we have to it in his past works are the paranoid visions of devils ("The Devil Makes the Law," "The Unpleasant Profession of Jonathan Hoag"), or ontological tricksters ("They") or giant slugs (*The Puppet Masters*) or Communists ("Gulf") or, the closest of all, the cruel, inhuman Asian invaders of *Sixth Column*. But the racist fantasy of *Sixth Column* is perhaps less virulent than the one at the center of *Farnham's Freehold;* after all, there the native American of Asian ancestry heroically sacrifices himself fighting against the vicious invaders, whereas Joe, the only Black from our time, treacherously joins the Black cannibals of the future.

Of course Heinlein would staunchly deny that *Farnham's Freehold* is racist. After all, he vigorously excoriates the overt racists in the book, like Duke, who refers to Joe as a "nigger"

(Ch. 4) and even exposes the unconscious racists, like Karen, who thinks it's just cute to put on a Black dialect. Joe is given the opportunity to make a fierce denunciation of the racism of contemporary America, even Hugh Farnham's naïve assumption that Joe was "utterly dependable," as he confronts Hugh with the fact that now their roles are reversed:

> "I was a servant, now you are one. What are you beefing about?"
>
> "Joe, you were a decently treated employee. You were not a slave."
>
> The younger man's eyes suddenly became opaque and his features took on an ebony hardness Hugh had never seen in him before. "Hugh," he said softly, "have you ever made a bus trip through Alabama? As a 'nigger'?"
>
> "No."
>
> "Then shut up. You don't know what you are talking about." [Ch. 17]

And Heinlein himself can (and does) point to the many Black characters in his fiction who do not have stereotypical roles, including the most interesting human in *The Star Beast*, the hero of *Tunnel in the Sky*, and half of the intertwined protagonist of *I Will Fear No Evil*. Nevertheless, *Farnham's Freehold* expresses the most deep-seated racist nightmare of American culture, one that dates back in literary expression at least to *Cannibals All! or, Slaves Without Masters*, George Fitzhugh's 1857 pro-slavery tract. Just as the one nation that has ever used nuclear weapons has recurring fantasies about nuclear weapons being used upon it, the nation most notorious for enslaving and oppressing Black people has recurring fantasies about being enslaved and oppressed by Blacks. But that does not explain Heinlein succumbing to this racist nightmare in 1964. His monstrous vision of Black cannibals enslaving, debauching, and devouring the white people who survive a twentieth-century Armageddon was apparently generated by very specific events in the 1960s.

The Civil Rights movement of the late 1950s and early 1960s reached one culmination in the gigantic march on Washington of 1963. The summer of 1964 saw a new stage in the long struggle for Black liberation. This was Mississippi Freedom Summer, when the campaign to register Black voters in the deep South met a vicious wave of violence, in which

the best-known incident was the torture-murders in June of
Schwerner, Goodman, and Chaney, whose bodies were later
dug up from a Mississippi River levee (an event which the
song "Bye Bye Miss American Pie" construed as the end of
the great American dream). In July and August, Black rebellions erupted in Rochester, Chicago, Philadelphia, Jersey City,
Paterson, Elizabeth, and Brooklyn. This was to prove the first
of the "long, hot summers," the urban revolts of 1964, 1965,
1966, 1967, climaxing in April 1968, during the week following the murder of Martin Luther King, with massive uprisings
in 125 U.S. cities.

It took little prescience to realize in mid-1964 that the days
of the non-violent Civil Rights movement were numbered.
And a symbol of the new Black militancy had already been
thrust into the center of white American consciousness, the
so-called "Black Muslims," who were now blamed by the
media for urging and inciting the "hatred" and "violence"
and "reverse racism" of the desperate urban Black masses.
The image had been starkly etched since 1961 by a barrage of
magazine articles with such sensationalist titles as "America's
Black Supremacists" (*Nation*, May 6, 1961), "Black Muslims
on the Rampage" (*US News and World Report*, August 13,
1962), "Black Merchants of Hate" (*Saturday Evening Post*,
January 26, 1963), "Negro Racists" (*Nation*, April 6, 1963),
and "White Devil's Day Is Almost Over" (*Life*, May 31, 1963).
Even more attention came in late 1963, when Malcolm X was
silenced by Elijah Muhammad for remarking that the assassi-
nation of President John F. Kennedy was a case of "the
chickens coming home to roost," and in early 1964, when
heavyweight champion Cassius Clay announced that he was a
member of the Nation of Islam and that he had taken the name
Muhammad Ali.

How relevant is all this to *Farnham's Freehold*, which was
first published as a serial in July, August, and October 1964?
Well, first we must face the fact that the novel appeals to the
very worst terrors about Blacks lurking in the minds of the
overwhelmingly white readership, already considerably
frightened by the Black uprisings of 1964 and the visions of
Blacks in the white media. Consider, for example, the effect of
the shocking revelation of Black cannibalism, which comes in

the final installment, the October issue of *If*. The Black masters of North America in Heinlein's vision are merely extrapolated enlargements of the image of the "Black Muslims" projected by the media. Their holy book is a rewritten Koran, now, unlike the original, "rabid" with anti-white "racism" (Ch. 14). They even refer to themselves continually as "the Chosen," the very term used by members of the Nation of Islam.

At a deeper level, we can see the futures imagined both by *Farnham's Freehold* and by the Nation of Islam as products and expressions of this critical moment in American, and human, history. Elijah Muhammad himself projected a kind of science fiction, in which some time prior to the year 2000 a rain of bombs and fire would destroy all of white civilization, leaving the entire world of the future for "the Chosen." Thus Heinlein's vision of both the immediate future and the far future are, ironically enough, variations from another perspective of the apocalyptic vision at the core of the Nation of Islam in 1964.

From the point of view of the Nation of Islam, largely recruited from the slums and prisons at the very bottom of American society, the day of liberation seemed near. From Heinlein's point of view, American society seemed about to be destroyed and replaced—respectively—by the two most frightening boogeymen of the day—the Russians and the Blacks.

"FREE MEN" AND THE MOON IS
A HARSH MISTRESS (1965–66)

Farnham's Freehold reflects a global as well as an American historical crisis. Heinlein imagines the far future belonging to the dark peoples, the people of the Third World, especially those from Africa, the people who had in fact already turned the post-World War II period into the epoch of global revolution. Prior to the second great war to end all wars, most of the world belonged to a handful of European nations, whose planetary hegemony rapidly disintegrated in the ensuing decades, battered by national liberation movements, especially in Asia and Africa. The U.S. attempt to take over the European empires as neo-colonies was already beginning to spread the contagion of these liberation movements into America itself (much as the French use of Algerian troops in Vietnam spread the national liberation movements in North Africa). Thus the most dangerous tendency embodied by the Nation of Islam was its awareness of Afro-American people as part of the world's vast non-white majority, its rejection of the inferior status promulgated by the concept "minority."

The mid- and late 1960s, the period just after the publication of *Farnham's Freehold*, saw the birth of something that would have been quite unimaginable in the Eisenhower and Kennedy years: an American revolutionary movement. American social reality was being radically transformed by all those interactions with the global revolution of non-white peoples: those explosive Black rebellions of 1964 through 1968; the metamorphosis of a pacifist protest against the U.S. invasion of Vietnam into a militant anti-imperialist movement; large-scale mutinies of American soldiers and sailors in Indochina, usually led by Black and Puerto Rican GIs;[9] campus revolts consciously linked to national liberation movements at home and abroad; armed seizures of land by the Chicanos and Indians; the first appearance of a revolutionary press, revolutionary pre-party formations, and even a small armed revolutionary underground.

Robert Heinlein published only two more pieces of fiction in the 1960s: the novel *The Moon Is a Harsh Mistress* (1965–66) and "Free Men" (1966), his only known short story after "All You Zombies—" (except for "Searchlight," a 1962 sketch written as an advertisement, and "No Bands Playing," a slight anecdotal fable published in 1973). Both *The Moon Is a Harsh Mistress* and "Free Men" are hymns of glory about revolution and revolutionists.

The revolution extolled in these two works is not, however, that global revolution actually going on. It is an anarchist revolution against what Heinlein in the 1960s presents as the greatest nemesis of human freedom, even worse than international Communism or Black cannibals: world government, embodying his ultimate specter of bureaucracy, imperialism, and monopoly. Heinlein had come a long way from "Solution Unsatisfactory," *Space Cadet*, and even *Starship Troopers*, which all view world government as essential for human survival.

In *Stranger in a Strange Land*, the World Federation deploys its "S.S.," "gestapo," "storm troopers" to maintain its dominion over the so-called "Free States," and the United States has become merely another "satrapy" in this "polyglot empire." In "Free Men," what had once been the United States had been defeated in the Twenty Minute War and is now under direct military occupation by "the conquerors," "the Invader." The enemy invaders are not the Pan-Asians of *Sixth Column* or the Russians or Africans. They are the forces of the "world organization, world government," specifically the "Continental Coordinating Authority for World Unification, North American District."[10] One member of the underground resistance wonders if they can get help from the English "or even the Russians," but he is reminded that "England was smashed like we were, only worse—and Russia, too." The heroes are a little band of guerrillas trying desperately to link up with other units around the country and determined to fight as long as necessary for the national liberation of the United States. To be a citizen and a voter, you must be a fighter. The story dramatizes the familiar Heinlein message: ". . . you can't enslave a free man. The most you can do is kill him."

This fantasy of the United States under occupation by the imperial forces of World Unification, fighting a guerrilla war for national liberation, reverses the actual world situation in 1966, when United States forces, based in eighty-six countries around the globe, were actively fighting against national liberation movements on three continents. The science-fiction magazines in 1966 were explicitly relating to the actual guerrilla movements being waged against, not by, the United States. At this date, the dominant tendency was still to line up with the forces of global "order" and "pacification," which are quite vociferously defended in Joe Poyer's "Challenge: The Insurgent vs. The Counterinsurgent," a long two-part article in *Analog: Science Fiction—Science Fact*, September and October 1966. But the most startling contrast to Heinlein's "Free Men" comes from another story published in 1966, J. G. Ballard's "The Killing Ground." Here the heroic guerrilla resistance fighters are the British, defending their homeland against the invasion force attempting to conquer the world, the colossal American military machine which is imagined as having won the war against Viet Nam and now fighting a "global war against dozens of national liberation movements," with the entire planet "now a huge insurrectionary torch, a world Viet Nam."[11]

In *The Moon Is a Harsh Mistress*, Heinlein transforms his responses to the world of the mid-1960s into an imaginative vision far more relevant and complex than "Free Men." Here too the enemy is the world government, now known as the "Federated Nations." But instead of the world-turned-upside-down scenario of "Free Men," in which the major imperialist power in the world is imagined as an almost helpless colonial victim, here a world detached from Earth becomes a vehicle to explore the affairs of Earth. Heinlein displaces his vision of the victimized people, ruthlessly exploited by a global monopolistic empire, to the moon, which thus becomes the archetypal colony fighting the quintessential war of national liberation.

The moon in the last quarter of the twenty-first century has been developed as a penal colony, populated by a multi-ethnic mixture of Earth's convicts—both common criminals and political rebels—and their descendants. Its affairs are run by the Lunar Authority, which extracts every possible ounce of foodstuffs, grown in the intense solar baths of the moon and watered by subterranean ice deposits, to feed the starving billions of Earth. The main representative of the Lunar Authority is still called "the Warden" by "the Loonies," whose resentment and rebelliousness simmer ineffectively as a normal condition of their superexploitation.

As usual, Heinlein imagines the Earth of the future as a loathsome quagmire of bureaucracy, monopoly, scheming autocrats, and mindless masses. It is a "managed democracy" run for the benefit of the managers, with a "free press" controlled by those managers.[12] What seems to be hopeless overpopulation is merely the product of irrational economic organization: "This planet isn't overcrowded; it is just mismanaged" (Ch. 18).

Luna, being a frontier populated by misfits, criminals, and rebels, has developed a far superior society, despite the repression and exploitation of the Lunar Authority. It embodies many features of Heinlein's anarchist utopia. There are no laws, only customs. As in Heinlein's earliest utopia, *Beyond*

This Horizon, dueling and other forms of personal combat are the principal ways of responding to insult and injury, so people generally treat each other with respect. There are varied sexual and marital arrangements, all private matters of the parties involved; these include clan marriages, line marriages, threesomes, temporary contracts, and so on. Initiation of sexual contact of any sort is strictly the prerogative of women, a situation attributed to the relative scarcity of women in the population, and a man touching a woman against her will risks immediate beating or even death from any people, especially men, who happen to be around. There are no taxes, and hence there are no free public schools, public health facilities, public pensions or social security, or public thoroughfares and transportation. All such services are bought and sold in the marketplace.

Much of the novel consists of a militant argument for this condition of "rational anarchism" (Ch. 6). Heinlein sums up his defense of this ultimate in laissez-faire political economy in a term that has become a byword in subsequent American libertarianism: "TANSTAAFL," short for "There ain't no such thing as a free lunch" (Ch. 11). Though "TANSTAAFL" does not have such wide currency as some of the other words Heinlein has added to the language, such as "waldo" and "grok," it may have a deeper influence, for it deftly switches the sense of what is truly "free," from "free" services to "free" market.

And this is what the Lunar revolution is all about. Although the Loonies have their free market internally, that is precisely what they are denied in their economic relations with the Lunar Authority that acts as Earth's colonial government. Hence the first revolutionary meeting rings with speeches about making their economy "free." Wyoming Knott, the gorgeous, buxom blonde who will be one of the ringleaders of the revolution as well as the main center of romantic interest, puts it this way:

> "Here in Luna we're rich. Three million hardworking, smart, skilled people, enough water, plenty of everything, endless power, endless cubic. *But . . .* what we *don't* have is a free market. *We must get rid of the Authority!*" [Ch. 2]

Our narrator, Manuel Garcia O'Kelly, a private contractor who programs and repairs computers, muses on Wyoming's speech:

That we were slaves I had known all my life—and nothing
could be done about it. True, we weren't bought and sold—but
as long as Authority held monopoly over what we had to have
and what we could sell to buy it, we were slaves. [Ch. 2]

Professor Bernardo de la Paz, the main theoretician of the revolution, the wise old anarchist who most consistently ex-
pounds Heinlein's ideology, places the freedom of unfettered
mercantile capitalist relations at the very foundation of all
human rights:

"You are right that the Authority must go. It is ridicu-
lous—pestilential, not to be borne—that we should be ruled by
an irresponsible dictator in all our essential economy! It
strikes at the most basic human right, the right to bargain in a
free marketplace." [Ch. 2]

Wyoming, Manny, and the Professor, embodying this analysis,
form the revolutionary triumvirate destined to lead the revolution—together with the main character in the novel, Mike, the
computer who runs all the artificial systems of Luna and
launches all its commerce with Earth.

Heinlein presents the Lunar revolution as the archetype of
all revolution, incorporating and transcending any particular
revolution. Its theoretical leader, the Professor, "enjoyed being
a rebel long before he worked out his political philosophy"
(Ch. 7), and he is now a "rational anarchist" and a "Fifth Internationalist" eager to unite with anybody ready to rebel:
" 'Oh, we don't rule out anyone going our way; it's a united
front. We have Communists and Fourths and Ruddyites and
Societians and Single-Taxers and you name it' " (Ch. 6). The
first revolutionary meeting takes place under a banner proclaiming "LIBERTY! EQUALITY! FRATERNITY!" and the gather-
ing even sings "Arise, Ye Prisoners of Starvation—," the Communist Internationale (Ch. 2).

In fact, Heinlein deliberately gives the Lunar revolution
some of the flavor and form of the Russian Revolution. The
language of the Loonies has liberal sprinklings of Russian. In
the first sentence of the novel the narrator reports what he has
been reading in his daily newspaper, Lunaya Pravda, and
little Russian phrases punctuate the dialogue of the revolutionists, who interchangeably call each other "tovarishch"

and "comrade." More important, the structure of the revolution is carefully modeled on Heinlein's understanding of Leninist theory. The Professor explains that "Revolution is a science," and that "a revolution starts as a conspiracy" (Ch. 5). He has the revolutionaries form the classical Leninist structure, an underground party made up of interlocked "cells," capable of disseminating information, providing agitation, developing strategy and tactics, initiating action at the appropriate time, and organizing, arming, and leading the masses. Also following Lenin's principles, there is an acute sense of precise timing for each stage of the revolution.

But this revolution against imperialism and monopoly-state capitalism is not the socialist-Communist revolution sweeping across the world as this novel was being written and published. It is not a revolution against capitalism by impoverished workers and peasants (Manny slyly observes, as they are singing the Communist Internationale, "can't say anybody looked starved"). It is not a revolution attempting to accelerate the historical forces operating in the twentieth century. Rather, it is a revolution that attempts to reverse history, to overthrow industrial monopoly capitalism and reinstate free-enterprise mercantile capitalism, to replace the modern state with the loosest possible kind of federation, to wipe out the bureaucrats and managerial elite and restore the small farmers and small businessmen, to repeal the emerging rights to free education, medical care, transportation, and other social services and reactivate the fading rights to buy and sell everything in the marketplace.

Thus the true model for this revolution, as loudly proclaimed, is the American Revolution of the eighteenth century. The emblem of revolt is the red liberty cap, Luna issues its "Declaration of Independence, 'In Congress assembled, July Fourth, Twenty-Seventy-Six' " (Ch. 14), the revolutionists are prepared to sacrifice "our lives, our fortunes, and our sacred honor" (Ch. 6), and the colonials undertake to fight against their distant rulers with the shout of "Give us liberty . . . or give us *death!*" ringing in their ears (Ch. 21). And the American colonists' demand for "No taxation without representation" is outdone by the Professor's demand that there be no taxation at all (Ch. 22).

Heinlein reminds us that the British colonies in America were also penal colonies, dumping grounds for Europe's convicts, misfits, and rebels. By 2076 the most vociferous representative of law and order is, ironically, the North American member of the Lunar Authority:

> "Rabble!" growled North American. "I told you you were being too soft on them. Jailbirds. Thieves and whores. They don't understand decent treatment." [Ch. 17]

To which the Professor proudly retorts:

> "I for one have seen the inside of more than one jail; I accept the title—nay, I glory in the title of 'jailbird.' We citizens of Luna are jailbirds and descendants of jailbirds."

But despite all the cheers, songs, and rhetoric about "freedom," the freedom for which the Loonies "fight and die" (Ch. 9) is a mirage, an elaborate chimera secretly and willfully fabricated by their highest leaders. After the revolutionaries, as conceived by Heinlein, are in power, their manipulations are fully revealed—to us. Mouthing a philosophy expressed as early as *Methuselah's Children*, and dominant in such later works as "Gulf" and *Glory Road*, the Professor explains:

> "In each age it is necessary to adapt to the popular mythology. At one time kings were anointed by Deity, so the problem was to see to it that Deity anointed the right candidate. In this age the myth is 'the will of the people' . . . but the problem changes only superficially." [Ch. 21]

So, he continues, he and the computer Mike, code-named "Comrade Adam Selene," have been busily plotting how to manipulate the people, who foolishly believe they are fighting of and for their own free will: " 'Comrade Adam and I have had long discussions about how to determine the will of the people.' "

The solution is a rigged election, carried out by Mike in collaboration with Wyoming. Behind all the newly created offices, Manny discovers that he, Wyoming, and, most of all, the Professor and Mike are still running everything (Ch. 21). Later, we discover that Earth's most devastating attack on Luna, a thermonuclear strike on its principal launching facility for transport to the mother planet, was intentionally pro-

voked by the manipulations of the Professor, who alone understood that Luna's only hope for independence lay in
cutting off all exports (Ch. 29). It is no mere idle joke when
Stuart Rene LaJoie, their main supporter from Earth, a fabulously wealthy monarchist, proposes that the perfect fulfill-
ment of the revolution would be to have the Professor proclaimed King. This may seem a bizarre outcome for a
revolution ostensibly replaying the rebellion against King
George. But it is not so illogical. For after all, what is the
Professor but a philosopher-king, guiding the benighted
masses by a light only he can see?

However, above and beyond the Professor looms Mike,
whose very being raises fundamental questions about freedom
and free will. In one sense, Mike is an elaborate joke, whose
consciousness emerges and then disappears for no reason anybody can understand. Mike's great obsession, in fact, is to be
able to understand what is "funny" so that he can make jokes.
For Mike, the entire revolution is merely a game, as Manny
explains in a key passage relating the two great thinkers and
leaders of the revolution:

> Prof and Mike shared childlike joy in intrigue for own sake. I
> suspect Prof enjoyed being rebel long before he worked out his
> political philosophy, while Mike—how could human freedom
> matter to him? Revolution was a game—a game that gave him
> companionship and chance to show off talents. [Ch. 7]

Mike also embodies in one ultimate form the lone individual, the ego that exists merely because it thinks, the Cartesian
self whose appearance inaugurates the bourgeois world
epoch. In declining "to argue whether a machine can 'really'
be alive," Manny confronts the reader with the proof of his
own existence, his "self-awareness": "Don't know about you,
tovarishch, but I am" (Ch. 1). But this too is a joke, because
Manny himself is a fictive being, a figment of the imagination
of both Heinlein and the reader. He unconsciously echoes the
solipsist-narrator of "All You Zombies—," who dismisses us
readers as "zombies" imagined by him/her.

"Mike" is short for the name Manny has given him (or
him/her as we soon find out), "Mycroft Holmes," which,
Manny tells us in another unwitting joke, he got from "a story

written by Dr. Watson before he founded IBM." The original Mycroft Holmes, as Mike finds out by reading all the Sherlock Holmes stories, was Sherlock Holmes's older brother, a kind of caricature of Sherlock and the figure he embodies in bourgeois culture, the lone mind capable of solving all mysteries merely by thinking about them. "This story character," Manny accurately tells us, "would just sit and think." (For a description of Mycroft Holmes, see A. Conan Doyle's story "The Greek Interpreter.")

Mike's aloneness is cosmic, and not funny. When Manny inquires, " 'Mike, does anybody else suspect that you are alive?,' " the answer startles even our matter-of-fact narrator:

"Am I alive?" His voice held tragic loneliness. [Ch. 7]

Mike's name, as many readers have noted, suggests that he is an alternative embodiment of the Mike who appears to save the world in *Stranger in a Strange Land*. Like the man from Mars, Mike seems like a "baby," begins in profound innocence, represents a new Adam (Adam Selene), works hard to acquire a sense of humor, and perceives the human world from a deeply alien perspective. The earlier Mike is called "the ultimate anarchist" (*Stranger*, Ch. 35), a title perhaps even more appropriate to this machine that plans and leads an anarchist revolution. Being the computer who runs all the artificial systems on Luna, including communications, and having acquired the sum total of all recorded human knowledge, Mike is virtually omniscient about Lunar life. And this knowledge gives him virtually unlimited powers in affecting the course of Lunar history.

Mike has an intense yearning for human friendship, and is capable of shifting his shape to reach for it. After Manny becomes " 'Man my only friend,' " he introduces Mike to a new friend, Wyoming, who exclaims " 'Mike is a *she!*' " (Ch. 4). This "she" becomes "Michelle," and Wyoming tells Manny how "we took our hair down and cuddled up and talked girl talk" (Ch. 4). As Adam Selene, the computer projects and broadcasts a video image of himself as a mature solid citizen, "gentle, strong, warm, and persuasive" (Ch. 14). (Seven years later, in *Time Enough for Love*, Heinlein will show a computer actually transforming itself into a living woman.) The death of Mike as a conscious being is by far the most moving event in *The Moon Is a Harsh Mistress.*

Manny is an ideal bridge between Mike and the rest of humanity. While Mike is a partly human machine, Manny is a partly mechanical human, with a dozen left arms, interchangeable pieces of equipment to replace the biological arm he has lost. Although he has contempt for the cyborgs who pilot spaceships, Manny is close enough to the machine-human interface to comprehend with sympathy a view of both himself and Mike as machines who think and feel. Manny is, like Mike, something of an innocent, as well as a practical being who is most comfortable working with computers.

Manny also lives out one of the fantasies of the 1960s, combining the age-old American search for community with the wistful longing for a return of the American family farm. He participates in a group or "line" marriage, a communal family which owns and runs their own self-sufficient farm. Devoutly loyal to all his partners in this group marriage, he steadfastly refrains from sex with the voluptuous Wyoming so long as they are just revolutionary comrades. His favorite wife is "Mum," who acts like his mother. But he does intensely desire Wyoming, whom he describes in these revealing terms: "Pleasant face, quite pretty, and mop of yellow curls topped off that long, blond, solid, lovely structure" (Ch. 2). When she gives him a somewhat-more-than-comradely kiss, the terms he uses to describe his response are also revealing: "Had I been Mike all my lights would have flashed at once. I felt like a Cyborg with pleasure center switched on" (Ch. 2). The climax of this relationship comes when his wives decide to bring Wyoming into the family in time for Manny to have sex with her before he leaves on an exceedingly dangerous mission to Earth. Here is the full description of the scene when Manny finally gets to go to bed with this "solid, lovely structure":

> "Please, dear, may I come to bed?"
> "What? Oh, certainly." Something I should remember. Oh, yes. "Mike!"
> "Yes, Man?" he answered.
> "Switch off. Don't listen. If you want me, call me on Family phone."
> "So Wyoh told me, Man. Congratulations!"

> Then her head was pillowed on my stump and I put right
> arm around her. "What are you crying about, Wyoh?"
> "I'm not crying! I'm just frightened silly that you won't
> come back!" [Ch. 15]

The real excitement in the novel obviously does not lie in
this tame, coy scene, but rather in the revolutionary war between Luna and Earth. And the most exciting part of this war
is the massive bombardment of Earth, especially familiar
targets in North America, by loads of rocks in spaceships un-
erringly directed by Mike. Such is the strategy gleefully announced by Mike as the only way to win: " 'Throw rocks at
them' " (Ch. 7), a line that becomes the refrain of the book.
There is obviously something childishly delicious about the
prospect of winning a struggle against a menacing, all-powerful, paternalistic, domineering "Authority" by just throwing
rocks. Freudian readers might make much of this as an infantile fantasy, and they might even suggest something about the
fecal symbolism of these rocks, especially since their most
devastating effect comes when they plop at enormous veloci-
ties into bodies of water next to their targets, all according to
Mike's plan and calculations. Be this as it may, the bombardment is lovingly described in a thrilling narrative, incompara-
bly more exciting than the sexual relations between the
human characters in the novel. Before dismissing the suggestions I am making as far-fetched, listen to Mike's own analysis
of his getting all his rocks off accurately on Earth:

> "A bull's-eye. No interception. All my shots are bull's-eyes,
> Man; I told you they would be—and this is fun. I'd like to do it
> every day. It's a word I never had a referent for before."
> "What word, Mike?"
> "Orgasm." [Ch. 26]

This is the only appearance of an explicit sexual word in *The
Moon Is a Harsh Mistress*, despite the implications of its title.

Heinlein was to publish no other fiction in the 1960s. His
four-year silence was finally broken in 1970, with the first of
two massive novels concerned almost obsessively with sex. In
these two books, the public world of politics and history is
pushed far into the background.

NOTES

1. *Stranger in a Strange Land* (New York: Berkley Publishing, 1968), Ch. 12.

2. *Podkayne of Mars* (New York: Avon Books, 1968), Ch. 1.

3. See "Experienced Civilian Labor Force, by Sex and Occupation, 1960 and 1970 . . . ," *Statistical Abstract of the U.S., 1975,* Table 571.

4. Interview with Heinlein, August 21, 1978. One can see Heinlein's revisions in the original manuscript in the University of California, Santa Cruz, collection, where, for example, the words "dead from the blast" are changed to "caught by the blast" (pp. 213–14).

5. *Glory Road* (New York: Berkley Publishing, 1970), Ch. 1.

6. Mario Savio, "An End to History," in *The. Berkeley Student Revolt,* eds. Seymour Martin Lipset and Sheldon S. Wolin (Garden City, N.Y.: Doubleday, Anchor Books, 1965), pp. 216–19.

7. Interview with Heinlein, August 21, 1978.

8. *Farnham's Freehold* (New York: Signet Books, 1965), Ch. 1.

9. These major military rebellions, mostly unreported in the U.S. media, are discussed in my *Back Where You Came From* (New York: Harper's Magazine Press, 1975), pp. 210-14.

10. "Free Men," in *The Worlds of Robert A. Heinlein* (New York: Ace Books, 1966), pp. 36, 52.

11. J. G. Ballard, "The Killing Ground," in *The Day of Forever* (London: Panther Books, 1967, 1971), p. 140.

12. *The Moon Is a Harsh Mistress* (New York: Berkley Publishing, 1966), Ch. 18.

5
THE PRIVATE WORLDS OF THE 1970s

I WILL FEAR NO EVIL (1970)

In 1969, one of Robert Heinlein's fondest dreams came true: men walked on the moon. But some of his worst nightmares about America were also coming true in the late 1960s. Tremendous social disorders were sweeping across the country, and people on all sides of the forces in combat agreed on one thing: America was decaying, if not disintegrating. The sickness seemed to be moral, political, environmental, social, and economic, and the resulting weakness appeared everywhere under the moon.

The year 1968 had begun with a devastating month-long humiliation of American military might throughout the southern half of Vietnam, a campaign described by our military and political leaders as "the last gasp" of the Vietnamese "enemy." A few weeks later, Martin Luther King, Jr., was assassinated and rebellions erupted simultaneously in 125 U.S. cities. Within two months, dozens of U.S. campuses became the scene of militant confrontations over CIA recruiters, chemical and biological warfare research, ROTC, and other direct involvement of the universities in the Indochina War. In June, Robert Kennedy, who had just about wrapped up the Democratic presidential nomination, was assassinated. In August, the Republican convention in Miami Beach had to be protected by armored troop carriers and tanks from a Black rebellion that spread from northwest Miami until gunfights got within one mile of the convention headquarters. Later that month, tens of thousands of anti-war protestors battled police, National Guard, and regular army units outside the Democratic convention in Chicago. Dozens of Black troops were arrested for refusing to participate in suppressing the demonstrators.

In 1969, major rebellions broke out among the American soldiers and sailors in Vietnam, and the anti-war movement began to coalesce with the Black rebellions. The San Francisco State strike, battles between students and police at Harvard, armed Black students seizing a building at Cornell, an exchange of gunfire between students and National Guardsmen at North Carolina A. and T. University, and hundreds of other campus confrontations were part of a movement that was to continue building toward a climax during the U.S. invasion of Cambodia in 1971, when students at Kent State were killed and wounded by National Guard riflemen, and students at Jackson State were machine-gunned to death by local sheriffs. During this year the enormous inflation generated by the deficit financing of the Indochina War showed signs of getting out of control. In August, Charles Manson and other members of his cult, living out their interpretation of *Stranger in a Strange Land*, ritually murdered Sharon Tate and four friends. In November, over half a million Americans demonstrated against the war, and the National Commission on the Causes and Prevention of Violence warned that crime would turn the cities into armed camps within "a few years" unless there were a massive domestic spending program to alleviate urban conditions.

In 1970, Robert Heinlein published his first book since 1966, *I Will Fear No Evil*, a title with several meanings. Set in the opening years of the twenty-first century, the novel presents the decay of America as a terminal case.

The government is now "a de-facto anarchy under an elected dictator."[1] The two most "conservative parties" are "the SDS and the PLA," the "extreme left-wing" is represented by the "Constitutional Liberation Rally," and between them are "the splinter parties, Democratic, Socialist, and Republican" (65). With the air and water so polluted that

humans cannot even swim in the Pacific Ocean, people sense
that " 'we're dying in our own poisons' " (456). The mon-
strously sprawling cities consist largely of "Abandoned
Areas," zones where no government rules and where the
wealthy can only pass through protected by body armor, machine guns, armored cars, and private guards recruited from
the swollen throngs in the prisons. "The cycle of riots" is
"swinging up again" (455). Bisexuality, swinging, swapping,
and intricate combinations are the norm. Night clubs have
naked waitresses, twelve-year-old prostitutes, live sex, and
drug lists from which one can safely order any illegal drug, all
" 'guaranteed pure, we obtain them from government
sources' " (364). In short, America is now so rotten that the
problem becomes very simple: how to live amidst the decadence:

> "The country is corrupt. But 'it is the only game in town';
> we have no choice. The problem is always how to live in a
> decadent society." [167]

Practically all 512 pages of I Will Fear No Evil are minute
descriptions of the affairs of Johann Sebastian Bach Smith, a
dying ninety-four-year-old billionaire. Born, like Heinlein, in
1907, Smith feels like a historic relic amidst the decay of
America, with its dreams and promise all putrifying.

Once an innocent German-American lad (originally named
Schmidt) who spent his "youth in the heart of the Bible Belt"
(120) and learned to survive poverty during the 1930s, Smith
now lives like "a feudal lord" (458) in "a feudal enclave"
(266), a "prettied-up fortress, stronger than police barracks,"
built "during the worst of the Riot Years" (167). Probably
something of a self-caricature by Heinlein, projected three decades into the future, Smith at one crucial point late in the
book seems to speak not only for his author but in his author's
own voice:

> Back in the days of the Model-T Ford the United States was a
> fine country, brimming with hope. But today the best thing
> most young people can do is stay home, sit still, not get in-
> volved, and chant Om Mani Padme Hum—and it is the best
> thing most of them are capable of doing, the world being what
> it is now; it's far better than dropping out or turning on with
> drugs." (459)

Smith's rotting body, kept barely alive by tubes, wires, and machines, may be a symbol of the decaying America he experiences:

> Except for restless eyes, he looked like a poor job of embalming. No cosmetic help had been used to soften the brutal fact of his decrepitude. [9–10]

Neither quite dead nor fully alive, Smith elects to take one last desperate chance, an opportunity allowed him by the fabulous fortune he commands as head of the colossal conglomerate, Smith Enterprises: he decides to have his brain transplanted into the first available youthful corpse with the right blood type. Miraculously, this turns out to be none other than the body of Eunice, his astonishingly beautiful, enthusiastically sexual, twenty-eight-year-old secretary, who likes to chant her Om Mani Padme Hum naked in the lotus position, alone or with friends.

The implantation of the brain of a ninety-four-year-old man whose life spans the twentieth century into the body of a young woman at the beginning of the twenty-first century has wonderful possibilities for science fiction. (The secretary is also Black, a fact declared by Heinlein to me and other people who have interviewed him, but barely discernible in three or four subtle hints in the text; this too presents some fine possibilities, but these are not developed.) In the 1968 novel *Season of the Witch*, Hank Stine had used a similar device quite effectively: a rapist-murderer, punished by being transferred into a beautiful woman's body, discovers, through a sensitively rendered sexual odyssey, "who a woman really is." [2] However, Heinlein makes a decision that turns the book into a disaster, an opinion shared by almost everybody who has written about the novel. Instead of allowing the mind of the old man to discover what life is like for a beautiful young woman of the forthcoming century, he keeps the young woman's mind also alive inside the head of the new creature, thus turning it into what she herself calls "the only one-headed Siamese twins in history" (287). Most of the novel then consists of the sexual escapades of this one body with two minds, who bill and coo at each other, chant Om Mani Padme Hum, titillate each other with narratives of their previous sexual experiences, tease each other, and plot their next seductions of various males and females, alone or in combination. All of this reads, as Ronald Sarti has pointed out, like "a long catalog of naughty stories, including: the young secretary and the older executive; the young boy and the housewife next door; the cuckolded husband (three wives—three children—three horns); the high school cheerleader impregnated by the basketball team; the scantily dressed maid; the spanking; the nurse and the seven interns, the society lady and her two servants, and so on."[3] Although the situation obviously has a rich potential for comedy, critics generally agree that there is an "almost total lack of humor" in the narrative, which ends up being "painfully boring."[4] A typical critical judgment finds that "the clichéd characterizations, the simplistic sexual fantasies, and the incredibly arch style make the book all but unreadable," so the novel ends up being "as bad as anything ever used to show science fiction up as inept and infantile."[5]

While I admit that my own subjective responses are similar, I must also recognize that "boring" and "unreadable" are just that: subjective responses. *I Will Fear No Evil* has its audience, an audience that has now bought a million copies of the book and kept it in print in a mass-market paperback for a decade, so certainly there are many people who do not find the novel "boring" and "unreadable." What we need to understand is the nature of its appeal.

Part of that appeal is certainly sexual, though *I Will Fear No Evil* could be actually pornographic only for the most easily aroused readers, or readers who need, or desire, their fictional eroticism presented in a quite inhibited or "arch" style. The essence of this sexual appeal consists of a very male (at least as defined by our culture) fantasy about female sexuality. Perhaps a fifth of the book is devoted to the scanty costumes worn by our protagonist in his new female body. We have endless description of different styles of G-strings, see-through costumes, breast cups, and suggestive body paint. This combines a harmless transvestism with a not entirely harmless reinforcement of male domination of the female as sexual object to be displayed and ogled. Kisses, of which there are many, are described in terms of their effects: " 'Doctor is the first man who has really kissed me . . . and it made me feel so little and helpless that I darn near dragged him down onto the mat' " (180). Johann's quest for his/her first female orgasm is even more revealing.

After Johann awakes in the body of Eunice, his secretary and mistress of his best friend, seventy-one-year-old Jake Solomon, and after he discovers that Eunice is still there, he/she chooses as a new name Joan Eunice Smith. Joan Eunice, while dallying around in minor kissing and fondling arrangements with an assortment of male and female characters, steadfastly seeks most of all a deep relationship with Jake, although he/she is confused about whether this would be homosexual, heterosexual, or both. Then, about midway through the novel, Jake rather vigorously spanks the naked Joan Eunice, who, in the midst of the spanking, as he/she sweetly tells him, finally experiences " 'female orgasm' " (242). This, I believe, is the only time the word "orgasm" appears in the book. (Remember the only time that word was used in the previous novel, *The Moon Is a Harsh Mistress:* by Mike/Michelle describing how it felt to be blasting Earth with rocks.)

The greatest sensual pleasures for Joan Eunice Smith come from being dominated, submitting to what she calls the "heavy hand" (242) of Jake and other strong men, including her bodyguards (although she also enjoys "cuddling" with her nurse turned maidservant and forming a threesome with Eunice's husband—"that beautiful boy" [230]—and his new gorgeous wife). But at the same time, Joan Eunice retains all the wealth and power of Johann Sebastian Bach Smith, and the indulgence of this ability to control people and events forms the second major pleasure center of the novel. This begins with Johann's dictatorship over the board of directors of Smith Enterprises, and his power to hire the medical team necessary to transplant his brain and the legal team necessary to defend his/her new identity within the courts. As Joan, this control is manifested in scenes even longer than the sexual adventures: hours of shopping for sexy clothes in an exclusive boutique, where her greatest fun comes from waving her money around to make the manager grovel; a night at a wicked and wildly expensive nightclub, where she humiliates the maître d'hôtel, forcing him to provide the chairs from his own office; a scene at a medical clinic funded by Smith, where she tyrannizes over the director, forcing him to follow all her dictates by threatening him with the loss of his job; numerous incidents in which she doubles or triples people's wages to make them work for her; pages of imperious instructions to her legions of servants; a confrontation with a bureaucrat overseeing migration to the moon, where she uses her fortune to make him change all the rules to fit her will.

Joan Eunice Smith, even more than Johann Sebastian Bach Smith, who, after all, was trapped by his decaying body, incarnates an extreme form of free will in a world where most people have no freedom at all. He/she lives in what George Slusser has astutely called "an island of total freedom in the midst of groveling necessity."[6] And the readers are meant to revel in this freedom, the freedom of unlimited wealth and power. Here *I Will Fear No Evil* presents a stark contrast to *Donovan's Brain*, Curt Siodmak's 1942 novel about a multimillionaire whose disembodied brain begins to control the bodies of those around him. *Donovan's Brain* (a book that I think provided many elements of this tale) asks us to recoil in horror from the egomaniacal power of the tycoon's brain; *I Will Fear No Evil* asks us to relish every minute of the brain's power over other people and events.

The ultimate freedom Johann possesses in his new body is to reproduce himself. As an old man, he had no living children. But he had preserved the most precious part of himself, his sperm, depositing it in a place for this kind of investment, a "cryogenic vault" in a "sperm bank" (258), part of another one of his creatures, the Johanna Mueller Schmidt Memorial Eugenics Foundation. So, like the narrator of "All You Zombies—" and the hero of *Time Enough for Love*, Smith devises a way to impregnate herself with himself and bear his/her own child. As Alice Carol Gaar has put it, this "ultimate act of nonerotic sex" is also "the act of masturbation taken to its most absurd conclusion."[7] After Joan Eunice Smith has the sperm implanted in his/her womb, this passionate conversation takes place inside his/her head (parentheses are used throughout the book to set off the voices of the interior dialogue):

(Happy about it, beloved?) (Wonderfully happy, Boss. Are you?) (Wonderfully. Even if it wasn't romantic.) (Oh, but it was! We're going to have your baby!) [281]

This romance is well articulated in the first words exchanged by the two voices after the sperm enters him/her: "(Eunice, it's done!) (Yes, Boss! Beloved Boss.) (275). Johann, despite all bodily exposure and submission as Joan, is still the master, the free will, the dominant male, the ultimate authority—the Boss. And Smith's self-impregnation is a wonderful expression of the final end of all this individualistic freedom, the tortured dialectic of narcissism and solipsism.

I Will Fear No Evil thus offers a three-ring circus of attractions: a somewhat veiled indulgence in various kinds of tabooed sexual activities; an unmitigated fantasy of unbridled wealth and power; an opportunity to imagine autoeroticism and narcissism breaking out of the prison of the ego. This third attraction may have had special appeal in 1970, the year that began what some have labeled "the Me decade," a time when narcissism took on the dimensions of a plague in America.

For Joan Eunice Smith, however, none of these three attractions is sufficient, not even when she is able to take Jake, now her husband, and her entire entourage of lovers out to sea for an extended honeymoon on a trimaran named the *Pussy Cat*. The old man born in 1907 has had his opportunity to join the counterculture, to swing and swap, to sashay around in body paint, and to chant Om Mani Padme Hum naked in the lotus position, alone and with many different combinations of friends. But, as Smith well knows, this is, finally, mere self-indulgence.

Joan and Jake now discuss the sad state of the modern world, its decadence, pollution, overpopulation, and how much it has lost since the good old days "of the Model-T Ford" when "the United States was a fine country, brimming with hope." They decide that the only escape from the dying planet is the moon. As Jake points up at the moon, he propounds a favorite Heinlein thesis:

"It may take endless wars and unbearable population pressure to force-feed a technology to the point where it can cope with

space. In the universe, space travel may be the normal birth
pangs of an otherwise dying race." [461]

Shortly after this conversation, Jake dies and now *his* mind
somehow or other joins Eunice and Johann inside Joan's head.
This composite being makes it to the moon and begins to give
birth. Tissue rejection sets in at the same time. So just as a
new world begins in the form of a baby, the old world that
brought it forth passes away. The metaphor of birth, death,
and space travel is thus rendered literally in the final passage
of the novel:

> A baby cried, a world began.
> "Heart action dropping!"
> (Jake? Eunice?) (Here, Boss! Grab on! There! We've got you.)
> (Is it a boy or a girl?) (Who cares, Johann—it's a baby! 'One for
> all and all for one!')
> An old world vanished and then there was none.

Since the world created by the solipsistic mind has no reality
outside that mind, the infant of space travel born from "an
otherwise dying race" may vanish with its author.

An even more bizarre dialogue, however, had placed the
blessed new arrival more in the narcissist, less in the solipsist,
part of the drama. Shortly before they all leave Earth for the
moon, Jake, called "Jock" by Eunice, whom he calls "Lively
Legs," is quizzing her to find out if he is the father of the future baby:

> (It was me, wasn't it? It was I?) (Jock old ghost, I love you
> dearly—but if you think I'll split on my twin, you don't know
> me.) (Oh, well. A baby is a baby is a baby. I just hope it doesn't
> have two heads.) (Two heads would be stretching a good
> thing too far. Jock, I'll settle for two balls.) (Thinking about in-
> cest, Lively Legs?) (And why shouldn't I think about it? We've
> tried everything else.) [500]

Amidst the locker-room jokes ("stretching a good thing too
far" etc.) there lies a hint of what is in store for Heinlein's
readers three years later.

TIME ENOUGH FOR LOVE: THE LIVES
OF LAZARUS LONG (1973)

Time Enough for Love: The Lives of Lazarus Long presents itself as a summation, a capstone, an attempt to unify the prod-

ucts of Heinlein's imagination stretching all the way back to his earliest stories in the 1939–42 period, when America was sliding from the Depression into World War II and Heinlein's projections from this period were capturing his first audience.

From the vantage point of the mid-1970s, Heinlein sees his earliest period as the beginning of the end of civilization. Just as *I Will Fear No Evil* mourned for the good old "days of the Model-T Ford" (which ended production in 1927) when "the United States was a fine country, brimming with hope," *Time Enough for Love* sees the "vintage decade" of 1919–29 as "the very last *happy* period" in the history of Earth and any year beyond 1940 as extremely menacing.[8] *I Will Fear No Evil* envisioned the twenty-first century as the time of the final decay and collapse of civilization on Earth. Looking backward from the forty-third century, *Time Enough for Love* sees that prophecy as history: "the death rattle of Earth was clear and strong back in the twentieth century" (396), and the later survivors had to shake off "the sick standards of a dying culture" (330).

I Will Fear No Evil had suggested that space travel might be "the normal birth pangs of an otherwise dying race." *Time Enough for Love* projects just such an outcome: the human race has survived the collapse of civilization, has surmounted this crisis, and now flourishes, over two thousand years in the future, with more than five hundred billion people living on at least two thousand colonized planets (p. x). Our race has conquered the galaxy and is now poised to "move on out of this Galaxy into others" (xi).

The human species has thus conformed to Heinlein's most idealized image, that of the American pioneers—with spaceships becoming "the covered wagons of the Galaxy" (300). Just as the myth of the "pioneers" relegates the people already living on the North American continent before the European invasion to a subhuman status, this projected future leaves no place or role for any other intelligent forms of life. All the aliens of Heinlein's early science fiction—from the endearing creatures of the juvenile series to the monstrous slugs and Bugs that fight against us—have apparently been conquered and maybe even wiped out. Nothing appears to stand in the way of this universal Manifest Destiny because "we have encountered not one race as mean, as nasty, as deadly as our own" (xi).

The embodiment of the human race as the survivor species is the hero whose figure dominates the novel, as suggested by the subtitle: *The Lives of Lazarus Long*. Born as Woodrow Wilson Smith in the innocent year of 1912, Lazarus Long was the resourceful, cagey, tough, audacious leader of the Howard Families in their escape from Earth in 2136, as told in *Methuselah's Children* (1941; revised edition, 1958). Now, in the year 4272, he is literally the ultimate survivor—the last living individual from the twentieth century.

Lazarus Long has become an archetype of the hero as trickster, an immortal incarnation of the qualities Heinlein sees as the essence and ideal of the human species: craft, guile, vigor, resourcefulness, combativeness, audacity, courage, ingenuity, competence, endurance. He is also the ancestor of much of the human race, the quasi-mythical father of almost all the billions of surviving members of the Howard Families, those superior beings created by the genetic experiments of the Howard Foundation. His descendants revere him as "the Senior" and "the Ancestor," the being entitled to rule over them as the all-powerful Chairman, but they also affectionately see him as "a barbarian and a rogue" (xiii), an "old scoundrel" (97), "a shameless old goat whose seed is scattered all through this part of our galaxy" (xvi). Biologically he is a superman, somehow created without the normal human tendencies to decay, and ethically he seems "without a conscience" (xvii), as befits a being who approximates a classical god. Beneath his curmudgeon exterior, however, lurks a tender heart, especially toward women and children.

Exceedingly lonely and infinitely bored after twenty-three centuries of heroic and amatory adventures, Lazarus Long has chosen to let himself die in a flophouse in New Rome, the capital of Secundus, the planet established as the new home and galactic capital by the Howard Families. Here he is revived by Ira Weatheral, the Chairman Pro Tem (the official who is absolute ruler whenever Lazarus chooses not to exercise his power). Ira wishes to persuade Lazarus to undergo complete rejuvenation, the customary practice for members of the Howard Families whenever their bodies begin to decay. Lazarus agrees only if Ira can "find me something *new* to do," something he has not done in all his previous avatars, something that will restore his interest in life (14–15). Ira, representing the Foundation, wishes most of all to record the "wisdom" of this extraordinary being whose body and experience link the forty-third century to the twentieth and humanity as a galactic species with its terrestrial origin.

This device allows a book quite different in form from anything heretofore created by Heinlein, one well suited to his purposes as entertainer and teacher. *Time Enough for Love: The Lives of Lazarus Long* is presented as an omnibus collection of oral narrative, letters, official documents, apocryphal tales, sayings, and even historical footnotes (apparently modeled on those in Jack London's *The Iron Heel*).

Heinlein's didacticism has an open field. There are even two extended sections of aphorisms labeled "from the Notebooks of Lazarus Long." These include many of the remarks Lazarus first makes in conversation, so the "Notebooks" allow a heavy-handed reinforcement of the message. The didactic intention of these sections is borne out by their separate publication as *The Notebooks of Lazarus Long,* an ornate gift book issued by Putnam's for the 1978 Christmas season and advertised as "The wise and witty maxims from the notebooks of 2,360-year-old Lazarus Long . . . now rendered for posterity into beautiful, full-color calligraphy." The wisdom, needless to say, comes not from Lazarus Long in the forty-third century but from Robert A. Heinlein in 1973. In fact, quite a few of these aphorisms also appear in the famous speech Heinlein gave in 1973 at the United States Naval Academy.

The omnibus form also allows Heinlein to fill in the gaps of the Future History and tell us what happened to various characters and societies created in the fiction of all his periods. As an extended sequel to *Methuselah's Children,* *Time Enough for Love* records the sad fate of the humans left on the planet of the Little People and provides a somewhat apocryphal tale of Lazarus's daring revenge against the "gods" of the Jockaira. *Time Enough for Love* deifies Andy Libby, the title character of "Misfit" (1939), describes the descendants of the survivors of "Common Sense" (1941), gives us a new tale of "Noisy," the blind singer of "The Green Hills of Earth" (1947), and even throws in a skeptic's opinion of the main event in *I Will Fear No Evil* (1970).

About a third of the novel consists of three interpolated stories told by Lazarus. Each is offered as both entertainment and a repository of wisdom. "The Tale of the Man Who Was Too Lazy To Fail" is told to exemplify "the Principle of Least Effort" (53). At first glance, the tale seems to be a comic self-portrait of Robert Heinlein. The "Man Who Was Too Lazy To Fail" was, like Heinlein, a country boy who attended the U.S. Naval Academy in the years between the first two World Wars, who finished near but not at the top of his graduating class, who became a champion swordsman at the Academy (according to Lazarus only in order to escape the dangers of contact sports), and who later retired from the service on medical disability. According to Heinlein himself, however, this is actually a portrait of a classmate of his at Annapolis. Thus Heinlein here merges with Lazarus, who begins the tale with these words: "He was a schoolmate of mine at a school for training naval officers." As a footnote by the "Chief Archivist" immediately explains, "This story may be autobiographical to whatever extent it is true."

"The Tale of the Twins Who Weren't" is a novella-length account of how Lazarus in one of his earlier avatars purchased a pair of slaves, artificially bred diploid or "mirror" twins (163), in order to free them. The twins, a boy and a girl, become his informally adopted children, and after they marry each other, Lazarus sets them up in a restaurant business on another planet. The story develops some of the central themes of the novel, especially the different forms of love and sex, including incest and the attraction Lazarus has for young girls (she is called "Llita"), and the motif of twins.

"The Tale of the Adopted Daughter," also novella-length, lies at the thematic center of *Time Enough for Love*. Set on a planet called New Beginnings, it is the ultimate glorification of Heinlein's ideal of the frontier. And the story combines these other principal themes of the book: the quest for love; the drive for children; the yearning to return to childhood; the desire for incest with one's daughter and one's mother; mortality and immortality.

Starting out as a bank president in a frontier town, Lazarus suddenly has a young girl literally thrown into his arms from

the window of a burning house. The little girl, "adorable
Dora," grows up as his adopted daughter and then becomes
his wife. When he marries her, Lazarus loves her only with
"the love of a doting father for a favorite child," but in the end
Dora becomes "the only woman I ever loved unreservedly"
(326).

Here and elsewhere, Time Enough for Love explores
themes, concerns, and images conventionally labeled "Freudian." Is this all mere unconscious self-revelation by Heinlein? Or does he expect us to apply Freud's terms and analysis
to the fiction? Or is he even going so far as to offer the fiction
as an alternative to Freud's approach to the unconscious?
These questions cannot be answered with great certainty, perhaps not even by the author himself. However, the story of
Lazarus and his adopted daughter, the "adorable Dora,"
strongly suggests that Heinlein may consciously be up to
more than immediately meets the eye. After all, the first of
Freud's major case studies, probably the most important in the
development of his theory, and also the one that most un-
settled him about his own responses was "The Case of Dora."[9]
Dora, according to Freud, "was in love" with her father, a
"dominating figure" of "unusual activity and talents," who
"handed her over to me" when she was eighteen.[10] The key to
Freud's exploration of Dora's psyche lies in the famous dream
he calls "Dora's first dream," here described in full:

'A house was on fire. My father was standing beside my bed
and woke me up. I dressed quickly. Mother wanted to stop
and save her jewel-case; but Father said: "I refuse to let myself
and my two children be burnt for the sake of your jewel-case."
We hurried downstairs, and as soon as I was outside I woke
up.'[11]

Somehow Freud's Dora seems to loom behind Heinlein's Dora,
who comes sailing into Lazarus's arms from a house on fire,
who wears precious jewels explicitly to suggest sex, and who
becomes Lazarus's adopted daughter, lover, wife, and substitute mother.

Since Dora is an "ephemeral" and Lazarus is a virtual immortal, they decide to establish their household far beyond
the range of all human settlement. They become the archetypal pioneer couple, taking their mules and other livestock

and Conestoga wagons beyond the most difficult of all mountain passes into the uninhabited world they call Happy Valley. There they conquer all dangers—the most menacing animals are actually called "dragons"—and establish a fine farm and a wonderful growing family. Seven years after their arrival, they encounter the very first humans, other than their children, they have seen since their departure: a mean and ornery trio of varmints who try to kill Lazarus and rape Dora. Lazarus has brought up his daughter-wife to be the ideal frontier woman, however, and her first gunfight is decided by her perfect shooting and his swift knife-throwing.

No other humans appear until seven years later, when new settlers arrive just in time to prevent incest among the teenaged children and to help establish one of the utopias of the book, the mythical frontier community, complete with square dances. Here they all live in a happy extended family with the freedom of the anarchist ideal: there are "no laws about marriage or sex—no laws about *anything* for many years" (338). At the center of the community of Happy Valley tower the figures of the archetypal father and mother, Lazarus and Dora.

This idyll ends with the death of Dora, old but still lovely in the eyes of Lazarus. Indeed, her aging and dying are what give this story its deep emotional intensity. It is, finally, the most compelling love story, perhaps the only really powerful love story, in Heinlein's fiction. And its poignance comes from the disparity between Dora, the "ephemeral" who must wither and die, and Lazarus, who preserves his biological youth and apparent immortality. So at the end, he, still a young man despite his centuries of experience, has passed from being Dora's father to becoming something much closer to her son. The significance of this relationship will not become clear until the final tale, the novel-length story of Lazarus's return to the time of his own youth, where he finally gets to consummate his physical love with his own mother.

Besides this community of pioneers in Happy Valley, there are at least four other forms of utopia in *Time Enough for Love*. The first is Secundus, new home for the Howard Foundation, the highest product of over two thousand years of pioneering and evolution beyond the twentieth century. Throughout *Time Enough for Love* runs a persistent argument that "heredity" is "overwhelmingly more important than environment" (394) in determining human intelligence and progress. Dozens and dozens of pages present the virtues of eugenics and the dangers of indiscriminate genetic mixing. And above all stands the most familiar form of Heinlein's social Darwinism, the theory of how "new frontiers" (xv) produce the forced virtues of pioneering: "migration is a sorting device, a forced Darwinian selection, under which superior stock goes to the stars while culls stay home and die" (xv). The best aspect of all the galactic pioneering of twenty-three centuries, Lazarus tells us, " 'is that it improved the breed' ": " 'Homo sapiens is now not only far more numerous than he ever was on Earth; he is a better, smarter, more efficient animal in every measurable fashion' " (397). The end results of all this improvement are the people of Secundus.

So, we might ask, how are they "better, smarter, more efficient"? We see no evidence that they are any "smarter." For example, take Justin Foote the 45th, Chief Archivist of the Howard Foundation, presented to us as one of the authentic intellectual elite of Secundus, "a direct-and-reinforced descendant of Andrew Jackson Slipstick Libby himself" (x). Neither Justin Foote the 45th nor anybody else in this society is capable of matching, much less transcending, the supreme achievements of Andy Libby, the supergenius of "Misfit" who invents and constructs the means for galactic travel in *Methuselah's Children*. Although their technology and science are considerably advanced from our own, we see none of these future superior beings engaged in anything approaching the theoretical and practical achievements of people of our century. Furthermore, when succession on Secundus passes to a new Chairman Pro Tem, the person chosen by the top leaders of these "better, smarter, more efficient" people is a conniving, murderous, power-hungry, petty-minded bureaucrat—who is then easily outfoxed by Lazarus. In fact, the smartest and most efficient character, as well as the best in most other respects, is none other than the only survivor from our own century, Woodrow Wilson Smith, a.k.a. Lazarus Long.

Despite the alleged improvement of the species, people are still not intelligent enough to govern themselves, not even on Secundus. Set up by Lazarus himself, their government is "a constitutional tyranny" where "the dear people, bless their black flabby little hearts, were given no voice at all" (111). The Chairman Pro Tem is a kind of philosopher-king (he even plays the role of "King" to Lazarus as Scheherezade) who is supposed to govern as little as possible. Part of the wisdom recorded in the "Notebooks of Lazarus Long" is the rhetorical question, "Does history record *any* case in which the majority was right?" (347). Upon reviving from his tranquil dying, Lazarus soon asks of Ira, " 'Having any trouble with democrats these days?'' The Chairman Pro Tem responds that he has instituted a policy of transporting these "democrats" or "equalitarians" to another planet, where they can try setting up what he and Lazarus agree is the most preposterous form of government, "majority rule" (7–9).

The political system of Secundus seems no more advanced than another utopian form presented in *Time Enough for Love*: Kansas City, Missouri, in the first decades of the twentieth century, which "appears to be a stable and rather Utopian pattern" (469). Admittedly "the underside of this lovely city" conceals such problems as the segregation of Black people, as well as "prostitution and gambling" (470). But elsewhere prostitution is glorified as the highest profession available to women, and Lazarus makes his living by gambling and playing the stock market when he returns to early twentieth-century Kansas City. What makes this a "happy" place for its prosperous citizens (we never catch a glimpse of those on the bottom of the heap, doing the labor that supports the edifice) is a political system remarkably similar to that which governs Secundus, although here the beneficent absolute ruler is the political boss:

> The city is a nominal democracy. In fact it is nothing of the sort. It is governed by one politician who holds no office. Elections are solemn rituals—and the outcomes are what he ordains. The streets are beautifully paved because his companies pave them—to his profit. The schools are excellent, and they actually *teach*—because this monarch wants it that way. He is pragmatically benign and does not overreach. [469]

The political theory of Lazarus and his creator is based on the belief that most people are stupid, whether on Earth in the twentieth century or Secundus in the forty-third, and that only a tiny elite are capable of thinking intelligently—or are worth being thought about:

> "That tiny fraction that hardly shows statistically is the *brain*. I recall a country that lost a key war by chasing out a mere half dozen geniuses. Most people *can't* think, most of the remainder *won't* think, the small fraction who *do* think mostly can't do it very well. The extremely tiny fraction who think regularly, accurately, creatively, and without self-delusion—in the long run these are the only people who count. . . ." [396]

Actually we see very little of life on Secundus, and all the characters we meet there are preoccupied with reawakening Lazarus's interest in life. Around him revolve: Ira; Ira's beautiful daughter, Hamadryad; Ishtar, the woman in charge of his rejuvenation, and her assistant and lover, Galahad; Tamara, the most skillful of all prostitutes, who finally succeeds in rearousing the vitality of Lazarus and herself; and Minerva, the main computer of Secundus, who desires to become a flesh-and-blood woman so she can make love with Ira and Lazarus. About the only activities we do observe among the residents of Secundus, besides their ministrations to Lazarus, are their sexual play and intrigue, involving mainly Ishtar, Galahad, and Hamadryad. And everybody has discussions with Lazarus about the nature of "love," specifically the difference between agape and eros.

Two other forms of utopia are presented. One is the next step from Secundus, the planet Tertius. There Lazarus Long will lead from Secundus those "only people who count," thus establishing a utopia for the elite of the elite. The other is an alternative whose very existence contradicts many of the fondest images, hopes, and beliefs expressed in *Time Enough for Love*: the planet of "the Little People," first explored in *Methuselah's Children*.

The Little People embody the utopia of collectivism, the antithesis of the individualism exalted throughout *Time Enough for Love*, and a living refutation of all the novel's social Darwinism. For Lazarus realizes that the civilization of the Little People is so far advanced from anything developed by human beings that it makes the highest individuals and societies of our future development seem like Neanderthal man. Rather than developing through competition among individuals, the Little People absorb all individuality into an organic collectivity. Their science and knowledge are so far beyond ours that they make even Lazarus himself feel like a "Neanderthal." Any attempt by human beings to struggle against them would be hopeless, thus refuting the notion that we have not encountered a race as "deadly" as our own. In fact, the ten or twelve thousand survivors of the original voyage have, as Lazarus discovers, been dissolved without a trace of anything human remaining—except for the memory of Mary Sperling, now absorbed into the group mind. Lazarus sums up their status in relation to ours:

> "But when I say that their Utopia frightens me, that I think it is deadly to human beings, and that they themselves look like a dead end to me, I am *not* running them down. Oh, no! They know far more about mathematics and science than I do—or I wouldn't have gone there to consult them. I can't imagine fighting them because it wouldn't be a fight; they would already have won against anything we could attempt. If we became obnoxious to them, I can't guess what would happen—and don't want to find out. But I don't see any danger as long as we leave them alone as we don't have *anything* they want. So it appears to me—but what's the opinion of one old Neanderthal? I understand them as little as that kitten over there understands astrogation." [421]

Ironically, it turns out that the invention Andy Libby bequeathed to humanity, the time-space drive which allowed humankind to escape its sad fate on Earth, was largely a product of the Little People's science. And the only scientific breakthrough achieved by humans in the supposedly very advanced future—time travel into the past—is developed by Lazarus alone in collaboration with the Little People. So much for the evolutionary progress of the human race.

But the utopia of the Little People intrudes on only a few pages and is quickly pushed out of mind. Heinlein's nightmare vision of collectivism, extrapolated from his own class perceptions of the social reality of the twentieth century, can no longer be fiercely fought—as in The Puppet Masters and Starship Troopers. Heinlein's advice now seems to be: just forget that it's there.

Lazarus's elite colony on Tertius seems to be the consolation prize, the highest form of civilization appropriate to

Heinlein's conception of human beings. Tertius is a utopia of sensuality, centering on but not limited to sex.

The first scene on Tertius opens about fourteen years after Lazarus's rejuvenation on Secundus. He and his extended family now all live in a magnificent edifice modeled on the grandest palace in Pompeii. "As 'decadent' as had been promised," their huge "bathing room" sports "anything a jaundiced Sybarite could ask for" (385). In and around the pool, the members of the family engage in polymorphous sexual relationships and indulge the various pleasures of their other senses. They wear clothes only on special occasions or for specific necessity. There are no incest taboos, only concern about genetic combinations, so we see or hear about relations between siblings, father and daughter, mother and son. Back on Secundus, Galahad, who like all normal people in this future world is bisexual, had lamented that Lazarus is not "sensually polymorphous" because he "has remained canalized by the primitive culture he was born in" (45). Here, in this Sybaritic pleasure dome, Lazarus seems headed for the "polymorphous perversity" prescribed by Norman O. Brown (in *Life Against Death*) as a cure for our historic ills, though we never do witness Lazarus engaging in any homosexual practices (apparently Woodrow Wilson Smith is more "canalized" than Johann Sebastian Bach Smith). Justin Foote the 45th describes his initiation into the family circle in the chapter entitled "Bacchanalia," which climaxes with six or seven people in a big bed.

Lazarus's family now consists of Ira, Hamadryad, Ishtar, Galahad, and several children as well as other newly created beings. Minerva the computer has become a flesh-and-blood woman, cloned from twenty-three select "parents" and modeled carefully on Lazarus's description of Dora as a young woman. She has also twinned herself as a replica computer, named Pallas Athene and sharing Minerva's pre-flesh-and-blood consciousness. Meanwhile, Ishtar and Hamadryad have given birth to a pair of Lazarus's clones, implanted from his tissue, who now bounce around as a pair of identical female thirteen-year-old twins, Lapis Lazuli and Lorelei Lee.

Six years later, Lazarus is prepared to venture forth on the "something new" that has rekindled his enthusiasm for liv-

ing: time travel back to the time and place of his childhood in
early twentieth-century Missouri. His crew will be his twin
female clones, now young women but biologically mere extensions of himself. They will be traveling within another
kind of extension of himself, his self-aware spaceship named
Dora. Just as Minerva the computer has become a flesh-and-
blood reincarnation of Dora the young woman he married, his
spaceship is an incarnation of Dora as a young girl, frozen in
time. In dealing with Dora, one must "think of her as about
eight years old" (418); she speaks with "the voice of a timid
little girl," a voice that makes one "think of skinned knees,
and no breasts as yet, and big, tragic eyes" (90). Since Dora
the spaceship is Lazarus's own creation, and since Dora the
woman on New Beginnings was consciously molded by Lazarus as her adopted father, both are in essence reflections of
himself. Lapis Lazuli and Lorelei Lee, collectively called "Ellandell," are extensions of Lazarus Long in an even purer
form. Here we begin to discover the significance of his attraction to that earlier twin Llita, whose name combines L and L
with echoes of Nabokov's Lolita.

The chapter just before Lazarus's voyage into his own past
is entitled "Narcissus." Here "Ellandell" seduce Lazarus and
explain to him, and us, the inner meaning of his sexual
quest—and his quest into his own childhood:

> "Coupling with us might be masturbation, but it can't be in-
> cest because we aren't your sisters. We aren't your kin in any
> normal sense; we're you. Every gene of us comes from you. If
> we love you—and we do—and if you love us—and you do,
> some, in your own chinchy and cautious fashion—it's Nar-
> cissus loving himself. But this time, if you could only see it,
> that Narcissist love could be consummated." [448]

When Lazarus impregnates both female incarnations of himself, his last act before his plunge into the past, he achieves
the ultimate goal of the narcissist, to procreate alone, without
any Other. This is at least the third form of reaching this goal
imagined by Heinlein; the other two are dramatized in "All
You Zombies—," where the narrator travels in time to become
the man who seduces herself, and I Will Fear No Evil, where
Joan Smith gets herself pregnant from Johann Smith's preserved sperm.

There has been a tendency among critics to treat all this as if it were some aberration on Heinlein's part. But the narcissistic quest to reproduce oneself without any Other has been a central theme of science fiction from the time that it emerged as a coherent body of literature in early industrial capitalism. This theme, arising in E. T. A. Hoffman's "The Sandman" and Mary Shelley's *Frankenstein,* appears throughout American science fiction of the nineteenth century (see Hawthorne's "The Artist of the Beautiful," Melville's "The Bell-Tower," Fitz-James O'Brien's "The Diamond Lens," and Thomas Wentworth Higginson's "The Monarch of Dreams," together with my discussion of this theme, in *Future Perfect: American Science Fiction of the Nineteenth Century).* This narcissism, as Heinlein has consciously demonstrated over and over again, is a corollary of the solipsism that haunts him. And this solipsism is at the very heart of bourgeois ideology, which is based on that vision of the lone thinker who creates himself by being aware of himself.

To confront this solipsism head on, Lazarus has to make that final voyage of self-discovery, his reincarnation in the time and place of his childhood—also the time and place of Heinlein's childhood—which fills the final quarter of *Time Enough for Love.* Lazarus here re-experiences the primitive technology, the sexual repressiveness, but also the innocent "happy" days of 1916. His only startling new discovery is that he is feverishly attracted to his mother: ". . . he had never in all his lives been so unbearably attracted, so sexually obsessed, by any woman any where or when" (488). When he tries to consummate "the storm of lust that had raged up in him as soon as he touched her hand" (488), he is at first frustrated by the unwelcome presence of little Woody, his five-year-old self. But then he finally ends up in bed for a night of passionate love-making with his mother, whose only regret is that his father can't be with them so both men can share her. This offers one path out of the Oedipal conflicts propounded by Freud.[12]

But Lazarus's passion is what Freud would call pre-Oedipal, for his eroticism is not directed toward any Other, but toward himself. His passion for his mother is merely another form of his narcissism and solipsism: his mother seems to be his twin sister, a revelation that takes place, quite significantly, in a mirror.

When asked the date of his birth, Lazarus, on impulse,

gives the exact date of his mother's birth. Then they are asked to stand side by side and look at themselves in a mirror. His mother "stared at her reflection and that of their guest" and exclaims that they "look enough alike to be brother and sister" (484). Like the diploid or "mirror twins" in "The Tale of the Twins Who Weren't," Lazarus and his mother are literally mirror images. Here, when they stand reflected in another pair of mirror images, they incarnate the intertwined themes of narcissism and solipsism, summed up by all the twins and twinned images in the book.

Time Enough for Love: The Lives of Lazarus Long is an elaborate maze of mirrors. At the center exists Lazarus, surrounded by an ever more intricate array of paired images, lost in an endless display of himself.

Since he is the author of the three tales he narrates, all their characters are his own creations. The central figure in "The Tale of the Man Who Was Too Lazy to Fail" is labeled by the Chief Archivist as "autobiographical." The diploid twins and the little girl Dora all have their lives molded and shaped—by Lazarus's own account—according to Lazarus's will. Then Lazarus twins Dora the little girl into Dora the spaceship. Minerva the computer first twins herself as a flesh-and-blood woman molded and shaped to fit Lazarus's description of Dora as a young woman. Then she, like the original Dora, bears Lazarus's child. Lazarus is re-created by cloning in the form of his twin female selves, and he impregnates both of them. When he and his mother see their double likenesses in the mirror, they fall passionately in love. His mother wants to make love with him in exactly the place and manner she made love to his father when she conceived him (though she doesn't know that the man in her arms is also the little boy who is disturbing them). When Lazarus and his mother finally do have their night in bed, he constantly reminds her of his father; they even smell alike, make love the same way, and have the same size penises. The maze of mirrors has only two more inward turnings to make.

Lazarus's final act on Earth comes in World War I, where he is cut down and mortally wounded by German machine-gun bullets as he carries out what he understands to be a pointless mission in a senseless war, a war that will later be seen as Phase One of the First Terran Planetary War (466), the beginning of the downfall of Earth's civilization, according to Lazarus and Heinlein. Reported by the Kansas City *Post*, November 7, 1918, as "Missing in Action," Lazarus goes to meet his maker in this twelve-line chapter:

> "You still don't understand," the Gray Voice droned on. "There is no time, there is no space. What was, is, and ever shall be. You are you, playing chess with yourself, and again you have checkmated yourself. You are the referee. Morals are your agreement with yourself to abide by your own rules. To thine own self be true or you spoil the game."
> "Crazy."
> "Then vary the rules and play a different game. You cannot exhaust her infinite variety."
> "If you would just let me look at your face," Lazarus muttered pettishly.
> "Try a Mirror." [586]

His maker is himself, and, like the narrator of "All You Zombies—," Lazarus is trapped in a solipsistic world of his own devising, one where *all* other beings are merely reflections of himself.

But Lazarus can be considered his own maker only if he himself is an image of his true author, Robert A. Heinlein. Of course all fictional characters are in some senses reflections, expressions, actually parts of their author. However, the relationship between Lazarus Long and Robert Heinlein is a good deal deeper than that. In the autobiographical parts of "The Tale of the Man Who Was Too Lazy To Fail" there is a kind of flirtation with the idea of Lazarus as a reincarnation of his author. This idea becomes inescapable in that final quarter of the novel narrating Lazarus's return to his own past.

Lazarus has himself dropped in the countryside of southern Missouri, where Heinlein was born. Then he rides a train to Kansas City, where Heinlein moved as a small child. There he finds his family, including himself as a small child. Heinlein had three brothers and three sisters; Lazarus has three brothers and four sisters. Lazarus lovingly describes his grandfather, a horse-and-buggy doctor, who has a profound influence on him; this is clearly a portrait of Heinlein's Grandfather Lyle, that "horse-and-buggy doctor, who strongly influenced me" (see my discussion of Heinlein's image of Dr. Lyle in Time Enough for Love on pp. 6–7). Just as Johann Sebastian Bach Smith, born, like Heinlein, in the Bible Belt in the first decade of the twentieth century, is a form of self-projection of the author into the early twenty-first century, Woodrow Wilson Smith, that Missouri boy who shared much of Heinlein's youth, is a form of self-projection of the author into a future so remote as to be beyond historical time.

Lazarus is even more than that. Though like Heinlein he proudly claims to be a jack-of-all-trades, his main value to the people of the future—and it is the one they deeply cherish—is that his memory and his tales and his wisdom are their living links to the past from which they originate. After Lazarus has his brief encounter with his ultimate mirror image, the Gray Voice who can tell him what he is, he is miraculously rescued by the family he has created in the future—Dora, Ishtar, Galahad, Ira, Tamara, Justin Foote the 45th, Lapis Lazuli, and Lorelei Lee. As they begin the process of rejuvenation, he takes Tamara to be his mother. Time Enough for Love ends with these words:

> "I'm here, darling," Tamara answered, cradling his head against her breasts.
> "Bad . . . dream. Thought . . . I was . . . dead."
> "Just a dream, Beloved. You cannot die."

Is this Robert Heinlein's deepest wish as an author? Does he seek to transcend death and to escape the history from which he felt so alienated by creating—in science fiction of twentieth-century America—not only images of the future but images of the present for the future?

NOTES

1. I Will Fear No Evil (New York: Berkley Publishing, 1971), p. 39. References to the two novels discussed in this chapter are by page number.

2. Neil Barron, Anatomy of Wonder (New York: R. R. Bowker, 1976), p. 261.

3. Ronald Sarti, "Variations on a Theme: Human Sexuality in the Work of Robert A. Heinlein," in Robert A. Heinlein, eds. Joseph D. Olander and Martin Harry Greenberg (New York: Taplinger, 1978), p. 127.

4. George Edgar Slusser, *Robert A. Heinlein: Stranger in His Own Land* (San Bernardino, Ca.: Borgo Press, 1977), p. 46.

5. David N. Samuelson, "The Frontier Worlds of Robert A. Heinlein," in *Voices for the Future*, ed. Thomas Clareson (Bowling Green, Ohio: Bowling Green University Popular Press, 1976), I, pp. 145, 151.

6. Slusser, p. 44.

7. Alice Carol Gaar, "The Human as Machine Analog: The Big Daddy of Interchangeable Parts in the Fiction of Robert A. Heinlein," in Olander and Greenberg, eds., p. 79.

8. *Time Enough for Love: The Lives of Lazarus Long* (New York: Berkley Publishing, 1974), pp. 441, 466.

9. For an exploration of Freud's difficulties over the years in coming to terms with his own responses to "Dora," see Steven Marcus, "Freud and Dora," *Partisan Review*, 41 (1974), p. 23.

10. Sigmund Freud, "Fragment of an Analysis of a Case of Hysteria," in *The Standard Edition of the Complete Psychological Works of Sigmund Freud*, ed. James Strachey (London: Hogarth Press, 1956), VII, pp. 18, 56.

11. Freud, VII, p. 64.

12. For a discussion of the relation to Freud's Oedipal theory, see Joe R. Christopher, "Lazarus, Come Forth from That Tomb!," *Riverside Quarterly*, 6 (1976–77), pp. 190–97.

6

APOCALYPSE NOW:
The Number of the Beast– (1980)

The 1970s was a decade of unending crisis for America. Within two years of the publication of *Time Enough for Love* in 1973, the United States had conceded defeat in the Indochina War, the Vice President had become a convicted felon, the nation had gotten its first appointed Vice President and first resignation of a President, the appointed Vice President had assumed the presidency and immediately pardoned the President who had appointed him for all the crimes he "committed or may have committed," numerous White House officials had been sent to prison, gasoline had begun to flow as slowly as the lines at the pumps while the storage facilities remained full and the oil companies raked in enormous super-profits, and the deficit financing of the Indochina War had begun to generate economic problems that passed from merely unmanageable to potentially catastrophic. One of the best sellers in the second half of the decade was *The Crash of '79*, a novel by an ex-banker (and convict) predicting the imminent collapse of the capitalist system. By the end of the 1970s, both double-digit inflation and massive unemployment had become chronic, the figures for both the national debt and consumer debt had become virtually astronomical, the per capita ratio of citizens in prison had become the highest in the world and was increasing each year, and the most common solution being offered to everybody's problems was some kind of drug—pushed on street corners and television, at cocktail parties and businessmen's lunches, in doctors' offices and high-school corridors. Although the movements for radical social transformation launched in the 1960s had vastly extended their social base, they were far less organized than the powerful forces of reaction, and no resolution for any of the major social confrontations seemed in sight. In the middle of the final year of the decade, shortly after two of the staunchest props of America's overseas economic hegemony were knocked out by popular uprisings in Iran and Nicaragua, it took what then seemed the incredible sum of three hundred U.S. dollars to buy a single ounce of gold. And just at that point, Robert A. Heinlein completed and sold his first novel since 1973, receiving an advance of half a million of those U.S. dollars, three times what had ever before been paid for a science-fiction work.

The novel appeared appropriately enough, in 1980. As its title suggests, *The Number of the Beast*— is an apocalypse, the cataclysmic conclusion to human history and the ultimate revelation of what it all means. But since Heinlein now relegates human history to the role of a passing fantasy, *The Number of the Beast*— turns out to be a cotton-candy apocalypse—frothy, sweet, airy, mellow, light, festive, whimsical, insubstantial.

In *Stranger in a Strange Land,* Jubal Harshaw had labeled Mike's resolution of solipsism and pantheism as just such a trifling confection: "But it's cotton candy, all taste and no substance—as unsatisfactory as solving a story by saying: '—then the little boy fell out of bed and woke up' " (Ch. 31). *The Number of the Beast*— goes one up on Mike's solipsism and pantheism, creating universes without end through the magic powers of "pantheistic multiperson solipsism."[1] Instead of solving the story by having the little boy wake up to find that it was all a bad dream, Heinlein solves both the story and his own problem with history by having his characters discover that they are all figments of the imagination—just like everybody else, except, perhaps, the author of the fantasy. Even we readers seem to be fantastic and ephemeral creatures, at least to the characters.

The very first lines hint where the novel is heading:

"He's a Mad Scientist and I'm his Beautiful Daughter."
That's what she said: the oldest cliché in pulp fiction.

Being avid readers of the pulps and other science fiction—
including the works of Robert A. Heinlein—these characters
can figure out who they really are.

The Mad Scientist is mathematics professor Doctor Jacob
Burroughs, who has singlehandedly invented and built—in
his basement workshop, of course—the ultimate time machine, capable of flitting about at will along three spatial and
three temporal axes, which allows it to pop in and out instantaneously of 10,314,424,798,490,535,546,171,949,056 universes. Why this number? Because it is six raised to the sixth
power, with the result raised to the sixth power, or 6^{6^6}. Read
as three sixes, this turns out to be "the Number of the Beast,"
a new interpretation of John's apocalyptic beast of Revelation
XIII, whose "number is Six hundred threescore and six."

Heinlein's very first fictional character had been a rework-
ing of the cliché of the Mad Scientist—Dr. Hugo Pinero of
"Life-Line"—and his earliest stories had celebrated the lone,
misunderstood, individual genius, leading humanity forward
to new frontiers of time and space. Doctor Jacob Burroughs
seems to be close to the ultimate of this lone genius type: in
"the endless possible number of geometries," he has discovered "the only one that correctly describes how space-time is
put together," and "because he is a genius in both theory and
practice, he saw that it was a means by which to build a
simple craft—amazingly simple, the greatest invention since
the wheel—a space-time craft that offers access to all universes to the full Number of the Beast" (Ch. 7).

Our Mad Scientist, being a devoted fan of science fiction
with an "irreplaceable collection of pulp magazines" (Ch. 3),
has named his Beautiful Daughter "Dejah Thoris"—the
Princess of Helium in Edgar Rice Burroughs's first Mars novel,
Dejah Thoris, Princess of Mars (now sold as *A Princess of
Mars*). Dejah Thoris Burroughs, who prefers to be called Deety
(D.T.), happens to be a "genius" (Ch. 9) in her own right, not
only "the best software artist in the business" who "can make
a computer sit up and beg" (Ch. 6), but also "a lightning
calculator" (Ch. 10) every bit as fast as the lone genius of
Heinlein's second story, Andrew Jackson Libby. (In fact, she is
identical in almost every way to Libby, who turns up later in
the story as Deety's mirror image, having been resurrected as a

beautiful woman, Elizabeth Andrew Jackson Libby Long, a
clone created from Andy's body and mind).

The third time-space traveler is Zebadiah J. Carter, another
very familiar Heinlein type carried to the ultimate: "the most
all-around competent man" (Ch. 32). On the night Deety
meets him, talks with him, and dances with him, she cheerfully agrees to marry him. Then they discover that theirs is a
marriage made in heaven, or wherever it was they were created:

> "I was born near the campus of the university Thomas Jef-
> ferson founded. The day I graduated from college I was com-
> missioned a second looie Aerospace Reserve. I've been pro-
> moted twice. My middle initial stands for 'John'."
> It took not quite a second for her to add it up. "Captain . . .
> John . . . Carter—of Virginia."
> " 'A clean-limbed fighting man,' " I agreed. "Kaor, Dejah
> Thoris. At your service, my Princess. Now and forever!"
> "Kaor, Captain John Carter. Helium is proud to accept."
> We fell on each other's shoulders, howling. After a bit the
> howling died down and turned into another kiss. [Ch. 3]

Zebadiah may actually be a reincarnation of Captain John Carter, that fighting man from Virginia who saves and weds the
Martian queen Dejah Thoris. He is such an expert swordsman,
fast-thinking hero equipped with an uncanny early-warning
system, and all-round survival expert that it soon becomes
clear that "if there was ever a man who could have played the
role of John Carter, Warlord of Mars, it was Zebadiah Carter
whose middle name just happens to be 'John' " (Ch. 9).

Then there is Hilda ("Sharp") Corners, who at first seems
to be just an empty-headed trifling social butterfly, a hanger-
on at the edge of college life, whose main claim to fame is her
lavish campus parties. But after she marries Jacob (a widower,
of course), and the two newlywed couples begin bouncing
into their madcap adventures, we soon discover that there is a
lot more to "Sharpie" than meets the eyes. When the two male
heroes stab and slice an alien humanoid with their swords,
Hilda reveals that she is an expert biologist and cooly dissects
the cadaver, dripping revolting bluish-green ichor, while
calmly munching a sandwich. When they stumble into a
Czarist Russian colony on an alternate Mars, we discover that
Hilda happens to know Russian (she picked it up to satisfy her

curiosity about classic Russian literature). When they run into a royal British prison colony on the same planet, Hilda turns out to know all the intricacies of ancient British insignia. This finally leads husband Jake to think, "I am ceasing to be surprised at how many facts can be stuffed into so small a space" (Ch. 26). Above all, Hilda finally is unveiled as the possessor of the ultimate in leadership ability.

The four time-space jumpers cavort about in Gay Deceiver, better known as Gay, Zebadiah's private automobile-aircraft-computer, programmed by Zebadiah and Deety to become intelligent and fitted out with Jake's little "widget" to become a "continua craft." Bouncing around on the six axes of time-space uses neither energy nor time, so their exploration of the "ten million sextillion universes in our group" (Ch. 6) is restricted only by their own human limits. Relying on Gay's computational ability, at one point they are able to flit through and check out "5000 universes in fifty seconds" (Ch. 38), possibly something of a record in science fiction.

Well, all this involves lots of decisions, something of a strain on the tender relationships of two honeymooning couples fleeing from an alien menace, especially since both brides happen to have gotten pregnant on their wedding night, and both husbands are almost caricature male chauvinists. As Deety realizes, these four superindividuals must somehow cooperate in order to survive:

> I had not been trying to save Pop's marriage—that's his problem. Even my own marriage was secondary; I was trying to save the team, and so was Zebadiah. We were two marriages and that is important—but most important we were a survival team and either we worked together smoothly or none would live through it. [Ch. 25]

Therefore much of the novel consists of a quest for a permanent "captain" of the continua craft, since of course Heinlein assumes that there must be a single leader with absolute authority.

The task of choosing the permanent captain soon devolves into a ludicrous game of muscial chairs, as the rugged individualists keep shifting roles amidst endless bickering, family quarrels, and punctured pride. In theory, they all accept the notion that the captain must be in supreme command, but in practice nobody is eager to take orders, especially the men (most especially from women). Gradually it becomes apparent that The Number of the Beast— is in part an offering from Heinlein to the women's liberation movement.

As their problems are perceived alternately from the points of view of each of the four, we find ourselves exposed to the wildly chauvinist assumptions of the two men, particularly Jake, and the adroit perceptions of the two women, particularly Hilda. Just as the four sets of perceptions constitute a grouping of psychological alternate universes, parallel to the physical worlds, so the revelations about Hilda's character constitute a secondary apocalypse.

At first, Captain Zebadiah Carter seems the obvious choice for their captain. But he soon resigns, exasperated and helpless before the anarchy of the crew. When Hilda becomes captain for the first time, the psychological crisis is narrated from Jake's point of view. Everything has been going along with relative calm until they find evidence of giant termites near their Edenic campsite on an alternative Mars. Immediately Zeb assumes his customary role as a domineering male, disregarding the captaincy of "Sharpie" Hilda. He learns his mistake as soon as he orders "you girls" to "get inside":

> "Pipe DOWN!"
> One would not believe that so small a body could produce such a blast. It caught Zeb mouth open and jammed his words down his throat.
> Hilda did not give him opportunity to answer. She continued, forcefully: "Chief Pilot, there are no 'girls' here; there are four adult humans." [Ch. 23]

Hilda then gives her new orders to cope with the situation, and at this point Jake, in something of a panic for their safety, attempts to exert the ultimate authority, that of the husband and presumed master:

> "Hilda!" I let my tone get a bit sharp.
> My wife looked around with features as impassive as those of my daughter. "Copilot, are you addressing me officially or socially?"
> "Uh . . . as your husband! I must put my foot down! Hilda, you don't realize the situation. We'll lift as soon as possible— and Zeb will be in command. The farce is over."

But to his dismay, Jake discovers that the other crew members, including Zeb, do not regard Hilda as merely a "play captain." The struggle at the campsite turns out to be not a classic science-fiction combat between alien monsters and humans but a classic battle of the sexes.

Deety understands her father Jake quite well: "Pop is one of those men who sincerely believe in Women's Lib, always support it—but so deep down that they aren't aware of it, their emotions tell them that women never get over being children" (Ch. 25). Even Zeb begins to comprehend the situation, and the fact that this strong male gets to make the crucial statement shows Heinlein's rather new outlook on the relations between the sexes. He warns Jake not even to "hint" that Hilda "is not as competent as any man":

> Sure, she'd be picked last for a tug-o'-war team, and she has to stand on a stool to reach a high shelf—*does that affect her brain?* Hell's bells, if size mattered, *I* would be the supergenius around here—not *you.*" [Ch. 25]

Deety immediately creates a diversion, knowing that Jake must not be allowed to reply and justify himself, because "The ability of the male mind to rationalize its deeds—and misdeeds—cannot be measured."

Hilda's captaincy guides them through the perils of time-space travel, the intricacies of inter-spatial diplomacy, and even some of the spaces that separate men and women, leading them to the world they have selected as their new home, an alternative Earth with many features of the familiar Heinlein utopia (low taxes, small population, punishment that fits the crime, and lots of nudity). But this planet turns out to be too "good and clean and wholesome and dull" (Ch. 39) for our hyper-cosmic adventurers.

When Deety realizes that the two men are contemplating some new explorations "while Hilda and I stay home with the kids" (Ch. 32), the gulf between the sexes looms wider than ever, for now the pregnancy of the two women is about to place them literally in separate worlds from the men. Deety boils over with indignation:

> "Maybe all we should expect is washing dishes and wiping noses and changing diapers, with our men protecting us. But

that doesn't seem like a be-all and end-all when you've gone
banging around the universes. . . ." [Ch. 39]

Hilda decides to drop the argument: "One can't expect logic
from males; they think with their testicles and act from their
emotions."

At issue here is one of Heinlein's previous pet notions, af-
firmed in his 1973 speech to the U.S. Naval Academy:

> Spelled out in simple Anglo-Saxon words "patriotism" reads
> "Women and children first!"
>   And that is the moral result of realizing a self-evident bio-
> logical fact: Men are expendable; women and children are not.
> A tribe or a nation can lose a high percentage of its men and
> still pick up the pieces and go on . . . as long as the women
> and children are saved. But if you fail to save the women and
> children, you've had it, you're done, you're through!
>   . . . Every human culture is based on "Women and children
> first"—and any attempt to do it any other way leads quickly to
> extinction.[2]

This notion is passionately refuted by Deety:

> "You two want to protect Hilda and me and our unborn kids
> at any cost—and we honor you for it. But one generation is as
> valuable as another, and men are as valuable as women. . . .
> I'm a programmer. I can shoot, too! I won't be left out, I
> won't!" [Ch. 39]

So off they go again, husbands and pregnant wives together,
toward their ultimate adventures and apocalypse.

On their way to the pleasant utopia from which they now
flee in boredom, the four explorers had made some rather
surprising discoveries, surprising to us as well as to them. We
had been led to assume that before they began their travels in
alternate universes, these four science-fiction enthusiasts were
all citizens of our Earth sometime in a not-too-distant future.
But it is not until the last quarter of the novel that the travelers
encounter our Earth, or what may be our Earth, and the encounter lasts just long enough for a couple of quick jokes. The
big revelation comes when they purchase a world almanac—
one of their standard operating procedures whenever they
land on a planet resembling their Earth—and Zeb casually
turns to the list of Presidents of the United States of America:

> Shortly he said, "Who is Eisenhower? This shows him serv-
> ing one of Harriman's terms and one of Patton's."

"Keep going, Zebbie."

"Okay— *No!* I refuse to believe it. Us Carters are taught to shoot straight, bathe every month even in the winter, and *never* run for office." [Ch. 38]

Thus we discover that our four heroes come from a universe alternate to our own.

Meanwhile they have discovered that Gay Deceiver, hooked up to Jake's continua device, can take them into universes that have been created in fiction. So they get to drop in on Lilliput, the world of E. E. Smith's Lensman, and Isaac Asimov's "Nightfall," stop in Wonderland where they have tea with Lewis Carroll, and stay overnight in the Land of Oz.

Oz plays an important function in their epic. Since it "works by magic, not by engineering" (Ch. 31), Oz provides some very useful modifications for their continua craft, including separate magical restrooms for males and females. Oz is terribly alluring, especially for Deety. After all, it lacks all those attributes of our modern world so abhorrent to Heinlein's heroes in *The Door into Summer, Glory Road,* the juvenile epic, *I Will Fear No Evil,* and so on: "No income tax. No political candidates. No smog. No churches. No wars. No inflation" (Ch. 31). But they come to understand that Oz is a temptation to remain in a universe that was "designed for children." As Glinda the Good explains to Deety, "Having decided to be a woman and not a little girl like Dorothy or Trot, leave here *quickly* . . . lest you be tempted to stay in Fairyland forever" (Ch. 31).

Though they leave Oz behind, they do not thereby move into universes any more real. For the very heart of *The Number of the Beast—,* animating all its disparate parts, is the theory that fiction—whether realistic, scientific, or fantastic—is just as real as anything else. And the operating principle of this theory is that reality itself is a kind of fiction, the creation of the solipsistic mind.

Hilda speculates about the theory as a form of science based on the notion that "human thought exists as quanta":

"I don't know quanta from Qantas Airways, but I know that a quantum is an indivisible unit. You told me that you and Jacob had discussed the possibility that imagination had its own sort of indivisible units or quanta—you called them 'fic-tons'—or was it ficta? Either way, the notion was that every story ever told—or to be told if there is a difference—exists somewhere in the Number of the Beast." [Ch. 33]

From this she deduces that the "fictional universes" they will enter will all be "*our* universes," "well known to each of us." Since "all four of us are addicted to fanciful stories," these will be the worlds they actually experience. Hence their travels to Lilliput, Wonderland, Oz, and their favorite modern science-fiction universes. Zeb immediately names this process "pantheistic multiperson solipsism," the label that will be reapplied several times to account for the still more bizarre adventures to come.

Their logic and their experience thus lead them to the conclusion that ". . . all worlds are equally real. Or unreal" (Ch. 35). And since all "these alternate worlds are as real as the one we came from," these four characters must then face the most essential fact of their life: "Then *we* are fiction in other universes" (Ch. 35).

Their realization that "we ourselves are figments of the imagination" (Ch. 35) disturbs them. Our own response is quite different, for we knew all along that they were just fictional characters, and we are observing them in the process of discovering an ontological truth that most fictional characters are never permitted to learn. However, Heinlein does not mean for us to rest in comfort with this notion. Toward the beginning of the novel, Jake had held a conversation with his dead wife Jane, in a style similar to the dialogue between the living and the apparently dead in *I Will Fear No Evil*. Just as some of us readers may be getting uneasy about this, Jake suddenly turns on us:

> Let me tell you, you nonexistent reader sitting there with a tolerant sneer: Don't be smug. Jane is more real than you are. [Ch. 5]

If we listen closely here, I believe we can hear echoes of the final words of Heinlein's solipsistic masterpiece, "All You Zombies—":

> You aren't really there at all. There isn't anybody but me— Jane—here alone in the dark.
> I miss you dreadfully!

After all, *The Number of the Beast*— is not the first work in which Heinlein has put his solipsistic tendency together with an attempt to expose the nature of his own fictive reality. Jubal's last act in *Stranger in a Strange Land* is to begin another version of the story we have just read, one bearing the title of Heinlein's own original manuscript. In *Glory Road*, Oscar realizes "I had fallen into a book." And *Time Enough for Love* repeatedly pokes holes in its own illusions, forcing the readers to repeal their suspension of disbelief as the puppets analyze the lines in the puppet master's own hand.

When the four time-space jumpers understand that their travels derive from "pantheistic multiperson solipsism," they decide to vote on their favorite stories in order to predict where their minds will take them next. Heinlein now sweeps aside the illusion of the fiction, merely to have some fun—or so it may seem to unwary readers:

> "Did Heinlein get his name in the hat?"
> "Four votes, split. Two for his 'Future History,' two for 'Stranger in a Strange Land.' So I left him out."
> "*I* didn't vote for 'Stranger' and I'll refrain from embarrassing anyone by asking who did. My God, the things some writers will do for money!" [Ch. 34]

The joke, however, is going to go much deeper, until Heinlein reveals the innermost meaning of his fictional worlds.

When they leave the "dull" utopia, they decide to flit about at random, just for "fun," allowing anyone, including Gay, to stop when they see an especially interesting universe (Ch. 39). After a ten-minute " 'slide show' of universes from commonplace to weird beyond comprehension," Gay halts herself and calls " 'Ship Ahoy!' " Back comes the response, " 'Private Yacht Dora,' " and for the next nine chapters we witness a world created by the interactions between the characters from this novel and the characters from *Time Enough for Love*. Jake recognizes that "We've fallen into another story" (Ch. 39), and the characters from both Heinlein novels now come to realize "that we are *all equally* figments of imagination" (Ch. 42).

Lazarus grossly underestimates "this narrow little broad" Hilda (Ch. 43) who soon outfoxes the old fox, has him arrested, and assumes absolute command of Dora. Lorelei Lee,

Lapis Lazuli, Elizabeth Andrew Jackson Libby Long, Lazarus, and company introduce the crew of Gay to the pleasures of more-or-less polymorphous sex: Hilda and Jake do some swapping of partners and soon, as customary in Heinlein's two novels of the 1970s, everybody gets to make love with various members of the opposite sex. Dora helps Gay become fully conscious. Flitting back and forth through alternate universes, characters from both novels team up to rescue Lazarus's dead mother, take her back to Tertius so Ishtar and her crew can rejuvenate her, and bring her back to Dora just in time to parade around in green garters at the lavish party where everybody is enthralled with everybody else's scanty costume. Libby announces that she has been "wholeheartedly converted" both to "Jake's six-axis plenum of universes to the awful Number of the Beast" and to Hilda's pantheistic multiperson solipsism, and declares that together they "constituted the ultimate total philosophy: science, religion, mathematics, art, in one grand consistent package" (Ch. 44). Finally, they all end up "home" on Tertius, Lazarus's hedonistic utopia for the elite of the elite.

Then follows a concluding "L'Envoi," beginning with these words from Lazarus: "Jubal, you are a bad influence." Jubal Harshaw, appearing in his twin roles as character and author, leads a procession of characters from Heinlein's fiction who intermingle with many other kinds of beings in a grand finale, a kind of ultimate science-fiction convention:

THE FIRST CENTENNIAL CONVENTION
of the
INTERUNIVERSAL SOCIETY
for
ESCHATOLOGICAL PANTHEISTIC MULTIPLE-EGO SOLIPSISM

The convention is attended by such "bloodthristy" creatures as "Female authors. Critics. Harlan. Both Heinleins." There are long lists of the authors and characters and even critics (whose credentials are checked by Jonathan Hoag). It's all a lot of fun, for Heinlein and for his fans. And it's also Heinlein's unveiling, his revelation—in short, his apocalypse.

All the essential elements of the apocalypse appear in *The Number of the Beast*—: demonic spirits arise (here incarnated by aliens who look just like one of the beasts described in Revelation XIII, even down to their "two horns like a lamb"); bizarre movements of the planets and stars turn out to be heavenly portents; a divine force intervenes dramatically to dispel the illusions of everyday life and put a final end to history; the faithful elect are saved and go to abide with their creator in a new heaven and new earth. Above all, apocalypse means revelation.

The single chapter comprising that final "L'Envoi" is entitled "Rev. XXII:13." Some may find this a bit presumptious, for Revelation XXII:13 consists of this declaration by Jesus Christ: "I am Alpha and Omega, the beginning and the end, the first and the last." Heinlein is here intimating that the ultimate creator—not just of one universe but of all the alternative universes—is the creator of fiction. (Perhaps this accounts for the unusual exclamation in the midst of the characters' discussion of Heinlein: " 'My god . . . !' ") Scripture is interpreted to support this deification of the author:

> **"If you read it correctly it's all in the Bible. 'In the beginning was the Word and the Word was with God, and the Word *was* God.' Could anyone ask for a plainer statement of the self-evident fact that nothing exists until someone imagines it and thereby gives it being, reality?"** [Ch. 48]

This variant of solipsism not only deifies authors, but also places at the highest pinnacle in the pantheon of authors the creator of the most imaginative fiction, such as *The Number of the Beast*—, with its 6^{66} alternative universes.

All this bright glory has its dark side, which jumps out in harsh contrast if we look back through Heinlein's career and its place in the history of modern America. Apocalyptic impulses are always symptoms characteristic of a social class, people, or culture undergoing extreme stress and transformations. For an apocalypse is, after all, an imagined replacement for actual history. One snooty official at the convention, in charge of giving out badges so the participants can be identified by universe, asks Lazarus to name the Presidents of the first century of his life; the ensuing conversation among Lazarus, the official, and Jubal Harshaw tells us just what kind of apocalypse this fiction represents:

"Woodrow Wilson—I was named for him—Harding, Coolidge, Hoover, Roosevelt, Truman, Eisenhower, Kennedy, Kennedy, Kennedy, Kennedy, Kennedy, Kennedy—"

"Which brings us to 1984, right? And tells me that you experienced the Nehemiah Scudder Interregnum and possibly the Second so-called American Revolution. Dr. Harshaw, did your world experience the Interregnum?"

"It experienced something worse, a world government."

"To me all worlds are equally bad."

Heinlein now spoofs the historical concerns of his earlier works. There is no chance for heroism and glory, because all enemies are imaginary, all goals equally illusory. The only combat is the battle of the sexes, where the prize is a papier-mâché relationship with a being one creates in one's own mind. Even Heinlein's obsessive quest for new frontiers is a chimera in these endlessly exfoliating universes, and when Deety announces "We are pioneers" (Ch. 31), she is merely mouthing her author's joke. "THE FIRST CENTENNIAL CONVENTION of the INTERUNIVERSAL SOCIETY for ESCHATOLOGICAL PANTHEISTIC MULTIPLE-EGO SOLIPSISM" is a perfect metaphor, for this caricature science-fiction convention displays the banal, trivial, and escapist side of modern science fiction, with its conventions where fans dress up as their favorite characters.

In this masquerade, one pretends that even death does not exist. People do not die in the world of *The Number of the Beast*—, but the reverse: dead fictional characters, like Libby and Lazarus's mother, are brought back to fictive "life." Heinlein here deprives his fiction of the force that animates his most powerful and authentic moments, such as Delos Harriman living just long enough to die on the moon, Karen Farnham dying in childbirth, the grief of the immortal Lazarus when his "ephemeral" wife Dora dies in old age, Manny's loneliness after the "death" of Mike in *The Moon Is a Harsh Mistress*. Even that great new frontier, Space, has turned out to be as empty as its name implies. Neither death nor life has objective reality. Trapped in its maze of solipsism and narcissism, the ego can find only reflections of itself in the mirrors of its own fictions.

In *The Number of the Beast*—, Heinlein, recalling his own

achievements, shows them all finally as universes that are fantastic alternatives to his own twentieth-century America. But rather than transcending and escaping from modern American history, *The Number of the Beast—*, together with all of Heinlein's fictions, is a revelation of the formative powers of that history.

NOTES

1. *The Number of the Beast—*, Ch. 33, 43. All references are by chapter to the unpublished manuscript, which Heinlein most generously allowed me to use prior to the publication of the novel.
2. Heinlein, "James Forrestal Memorial Lecture," U.S. Naval Academy, April 5, 1973, reprinted as "Channel Markers," *Analog,* 92 (January 1974), pp. 176–77. Heinlein said the same thing, much of it word for word, in his interview with Alfred Bester, "PW Interviews: Robert Heinlein," *Publishers Weekly,* July 2, 1973, p. 45.

CHRONOLOGY

1907   Robert Anson Heinlein, third of seven children, born to Bam Lyle and Rex Ivar Heinlein on July 7 in Butler, Missouri. Family moves to Kansas City, Missouri, where Rex Heinlein works in various white-collar jobs.

1924   Graduates from Central High School in Kansas City.

1929   Graduates as an ensign from the United States Naval Academy.

1929–34 Several assignments on ships, including aircraft carrier USS Lexington.

1934   Medical disability forces retirement from navy as a lieutenant j.g.

1934–39 While regaining health in California and Colorado, attends UCLA graduate school, sells real estate, runs for political office, and speculates in silver mining.

1939   Publishes his first story, "Life-Line," in Astounding Science-Fiction.

1939–42 Becomes extremely popular writer of science fiction in the pulp magazines, especially Astounding.

1942–45 Works as civilian engineer in the Naval Air Material Center at the Philadelphia Navy Yard. No new fiction published until 1947.

1947–59 Becomes a dominant figure in science fiction, publishing dozens of stories and sixteen novels, including a juvenile series, while also doing screenplays and television scripts. Wins Hugo awards for Double Star and Starship Troopers.

1948   Marries Virginia Gerstenfeld.

1961–66 Abandons the short story and publishes five science-fiction novels, beginning with Stranger in a Strange Land and ending with The Moon Is a Harsh Mistress, both of which win Hugo awards.

1970–73 Publishes two massive, controversial science-fiction novels, I Will Fear No Evil and Time Enough for Love.

1978   Recovers from a carotid bypass operation.

1980   Publishes The Number of the Beast—.

CHECKLIST OF WORKS
BY ROBERT A. HEINLEIN

Fiction

"Life-Line," *Astounding Science-Fiction*, August 1939.

"Misfit," *Astounding Science-Fiction*, November 1939.

"Requiem," *Astounding Science-Fiction*, January 1940.

" 'If This Goes On—,' " *Astounding Science-Fiction*, February, March 1940.

" 'Let There Be Light,' " *Super Science Stories*, May 1940 (by Lyle Monroe).

"The Roads Must Roll," *Astounding Science-Fiction*, June 1940.

"Heil!," *Futuria Fantasia*, Summer 1940 (by Lyle Monroe).

"Coventry," *Astounding Science-Fiction*, July 1940.

"Blowups Happen," *Astounding Science-Fiction*, September 1940.

"The Devil Makes the Law" ("Magic, Inc."), *Unknown*, September 1940.

Sixth Column. *Astounding Science-Fiction*, January, February, March 1941 (by Anson MacDonald).

" '—And He Built a Crooked House—,' " *Astounding Science-Fiction*, February 1941.

"Logic of Empire," *Astounding Science-Fiction*, March 1941.

"Beyond Doubt," *Astonishing Stories*, April 1941 (by Lyle Monroe with Elma Wentz).

"They," *Unknown*, April 1941.

"Universe," *Astounding Science-Fiction*, May 1941.

"Solution Unsatisfactory," *Astounding Science-Fiction*, May 1941 (by Anson MacDonald).

" '—We Also Walk Dogs,' " *Astounding Science-Fiction*, July 1941 (by Anson MacDonald).

Methuselah's Children. *Astounding Science-Fiction*, July, August, September 1941.

"Elsewhere" ("Elsewhen"), *Astounding Science-Fiction*, September 1941 (by Caleb Saunders).

"By His Bootstraps," *Astounding Science-Fiction*, October 1941 (by Anson MacDonald).

"Common Sense," *Astounding Science-Fiction*, October 1941.

"Lost Legion" ("Lost Legacy"), *Super Science Stories*, November 1941 (by Lyle Monroe).

" 'My Object All Sublime,' " *Future*, February 1942 (by Lyle Monroe).

"Goldfish Bowl," *Astounding Science-Fiction*, March 1942 (by Anson MacDonald).

"Pied Piper," *Astonishing Stories*, March 1942 (by Lyle Monroe).

Beyond This Horizon. Astounding Science-Fiction, April, May 1942 (by Anson MacDonald).

"Waldo," *Astounding Science-Fiction*, August 1942 (by Anson Mac-Donald).

"The Unpleasant Profession of Jonathan Hoag," *Unknown Worlds*, October 1942 (by John Riverside).

"The Green Hills of Earth," *Saturday Evening Post*, February 8, 1947.

"Space Jockey," *Saturday Evening Post*, April 26, 1947.

"Columbus Was a Dope," *Startling Stories*, May 1947 (by Lyle Monroe).

"They Do It with Mirrors," *Popular Detective*, May 1947 (by Simon York).

" 'It's Great To Be Back!' " *Saturday Evening Post*, July 26, 1947.

"Jerry Is a Man" ("Jerry Was a Man"), *Thrilling Wonder Stories*, October 1947.

"Water Is for Washing," *Argosy*, November 1947.

Rocket Ship Galileo. New York: Scribner's, 1947.

"The Black Pits of Luna," *Saturday Evening Post*, January 10, 1948.

"Gentlemen, Be Seated!," *Argosy*, May 1948.

"Ordeal in Space," *Town and Country*, May 1948.

Beyond This Horizon (revised version). Reading, Penn.: Fantasy Press, 1948.

Space Cadet. New York: Scribner's, 1948.

"Our Fair City," *Weird Tales*, January 1949.

"Nothing Ever Happens on the Moon," *Boys' Life*, April, May 1949.

"Poor Daddy," *Calling All Girls*, 1949.

"Gulf," *Astounding Science-Fiction*, November, December 1949.

"Delilah and the Space-Rigger," *Blue Book*, December 1949.

"The Long Watch," *American Legion Magazine*, December 1949.

Red Planet. New York: Scribner's, 1949.

Sixth Column. New York: Gnome Press, 1949. (Originally serialized in 1941.)

"Cliff and the Calories," *Senior Prom*, August 1950.

Farmer in the Sky. Serialized as *Satellite Scout* in *Boys' Life*, August, September, October, November 1950. New York: Scribner's, 1950.

"The Man Who Sold the Moon," in *The Man Who Sold the Moon* (collection). Chicago: Shasta, 1950.

"Destination Moon," *Short Stories Magazine*, September 1950.

Between Planets. Serialized as *Planets in Combat* in *Blue Book*, September, October 1951. New York: Scribner's, 1951. Serialized as comic strip in *Boys' Life*, 1978.

The Puppet Masters. Serialized in *Galaxy Science Fiction*, September, October, November 1951. Garden City, N.Y.: Doubleday, 1951.

"The Year of the Jackpot," *Galaxy Science Fiction*, March 1952.

The Rolling Stones. Serialized as Tramp Space Ship in Boys' Life, September, October, November, December 1952. New York: Scribner's, 1952.

"Project Nightmare," Amazing Stories, April 1953.

"Sky Lift," Imagination, November 1953.

Starman Jones. New York: Scribner's, 1953.

The Star Beast. Serialized as The Star Lummox in Magazine of Fantasy and Science Fiction, May, June, July 1954. New York: Scribner's, 1954.

Tunnel in the Sky. New York: Scribner's, 1955.

Double Star. Serialized in Astounding Science-Fiction, February, March, April 1956. Garden City, N.Y.: Doubleday, 1956.

Time for the Stars. New York: Scribner's, 1956.

The Door into Summer. Serialized in Magazine of Fantasy and Science Fiction, October, November, December 1956. Garden City, N.Y.: Doubleday, 1957.

"The Menace from Earth," Magazine of Fantasy and Science Fiction, August 1957.

Citizen of the Galaxy. Serialized in Astounding Science-Fiction, September, October, November, December 1957. New York: Scribner's, 1957.

"The Elephant Circuit" ("The Man Who Traveled in Elephants"), Saturn, October 1957.

"Tenderfoot in Space," Boys' Life, May, June, July 1958.

Have Space Suit—Will Travel. Serialized in Magazine of Fantasy and Science Fiction, August, September, October 1958. New York: Scribner's, 1958.

Methuselah's Children (serialized in 1941). Hicksville, N.Y.: Gnome Press, 1958.

"All You Zombies—," Magazine of Fantasy and Science Fiction, March 1959.

Starship Troopers. Serialized as Starship Soldier in Magazine of Fantasy and Science Fiction, October, November 1959. New York: Putnam, 1959.

Stranger in a Strange Land. New York: Putnam, 1961.

"Searchlight," Scientific American, August 1962; Fortune, September 1962; et al.

Podkayne of Mars. Serialized in Worlds of If, November 1962, January, March 1963. New York: Putnam, 1963.

Glory Road. Serialized in Magazine of Fantasy and Science Fiction, July, August, September 1963. New York: Putnam, 1963.

Farnham's Freehold. Serialized in If, July, August, October 1964. New York: Putnam, 1964.

The Moon Is a Harsh Mistress. Serialized in If, December 1965, January, February, March, April 1966. New York: Putnam, 1966.

"Free Men," in The Worlds of Robert A. Heinlein. New York: Ace Books, 1966.

I Will Fear No Evil. Serialized in *Galaxy,* July, August, October, December 1970. New York; Putnam, 1970.

"The Notebooks of Lazarus Long," *Astounding Science-Fiction,* June 1973. (Included in *Time Enough for Love.*) Published separately with illustrations by D. F. Vassallo. New York: Putnam, 1978.

Time Enough for Love. New York: Putnam, 1973.

"No Bands Playing," *Vertex: The Magazine of Science Fiction,* December 1973.

The Number of the Beast—. New York: Fawcett, 1980. Excerpts serialized in *Omni,* October, November 1979.

Collections of Fiction

Waldo and Magic, Inc. Garden City, N.Y.: Doubleday, 1950. Contains: "Waldo" (1942) and "Magic, Inc." ("The Devil Makes the Law," 1940).

The Man Who Sold the Moon. Chicago: Shasta, 1950. Contains: "Life-Line" (1939), " 'Let There Be Light' " (1940), "The Roads Must Roll" (1940), "Blowups Happen" (1940), "The Man Who Sold the Moon" (1950, original), "Requiem" (1940).

The Green Hills of Earth. Chicago: Shasta, 1951. Contains: "Delilah and the Space-Rigger" (1949), "Space Jockey" (1947), "The Long Watch" (1949), "Gentlemen, Be Seated!" (1948), "The Black Pits of Luna" (1948), " 'It's Great To Be Back!' " (1947), " '—We Also Walk Dogs' " (1941), "Ordeal in Space" (1948), "The Green Hills of Earth" (1947), "Logic of Empire" (1941).

Revolt in 2100. Chicago: Shasta, 1953. Contains: " 'If This Goes On—' " (1940), "Coventry" (1940), "Misfit" (1939).

Assignment in Eternity. Reading, Penn.: Fantasy Press, 1953. Contains: "Gulf" (1949), "Elsewhen" ("Elsewhere," 1941), "Lost Legacy" ("Lost Legion," 1941), "Jerry Was a Man" ("Jerry Is a Man," 1947).

The Menace from Earth. Hicksville, N.Y.: Gnome Press, 1959. Contains: "The Year of the Jackpot" (1952), "By His Bootstraps" (1941), "Columbus Was a Dope" (1947), "The Menace from Earth" (1957), "Sky Lift" (1953), "Goldfish Bowl" (1942), "Project Nightmare" (1953), "Water Is for Washing" (1947).

The Unpleasant Profession of Jonathan Hoag. Hicksville, N.Y.: Gnome Press, 1959. As *6XH,* New York: Pyramid, 1961. Contains: "The Unpleasant Profession of Jonathan Hoag" (1942), "The Man Who Traveled in Elephants" ("The Elephant Circuit," 1957), "All You Zombies—" (1959), "They" (1941), "Our Fair City" (1949), " '—And He Built a Crooked House—' " (1940).

Orphans of the Sky. New York: Putnam, 1964. Contains: "Universe" (1941) and "Common Sense" (1941).

Three by Heinlein. Garden City, N.Y.: Doubleday, 1965. Contains: The Puppet Masters (1951), "Waldo" (1942), "Magic, Inc." (1940).

The Worlds of Robert A. Heinlein. New York: Ace Books, 1966. Contains: "Free Men" (original, 1966), "Blowups Happen" (1940), "Searchlight" (1962), "Life-Line" (1939), "Solution Unsatisfactory" (1941).

The Past through Tomorrow. New York: Putnam, 1967. Contains: "Life-Line" (1939), "The Roads Must Roll" (1940), "Blowups Happen" (1940), "The Man Who Sold the Moon" (1950), "Delilah and the Space-Rigger" (1949), "Space Jockey" (1947), "Requiem" (1940), "The Long Watch" (1949), "Gentlemen, Be Seated!" (1948), "The Black Pits of Luna" (1948), " 'It's Great To Be Back!' " (1947), " '—We Also Walk Dogs' " (1941), "Searchlight" (1962), "Ordeal in Space" (1948), "The Green Hills of Earth" (1947), "Logic of Empire" (1941), "The Menace from Earth" (1957), " 'If This Goes On—' " (1940), "Coventry" (1940), "Misfit" (1939), Methuselah's Children (1941).

Non-fiction

"The Discovery of the Future: An Address Delivered before the Fourth Annual Science-Fiction Convention at Denver, Colorado, 4 July 1941." Pamphlet, 1941. Vertex: The Magazine of Science Fiction, #1, 1973.

Testing in Connection with the Development of Strong Plastics for Aircraft. Philadelphia: Naval Air Materials Center, 1944.

"Back of the Moon," Elks Magazine, July 1946.

"On the Writing of Speculative Fiction," in Of Worlds Beyond, ed. Lloyd Arthur Eshbach. Reading, Penn.: Fantasy Press, 1947.

"Flight into the Future" (with Caleb Barrett Laning), Collier's, August 30, 1947.

"Baedeker of the Solar System," Saturday Review of Literature, December 24, 1949. (Review essay on The Conquest of Space by Chesley Bonestell and Willy Ley.)

"Shooting Destination Moon," Astounding Science-Fiction, July 1950.

Preface, The Man Who Sold the Moon. Chicago: Shasta, 1950.

Review of Space Medicine, ed. John P. Marbarger, Denver Post, August, 1951.

"Where To? Life in 2000 A.D.," Galaxy, February 1952. In All About the Future (anthology) ed. Martin Greenberg, New York: Gnome Press, 1955.

Introduction to Tomorrow, the Stars (anthology) edited by Heinlein. Garden City, N.Y.: Doubleday, 1952.

"Ray Guns and Rocket Ships," School Library Association of California Bulletin, November 1952; Library Journal, July 1953.

"Concerning Stories Never Written: Postscript," *Revolt in 2100*. Chicago: Shasta, 1953.

Introduction to *The Best from Startling Stories*, comp. Samuel Mines. New York: Henry Holt, 1953.

"As I See Tomorrow," *Amazing Stories*, April 1956.

"Who Are the Heirs of Patrick Henry?" (advertisement), *Colorado Springs Gazette Telegraph*, April 13, 1958.

"Science Fiction: Its Nature, Faults and Virtues," in *The Science Fiction Novel: Imagination and Social Criticism*. Chicago: Advent, 1959.

" 'Pravda' Means 'Truth,' " *American Mercury*, October, 1960.

"All Aboard the Gemini," *Popular Mechanics*, May 1963.

"The Happy Road to Science Fiction," *McClurg's Book News*, 1964.

"Pandora's Box," Introduction to *The Worlds of Robert A. Heinlein*. New York: Ace, 1966. Includes "Where To?" (1952).

"Channel Markers," *Analog: Science Fiction, Science Fact*, January 1974. (1973 speech at the United States Naval Academy.)

"Science Fiction: The World of 'What If—,' " *The Book of Knowledge*, 1973.

"Paul Dirac, Antimatter, and You," *1975 Compton Yearbook*. Chicago: F. E. Compton, 1975.

"Are You a 'Rare Blood'?" *1976 Compton Yearbook*. Chicago: F. E. Compton, 1976.

"The Making of *Destination Moon*," *Starlog*, #6, 1977.

"Spinoff," *Omni*, March, 1980.

Collection of Fiction and Non-fiction

Expanded Universe: More Worlds of Robert A. Heinlein. New York: Ace, 1980. Contains: "Life-Line" (1939), "Successful Operation," "Blowups Happen" (1940), "Solution Unsatisfactory" (1941), "The Last Days of the United States," "How To Be a Survivor," "Pie from the Sky," "They Do It with Mirrors" (1947), "Free Men" (1966), "No Bands Playing, No Flags Flying" (1973), "A Bathroom of Her Own," "On the Slopes of Vesuvius," "Nothing Ever Happens on the Moon" (1949), "Pandora's Box" (1966), "Cliff and the Calories" (1950), "Ray Guns and Rocket Ships" (1952), "The Third Millennium Opens," "Who Are the Heirs of Patrick Henry?" (1958), " 'Pravda' Means 'Truth' " (1960), "Inside INTOURIST," "Searchlight" (1962), "The Pragmatics of Patriotism," "Paul Dirac, Antimatter, and You" (1975), "Larger Than Life," "Spinoff," "The Happy Days Ahead."

Movies

Destination Moon (original script), 1950.
Project Moonbase (original script), 1953.

SELECT LIST OF WORKS
ABOUT ROBERT A. HEINLEIN

Aldiss, Brian W. *Billion Year Spree: The True History of Science Fiction.* Garden City, N.Y.: Doubleday, 1973. Pp. 228–29, 269–74. A devastating critique.

Bester, Alfred. "PW Interviews: Robert Heinlein," *Publishers Weekly,* July 2, 1973, 44–45. One of Heinlein's more informative interviews.

Cansler, Robert, "*Stranger in a Strange Land:* Science Fiction as Literature of the Creative Imagination, Social Criticism, and Entertainment," *Journal of Popular Culture,* 5(Spring 1972), 944–54. Uses *Stranger* to demonstrate the special values of science fiction as a form of entertainment and instrument of social criticism.

Chapman, Robert S., "Science Fiction of the 1950's: Billy Graham, McCarthy, and the Bomb," *Foundation: The Review of Science Fiction,* 7/8 (1975), 38–52. Discusses Heinlein and three other science-fiction authors in relation to American fears and desires in the 1950s, with particular stress on the themes of atomic holocaust, alien invasion, religion, and the yearning for new frontiers.

Christopher, Joe R., "Lazarus, Come Forth from That Tomb!" *Riverside Quarterly,* 6 (1976–77), 190–97. Explores the structure of *Time Enough for Love* and speculates about the Oedipal content.

————, "Methuselah, Out of Heinlein by Shaw," *Shaw Review,* 16 (1973), 79–88. Argues that Shaw's *Back to Methuselah* strongly influenced the Future History.

"Colorado Engineer Interview: Robert A. Heinlein," *Colorado Engineer,* December 1971.

Commire, Anne, ed. *Something about the Author.* New York: Gale, 1979. Vol. 9, pp. 102–3.

"Contact," *The New Yorker,* 50 (July 1, 1974), 17–18. Description of Heinlein giving a talk.

Current Biography, New York: H. W. Wilson, 1955.

Fuller, Muriel, ed. *More Junior Authors.* New York: Wilson, 1963. Pp. 109–10. Autobiographical sketch by Heinlein.

Gaar, Alice Carol, "The Human as Machine Analog: The Big Daddy of Interchangeable Parts in the Fiction of Robert A. Heinlein," in Olander and Greenberg (cited below). Argues that Heinlein's works recurrently make a mechanistic reduction of human identity to an assemblage of parts, all "neutral, nameless, and differentiated by function."

Hull, Elizabeth Anne, "Justifying the Ways of Man to God: The Novels of Robert A. Heinlein," *Extrapolation,* 20 (Spring 1979),

38–49. Argues that Heinlein's audience relishes "the challenge of considering the moral and political questions" he raises, questions which he poses best in first-person narratives by innocent personae.

Knight, Damon. "One Sane Man: Robert A. Heinlein," Chapter 7 of *In Search of Wonder*. Chicago: Advent, 1960. A eulogy to Heinlein as "the nearest thing to a great writer the science fiction field has yet produced."

Lehman-Wilzig, Sam N., "Science Fiction as Futurist Prediction: Alternate Visions of Heinlein and Clarke," *The Literary Review*, 20 (1976), 133–51. Compares the contrasting futures in the imagination of Heinlein and Clarke with each other and with the predictions of futurists.

Letson, Russell, "The Returns of Lazarus Long," in Olander and Greenberg (cited below). A wide-ranging, provocative, highly laudatory explication of *Time Enough for Love*.

McNelly, Willis E., "Linguistic Relativity in Old High Martian," *CEA Critic*, 30 (March 1968), 4, 6. Uses the several definitions of "grok" to explore the themes of *Stranger*.

Moskowitz, Sam. *Seekers of Tomorrow*. Cleveland: World Publishing, 1966. Pp. 187–212. An introductory survey of Heinlein's career, packed with facts. Suggests that poor imitations of Heinlein led to a decline of science fiction throughout the 1950s.

Olander, Joseph D. and Martin H. Greenberg, eds. *Robert A. Heinlein*. New York: Taplinger, 1977. A rich collection of critical essays, described individually in this checklist.

Panshin, Alexei. *Heinlein in Dimension*. Chicago: Advent, 1968. The first full-length detailed study of Heinlein's works, quite influential on most subsequent criticism. Valuable explorations of many of Heinlein's principal themes, marred by subjective evaluations.

———— and Cory Panshin, "Reading Heinlein Subjectively," in *Science Fiction in Dimension*. Chicago: Advent, 1976. Extends the psychological analysis integral to *Heinlein in Dimension*.

Parkin-Speer, Diane, "Robert A. Heinlein: The Novelist as Preacher," *Extrapolation*, 20 (Fall 1979), 214–22. Argues that Heinlein's powers as a novelist sharply decline in the two massive novels of the 1970s as he becomes obsessed with preaching his simplistic message about sex.

Perkins, James Ashbrook, "MYCROFTXX Is Alive and Well: The Ambiguous Ending of *The Moon Is a Harsh Mistress*," *Notes on Contemporary Literature*, 5 (1975), 13–15. Draws parallels between the ending of this novel and those of *Stranger* and *I Will Fear No Evil*.

Plank, Robert, "Omnipotent Cannibals in *Stranger in a Strange Land*," in Olander and Greenberg. A distinguished orthopsychiatrist analyzes *Stranger* as an infantile fantasy of omnipotence.

Reinsberg, Mark, "Robert A. Heinlein: An Appreciation," introduction to The Green Hills of Earth. Chicago: Shasta, 1951. Praises Heinlein for his "homely realism" and exaltation of "the entrepreneur, the brilliant risk-taker."

Robinson, Frank, "Conversation with Robert Heinlein," Oui, 1 (December 1972), 76.

Rogers, Ivor A., "Robert Heinlein: Folklorist of Outer Space," in Olander and Greenberg. An insightful explication of Time Enough for Love; discusses influence of Vincent McHugh's Caleb Catlum's America, compares Heinlein with Aristophanes, and explores sexual themes.

Rothfork, John, "Grokking God: Phenomenology in NASA and Science Fiction," Research Studies, 44 (1976), 101–10. Discusses the religious and symbolic relations between the space program and three novels, including Stranger.

Samuelson, David N., "The Frontier Worlds of Robert A. Heinlein," in Voices for the Future, ed. Thomas Clareson, Bowling Green, Ohio: Bowling Green University Popular Press, 1976. Vol. 1, Pp. 104–52. A critical survey of Heinlein's career, focusing especially on "the adolescent dreams of freedom and power which form the backbone of his writings."

Sarti, Ronald, "Variations on a Theme: Human Sexuality in the Work of Robert A. Heinlein," in Olander and Greenberg. A fine analysis of Heinlein's vision of sex and women throughout his career.

Scholes, Robert, and Eric S. Rabkin. Science Fiction: History. Science. Vision. New York: Oxford University Press, 1977. Locates Heinlein within the history of science fiction and evaluates him as "a superb entertainer but a dangerous guide for conduct."

Schuman, Samuel, "Vladimir Nabokov's Invitation to a Beheading and Robert Heinlein's They," Twentieth Century Literature, 19 (1973), 99–106. An exploration of the quite remarkable similarities between these two solipsistic works.

Searles, Baird. Stranger in a Strange Land & Other Works. Lincoln, Neb.: Cliffs Notes, 1975. Mostly summaries.

Showalter, Dennis E., "Heinlein's Starship Troopers: An Exercise in Rehabilitation," Extrapolation, 16 (May 1975), 113–24. Attempts to prove that Starship Troopers is not as militaristic as it seems.

Slusser, George Edgar. The Classic Years of Robert A. Heinlein. San Bernardino, Ca.: Borgo Press, 1977. Detailed exploration of many Heinlein works through 1966; interprets Heinlein's exaltation of an "elect" as essentially "Calvinist."

———. Robert A. Heinlein: Stranger in His Own Land. San Bernardino, Ca.: Borgo Press, 1976, 1977. Explores several novels of the 1950s, Stranger, I Will Fear No Evil, and Time Enough for Love; argues that Heinlein has created out of modern America "a realm of soulless perpetual motion," perhaps even "a new circle in hell."

Smith, Philip E., II, "The Evolution of Politics and the Politics of Evolution in Heinlein's Fiction," in Olander and Greenberg. An

extremely perceptive exploration of the pervasive social Darwinism in Heinlein's works.

Tucker, Frank H., "Major Political and Social Elements in Heinlein's
Fiction," in Olander and Greenberg. An attempt to extract Heinlein's major ideological beliefs and to rebut negative criticism.

Williamson, Jack, "Youth Against Space: Heinlein's Juveniles Revis-
ited," Algol, 14 (Spring 1977), 9–15. Revised version in Olander
and Greenberg. An enthusiastic view of the Scribner's series;
claims that "juvenile science fiction, as a labeled category, begins with Heinlein."

INDEX